The Organizational
Behaviour Casebook

The Organizational Behaviour Casebook

edited by

Alan Berkeley Thomas

INTERNATIONAL THOMSON BUSINESS PRESS
I ⓣ P An International Thomson Publishing Company

London • Bonn • Boston • Johannesburg • Madrid • Melbourne • Mexico City • New York • Paris
Singapore • Tokyo • Toronto • Albany, NY • Belmont, CA • Cincinnati, OH • Detroit, MI

British Library Cataloguing-in-Publication Data
A catalogue record for this book is available from the British Library

First edition 1996

Produced by Gray Publishing, Tunbridge Wells, Kent
Printed in the UK by Clays Ltd, St Ives plc

ISBN 0-415-11850-6

International Thomson Business Press
Berkshire House
168–173 High Holborn
London WC1V 7AA
UK

International Thomson Business Press
20 Park Plaza
14th Floor
Boston MA 02116
USA

Contents

Acknowledgements		vii
Contributors		viii
Introduction		**1**
	Cases in organizational behaviour *Alan B. Thomas*	1
Part one	**Manufacturing organizations**	**11**
Case 1.1	Responding to reorganization at Northern Bakery *Allan Warmington*	13
Case 1.2	Growth in NuPlast, a small family firm *Neil Carruthers*	21
Case 1.3	Managing change at Fumac Ltd *Christian De Cock*	34
Part two	**Leisure service organizations**	**47**
Case 2.1	Climate and change at Chestertons Ales *Paul R. Sparrow*	48
Case 2.2	Modernizing the Royal Hotel *Graham Barlow*	61
Part three	**Financial service organizations**	**79**
Case 3.1	The rise and fall of Hamlet Insurance Company *Glenn Morgan*	81
Case 3.2	Culture and control at International Commodity Traders *Alan B. Thomas and Walter Skoly*	97
Case 3.3	Project Spectrum – implementing re-engineering in a bank *Christian De Cock*	110

Part four   **Government service organizations**   **123**

Case 4.1   Satisfying the customer/satisfying the staff at City
                Museum   126
                Alan B. Thomas

Case 4.2   Change in the police: a case of arrested development?   132
                Kevin C. Gaston

Case 4.3   'We've got no time for that: we've got people dying' –
                introducing IT to a social services department   149
                Heather Salt

Case 4.4   Performance, pay and privatization in the Civil Service   164
                Ian Tanner

Part five   **Spiritual service organizations**   **181**

Case 5.1   The diocese of Carbridge: crisis and change   183
                Anthony J. Berry

Case 5.2   Piety, power and progress   197
                Graham Barlow

Part six   **Organizing the unknown**   **213**

Case 6.1   Working in space: Skylab   214
                Alan B. Thomas

                Author index   **227**

                Subject index   **230**

Acknowledgements

The production of this book has been greatly assisted by the following: Sue Grey, at Manchester Business School, whose patience, good humour and hard work during the production of the manuscript has proved invaluable; Rosemary Nixon, who helped me to get the idea for the casebook off the ground and to sustain it through difficult times; Frania Weaver; and Steve Reed, who has seen the manuscript through the final stages to publication.

Our thanks to Michael Joseph Ltd for permission to reproduce the line drawing of Skylab which originally appeared on p. 124 of Tony Osman's *Space History* (1983).

Contributors

Graham Barlow teaches organizational behaviour and management development, specializing in project fieldwork, at the Manchester Business School.

Anthony J. Berry is Professor of Management Control at Sheffield Hallam University. He previously taught at the Manchester Business School.

Neil Carruthers is Fellow in Retailing at the Manchester Business School.

Christian De Cock is Lecturer in Management and Organizational Development at Royal Holloway, University of London, and previously undertook research at the Manchester Business School.

Kevin C. Gaston is Fellow in Organizational Behaviour at the Manchester Business School.

Glenn Morgan is Lecturer in Organizational Behaviour and Management at the Manchester Business School.

Heather Salt was formerly a Research Associate at the Manchester Business School and now researches and practices in psychotherapeutic counselling.

Walter Skoly is a commodity trader working in the City of London.

Paul R. Sparrow is Reader in International Human Resource Management at the University of Sheffield. He previously taught at the Manchester Business School.

Ian Tanner is Lecturer in Organizational Behaviour at the Manchester Business School.

Alan B. Thomas is Senior Lecturer in Sociology and Organizational Behaviour at the Manchester Business School.

Allan Warmington was formerly Lecturer in Organizational Development at the Manchester Business School.

Introduction

Cases in organizational behaviour

ALAN B. THOMAS

The use of cases as vehicles for teaching in management education has a long history originating in the formulation of the case method at Harvard Business School in the 1920s (Lundberg, 1993). Although few institutions have given the analysis of cases the central place in their pedagogy that Harvard, until recently, has done (Bongiorno, 1993), cases have nonetheless become a regular feature of the management education scene, especially in courses in strategy, business policy and organizational behaviour. Moreover, with the growth of management education in universities in Britain since the 1960s, there has been a growing demand for case materials which can be used in MBA and other management courses.

This book brings together fifteen cases which have been prepared by current or former members of the staff of the Manchester Business School (MBS) for use in the teaching of courses in organizational behaviour. Most of the cases have been written specifically for this volume, although a number of them have formed part of the syllabus of the organizational behaviour and design component of the MBA programmes at MBS for some years. As such they have been used in conjunction with a more traditional lecture course where they have provided the basis for small-group tutorial discussions. At MBS case analysis has come to be regarded, by students and teachers alike, as an essential part of the process of understanding organizational behaviour.

In producing this casebook it has been our intention not only to provide fresh materials for use by those who are already familiar with case teaching, but also to encourage those who are less familiar with, and perhaps even sceptical of, its value to venture into the field. Case teaching is not without its critics (e.g. Argyris, 1980; Mintzberg, 1989) and continues to be a focus of critical debate (Berger, 1983; Romm and Mahler, 1991; Smith, 1987; Stonham, 1995). Yet even where teachers are familiar with case teaching, most students, in our experience, are not. In this introduction, therefore, some general remarks on the nature, uses and limitations of cases as vehicles for learning about organizational behaviour, and approaches to their analysis are presented.

Cases and their uses

Organizational behaviour cases are, typically, written descriptions of a series of events, activities, processes and outcomes which have occurred in a real-life organization set in a particular social context at some point in history. They are problem-centred, depicting some difficulty or issue that the organization's members have encountered, and are intended to provide sufficient information about the issue at hand to enable the reader to generate an analysis of the problem, its likely causes and possible resolutions. The analysis of cases in organizational behaviour is thus a means whereby learners may come to sharpen their skills in interpreting and evaluating complex bodies of evidence and drawing reasoned conclusions from them. Such skills are surely sorely needed by members of contemporary organizations who must face increasing levels of uncertainty and complexity in their working lives.

The use of cases in teaching organizational behaviour has become widespread in recent years, and although case teaching, like every other teaching method, has its critics and detractors, it has retained a powerful and justifiable appeal both to teachers and learners.

For the teacher, the analysis of cases enables glimpses of 'reality' to be brought to what otherwise can be an arid encounter with the organizational world. Textbooks and lectures, the staple diet of much higher education, tend to deal in generalizations and abstractions: concepts, theories, frameworks, models, and so on. By confronting students with cases depicting 'real' organizational events and problems, the risk of isolation from the messy world outside the classroom and of academic 'irrelevance' can be offset. In addition, case analysis requires the active engagement of learners with the learning materials. Learners are required to formulate interpretations of the case materials for themselves, to seek out applications of the concepts, frameworks and theories presented by other means, to explain the occurrences described in the case, to diagnose problems and issues, and to offer thoughtful suggestions as to how the problems might have been avoided and what might be done about them. All this is central to the task of communicating the subject-matter of organizational behaviour and to the development of skill as an organizational practitioner.

In our experience, case analysis is also a popular learning method for students. Adult learners, in particular, generally welcome the opportunity to get close, as they see it, to the 'nitty-gritty' of organizational life. Since most adults have considerable experience of working in organizations, cases can provide a valuable basis for comparison and reflection. More than once we have heard learners respond to a case by saying that it bears a strong resemblance to some situation they have encountered in their own organization. Moreover, learners generally welcome the opportunity for participation in the learning enterprise which case analysis provides.

Case analysis can be seen as one key element in a trinity of learning resources. In their attempts to develop their understanding of organizational life, learners will typically be exposed to conceptual materials by means of texts, lectures and perhaps tutorials. But they also bring their own experiences, concepts and everyday theories to the learning task. Case analysis is a means whereby both the formal schemes of organizational behaviour and the personal schemes of learners can be brought together, tested and integrated. The hope, of course, is that learners will thus come to convince themselves of the value of organizational-behaviour thinking, by seeing how it can be used to illuminate the real world of organizational practice. Without this, there is the very real risk of ritual learning, in the extreme the memorization, often rather briefly, of a set of meaningless algebras soon to be forgotten once the demands of the assessment system have been satisfied.

The cases brought together in this book are teaching cases. As such they differ somewhat from research case studies both in terms of their method of creation, presentation and intent. Research cases are typically based on empirical investigation of one or more case units, using rigorous and explicit methodological procedures, and for the purpose of generating or testing theory (Eisenhardt, 1989; Yin, 1989). Although teaching cases are often derived from research inquiries, they are seldom explicit about their methods of construction. Nor can they be assumed to be unquestionably 'real'.

One of the key attractions of cases, especially to students, is their sense of being 'real', snapshots of the organizational world based on actual people, organizations and events. Yet it seems important not to be beguiled by the impression that cases, by seemingly 'telling it like it is', are purely objective descriptions of the world they portray. Cases are, first and foremost, texts which constitute someone's, the author's, attempts at sense-making (Weick, 1995). It is all too easy to forget this and to assume that a case simply describes things as they are. On the contrary, cases are only interpretable because authors conform to certain implicit and conventional rules of sense-making when writing their cases. Cases are thus inevitably biased in that, by including reports of some aspects of the world and excluding others, they facilitate some kinds of interpretation and disqualify or discourage others. So, for example, the materials necessary for a psychoanalytical interpretation of the behaviour depicted in the cases presented in this book is usually absent: had the authors been committed to such a frame of reference it would probably have been otherwise.

Case writers are in no different a position than everyday organizational members: they interpret the phenomena they encounter as best they can and offer accounts of them shot through with the basic assumptions of their culture and society. As Bromley (1986: 97) has put it:

> ... case studies are never merely a matter of collecting enough facts. The facts do not speak for themselves; they have to be spoken for. They are spoken for by what is, in effect, a 'theory', a form of argument by means of which the facts can be shown to be related to each other in a particular kind of way. To interpret facts in a particular way tends to rule out other interpretations and leads to implications which go beyond the information given ... A great deal of information is taken for granted as common knowledge about the world and about human nature. Added to this there are a great many reasonable assumptions which can be introduced as a matter of convenience to enable one to arrive at a satisfactory interpretation of a case.

We are reminded, then, that the social world, the world of organizations and organizational behaviour, is inherently ambiguous and open to alternative interpretations (Tsoukas, 1994). The social world we inhabit must be treated as an ambiguous figure for, as phenomenologists have pointed out (Spinelli, 1989), the world is intrinsically meaningless. We thus endow it with our own meanings using whatever symbolic resources that are available to us. 'What is going on?' is thus a question that can potentially be answered in many ways according to the frameworks, assumptions or metaphors (Morgan, 1986) that we bring to the task. Authors cannot escape from this situation any more than their readers can: to write at all requires the adoption of a framework, some point of view (Thomas, 1993).

Should we despair at this inevitable relativism? Surely not. On the contrary, it is our hope, and indeed our expectation, that these cases will be understood in a variety of ways. It cannot be claimed, then, that the cases presented here are entirely innocent descriptions of the organizational world. Far from it! Rather they are best seen as invitations to see things in particular ways, in effect in the ways that the case writers encourage and allow as well as discourage and disallow. As Morgan (1986) has pointed out, a way of seeing is also a way of not seeing.

The limitations of case analysis

Analysing a case can be likened to a process of dissection. In learning biology, school students have often been faced with the task of dissecting a frog. A specimen frog is slit open, its skin carefully peeled back and pinned so that its innards can be observed and investigated. This is undoubtedly a useful way of learning about frog anatomy and physiology unless, of course, you happen to be the frog! But it does have one significant drawback if your interest is in frog behaviour. For the frog that is subjected to dissection lacks that one essential quality vital to an understanding of its behaviour – life!

Case analysis shares this disadvantage in that the events depicted in a case are unamenable to manipulation by the analyst. In the real world, live frogs respond when they are stimulated just as people in organizational settings do. Any input into an organizational system – an action, recommendation, policy, procedure – produces a reaction of some sort, even if it is only that of being ignored! But case analysis does not permit such 'on-line' experimentation. The situation depicted in a case may no longer exist, learners have no direct access to it, and they almost certainly will never find themselves working in the organization described in the case. They are, in effect, dissecting a dead frog! This means that case analysis can only take us so far.

The well-known writer on management and organizations, Henry Mintzberg, has recently been highly critical of the use of case analysis in MBA teaching (Mintzberg, 1989). Although his remarks can best be understood in the context of American business-school education, where the Harvard 'case method', or something like it, has been widely adopted, they nonetheless offer a salutary warning about the misuse of case analysis.

Too often, he argues, students are encouraged to pronounce 'strategic decisions' on the basis of a few hours study of a twenty-page case document without ever having to implement those decisions or live with their consequences, without ever having to enter a factory or encounter a customer. The result is to foster remoteness and superficiality and the dangerous illusion on the part of learners that coping with organizational reality and analysing a case description are one and the same thing. To return to the frog analogy, learners may come to believe that there is little or no difference between a live frog and a dead frog, or even between a dead frog and a live human being.

As Mintzberg points out, however, the problem lies not so much with the use of cases for learning but with the way in which case analysis is approached. If, as is typical with the so-called 'case method' in management teaching, learners are required to take the role of management and to make recommendations for action, the risk of encouraging the managerial equivalent of *'chateau generalship'* seems substantial. Case analysis may then become 'part of the problem, not the solution' (Mintzberg, 1989: 88); like the generals, making life-and-death decisions about battle while ensconced in the comfort of their chateaux far from the gruesome realities of the front line, managers may come to think of themselves as primarily cool case analysts.

Cases may permit this way of teaching but they do not necessitate it. For the purposes of learning about organizational behaviour, we see the analysis of cases as less concerned with reaching decisions or with formulating recommendations than with developing understanding. And this understanding need not be restricted to the managerial perspective. Organizational behaviour is, or perhaps should be, a matter of concern to every organizational member, not simply managers. All too often cases adopt a managerial orientation as if organizational behaviour is only to be considered from a managerial point of view.

In the context of the 'case method', this managerial bias is clearly in evidence. Gragg (1954: 6 in Lundberg, 1993), for example, states that 'a case typically is a record of a business issue which actually has been faced by business executives' and is concerned with 'executive decisions', while Erskine *et al.* (1981: 10 in Lundberg, 1993) say that a case is 'normally written from the viewpoint of the decision-makers involved and allows the student to step figuratively into the shoes of the decision-maker or problem solver.' Similarly, Reynolds (1989: 9) writes that 'a good case almost puts the student into the position of the real-world manager, facing the challenge to make a decision and prepare a plan of action.'

To understand what is happening, why it is happening, the significance of what is happening, and how it could be otherwise is a difficult task, and one that takes the learner beyond any narrow concern with decisions. Even if learners have a vocational interest in their studies, perhaps aspiring to become managers, it seems clear that 'strategic decision-making' is only one aspect of the task of learning to be a manager. As Kotter (1982) has pointed out, it is rather disconcerting to think that a student undertaking a conventional case analysis makes more 'big decisions' in a few hours than a chief executive does in a lifetime!

In the context of policy research, Hakim (1987: 3–4) has suggested that it 'is ultimately concerned with knowledge for action, and the long-term aim is in line with the famous dictum that it is more important to change the world than to understand it.' Without taking this too literally, it seems a nonetheless questionable position. Whilst it may be *necessary* to change the world without understanding it, it hardly seems more *important* to do so. Indeed it might be argued that many important practical problems remain unsolved precisely because managers, in their various guises, persistently try to change things without understanding what they are doing.

In any event, in the course of a case analysis readers are not in a position to intervene in the situations portrayed. Although closure in the form of decisions is necessary for the purposes of everyday life, for the purposes of education this can be unhelpful. A decision-making orientation encourages convergent thinking whereas case analysis facilitates divergent thinking (Schumacher, 1978) involving the search for alternative interpretations and reframings. Since it is clear that the most significant problems facing managers are divergent in character and because cases are particularly potent vehicles for displaying this, the primary task of learners must be to understand them, to develop *usable understandings* (Turner, 1991). Thus while the 'questions for discussion' accompanying the cases in this book do sometimes invite the reader to formulate 'solutions' to the problems presented, in general the emphasis has been placed on encouraging diagnosis and conceptual analysis rather than on formulating specific recommendations for action.

Doing case analysis

Undertaking the analysis of a case for the first time is a daunting prospect for many students, the more so when it is realized that not only is there no clear statement of the problems in the case itself but also no right answers to them. Cases are by their nature complex and place considerable demands on the learner's resources.

Although there is no one best way to tackle a case analysis, certain guidelines can be suggested (see also Bromley, 1986; Easton, 1992).

1 Begin by skim-reading the case: the aim at this point is to gain an overall feel for the case, a general impression of its content and themes.
2 Formulate questions: interrogate the case by asking what is happening, why this is happening, what could happen next, who is doing or saying what, where and when is this happening?
3 Summarize key information: make summaries of key elements in note form, make summary calculations of quantitative data, create diagrams (organizational charts, activity flows, physical layouts, maps).
4 Construct an influence map: this is a difficult but valuable step in your analysis – try to depict the linkages between various elements of the case in order to clarify chains of influence (see Hogan, 1993).
5 Identify key concepts: relate the case materials to concepts, frameworks and theories that can be used to interpret the case materials.

6 Organize your analysis: this may take the form of a summary of the case material, a statement of key problems, conceptualization and explanation of the problems in terms of organizational-behaviour thinking, evidence to sustain your interpretations, limitations posed by lack of information, conclusions, and recommendations (if required).

Although case analysis may be undertaken by the student working alone, it is more usual and more productive for cases to be examined in group discussions. The case tutorial enables students to pool their ideas and to receive critical feedback from their fellow learners and tutors. In addition, case discussion facilitates the development of skills of analysis, presentation, and debate. Thorough preparation is, however, vital if the full potential of these discussions is to be realized.

Common pitfalls in case analysis include:

- Drawing conclusions without supporting evidence.
- Failing to recognize and take into account competing interpretations of events.
- Not utilizing organizational behaviour concepts in the course of the analysis.
- Not taking into account all relevant factors when diagnosing problems.
- Taking stated problems at face value rather than seeing them in their broader context or as the conjectures of organizational actors.
- Not specifying alternative courses of action and failing to evaluate their likely costs, benefits and consequences.
- Focusing on the symptoms of problems rather than their underlying causes.
- Treating statements of belief as if they were authoritative statements of fact.
- Giving undue weight to the opinions and statements of organizational authority figures.
- Specifying courses of action before analysing the causes of problems adequately.
- Specifying courses of action without considering their implementability – especially, adopting an omnipotent outsider's viewpoint which fails to take account of the powers, interests and capacities of the actors in the case situation.

These failings may often mirror, of course, those of organizational members themselves and so, somewhat ironically, may often form part of the analyst's diagnosis of a case!

Organization of the book

Fifteen cases are presented in this book, grouped into parts according to the organizations' main activities. Brief synopses of the cases are presented at the start of each part, in which the organizational setting, the main themes and questions, and related issues and concepts are outlined. Despite the diversity of settings and problems presented in the cases, a common underlying theme is that of change and its management.

All the cases are based on real-life instances although the identities of the case organizations have usually been disguised. With the exception of *Working in space: Skylab* (Case 6.1) and *Piety, power and progress* (Case 5.2) which have been constructed largely from published secondary sources, all the materials presented have been derived from first-hand experience, research and consultancy assignments. Wherever possible, verbatim quotations by participants have been included so as to allow organizational actors to speak for themselves, and as a reminder that organizational life is composed very largely of talk (Smircich, 1983).

Whilst some uniformity of presentation and organization has been imposed on the cases, they differ somewhat in style and tone according to the preferences of the authors. This variety has seemed to the editor to be beneficial in that it demonstrates the diverse character both of formal organizational analysis and of everyday organizational experience. So, for example, the *Royal Hotel* case (Case 2.2) is written more in the style of narrative fiction (which Alvarez and Merchan (1992) see as characteristic of the use of cases in business education) than in that of 'scientific' reportage; *Performance, pay and privatization in the Civil Service* (Case 4.4) includes extensive verbatim reports from organizational members; whereas *The rise and fall of Hamlet Insurance Company* (Case 3.1) and *Working in space: Skylab* (Case 6.1) have been organized along more conventional lines. Is there indeed a best way to write a case? The conventions which have been established by the dominant US school of case writers can hardly be regarded as the last word on the subject. Indeed the editor was tempted to include an 'anti-case' in the collection, which systematically subverts such conventions and, by so doing, makes them visible and open to critical scrutiny – but that must wait for another time.

As an accompaniment to the *Casebook*, a *Tutor Handbook* is available from the publishers to bona fide teachers of organizational behaviour. The *Handbook* consists of supporting materials written by the case authors and typically includes for each case: notes providing additional contextual material on the cases; suggested 'answers' to the case questions; and additional references which may be recommended to students or which may help the tutor to appreciate the case materials. Needless to say, the entries in the *Handbook* represent the authors' interpretations of the cases and how they might be understood. These need not, of course, constrain the choices available to tutors on how best to utilize the cases. Like most texts, cases may be read at many levels by different audiences and we hope that those presented here will be.

In general, when teaching organizational behaviour we prefer to use cases less as a way of focusing on the issues of the moment in favour of broad engagement with the perennial problems of organizational life. In principle, any of these cases can serve as a springboard for the illumination of the human project of organization. In that sense the cases themselves do not matter all that much; it is their potential as catalysts for thinking that provides their main justification, a potential that can best be realized by their creative use in the teaching process.

Note

The views expressed in this introduction are those of the editor and should not necessarily be taken to represent those of every contributor.

References

Alvarez, J.L. and Merchan, C. (1992) 'The role of imagination in the development of imagination for action', *International Studies of Management and Organization* 22: 27–45.

Argyris, C. (1980) 'Some limitations of the case method: experiences in a management development program', *Academy of Management Review* 5: 291–8.

Berger, M.A. (1983) 'In defence of the case method: a reply to Argyris', *Academy of Management Review* 8: 329–33.

Bongiorno, L. (1993) 'A case study in change at Harvard', *Business Week,* November 15, p. 33.

Bromley, B.D. (1986) *The Case Study Method in Psychology and Related Disciplines,* Chichester: John Wiley.

Easton, G. (1992) *Learning from Case Studies,* 2nd edn, Hemel Hempstead: Prentice Hall.

Eisenhardt, K.M. (1989) 'Building theories from case study research', *Academy of Management Review* 14: 532–50.

Erskine, J.A., Leenders, M.R. and Maufett-Leenders, L.R. (1981) *Teaching with Cases,* London, Ontario: University of Western Ontario, School of Business Administration.

Gragg, C.I. (1954) 'Because wisdom can't be told', in M.P. McNair (ed.) *The Case Method at the Harvard Business School,* New York: McGraw-Hill.

Hakim, C. (1987) *Research Design: Strategies and Choices in the Design of Social Research,* London: Unwin Hyman.

Hogan, E. (1993) 'Using a model for case analysis in case method instruction', in C.M. Vance (ed.) *Mastering Management Education: Innovations in Teaching Effectiveness,* Newbury Park, CA: Sage, pp. 59–69.

Kotter, J.P. (1982) *The General Managers,* New York: Collier Macmillan.

Lundberg, C.C. (1993) 'Case method', in C.M. Vance (ed.) *Mastering Management Education: Innovations in Teaching Effectiveness,* Newbury Park, CA: Sage, pp. 45–52.

Mintzberg, H. (1989) *Mintzberg on Management,* New York: Free Press.

Morgan, G. (1986) *Images of Organization,* Beverly Hills: Sage.

Reynolds, J.I. (1980) *Case Method in Management Development,* Geneva, ILO.

Romm, T. and Mahler, S. (1991) 'The case study challenge – a new approach to an old method', *Management Education and Development* 22: 292–301.

Schumacher, E.F. (1978) *A Guide for the Perplexed,* London: Abacus.

Smircich, L. (1983) 'Organizations as shared meanings', in L.R. Pondy, P.J. Frost, G. Morgan and T.C. Dandridge (eds) *Organizational Symbolism,* Greenwich, CN: Jai Press, pp. 55–65.

Smith, G. (1987) 'The use and effectiveness of the case study method in management education – a critical review', *Management Education and Development* 18: 51–61.

Spinelli, E. (1989) *The Interpreted World: An Introduction to Phenomenological Psychology*, London: Sage.

Stonham, P. (1995) 'For and against the case method', *European Management Journal* 13: 230–2.

Thomas, A.B. (1993) *Controversies in Management*, London: Routledge.

Tsoukas, H. (1994) 'Introduction: from social engineering to reflective action in organizational behaviour', in *New Thinking in Organizational Behaviour*, Oxford: Butterworth-Heinemann.

Turner, R.H. (1991) 'The many faces of American sociology: a discipline in search of an identity', in D. Easton and C.S. Schelling (eds) *Divided Knowledge*, Newbury Park, CA: Sage, pp. 59–85.

Vance, C.M. (1993) *Mastering Management Education: Innovations in Teaching Effectiveness*, Newbury Park, CA: Sage.

Weick, K.E. (1995) *Sensemaking in Organizations*, Thousand Oaks, CA: Sage.

Yin, R.K. (1989) *Case Study Research*, Newbury Park, CA: Sage.

Part one

Manufacturing organizations

Case 1.1

Responding to reorganization at Northern Bakery

This case is set in a large bakery which is part of one of the major national bakery groups. In response to changes in market structure and intensified competition, the bakery's management has instituted a reorganization of the bakery's sales structure in order to improve efficiency and the standard of customer service. The bakery group's internal consultancy organization is conducting an investigation to assess the effects of the changes. Its preliminary conclusions are equivocal about the success of the reorganization.

The case focuses in particular on the effects of the changes in the bakery organization's structure on the motivation and behaviour of three staff groups: the district sales managers, the supervisors and the salesforce. What effects would the changes have on the performance of the bakery sales function? Readers are invited to examine these issues in the light of current theories of motivation. Issues of organizational structure, environmental change, employee rewards, training and development, management control, supervisory behaviour, group relations and change management can also be explored during the case analysis.

Case 1.2

Growth in NuPlast, a small family firm

This case traces the growth and development of a small family-owned firm engaged in the wholesale distribution and manufacture of a variety of consumer products from its establishment in the 1930s up until the early 1990s. A detailed account is provided of the circumstances facing the firm at the various stages of its development, the perceptions and decisions of its chief executive, the organizational and managerial changes that were instituted in response to changes in the firm's internal and external environments, and the problems currently faced by the firm.

The case focuses on issues of leadership and management style in the context of family control as well as theoretical approaches to the understanding of organizational growth, evolution and change. Management succession in the family firm, strategy and structure, the significance of organizational leadership, and management control problems are also raised by this case.

Case 1.3

Managing change at Fumac Ltd

Fumac Ltd is a medium-sized manufacturing organization in the engineering industry. In response to the burgeoning 'quality movement' of the 1980s, Fumac introduced a number of quality initiatives, such as materials requirement planning (MRPII) and total quality management (TQM), to what until then had been a rather traditional, hierarchical organization. A firm of external consultants has been appointed to review the success of the change initiatives.

The case examines the organization's attempts to implement TQM and an associated 'rightsizing' programme and, in particular, its effects on one department, the technical department. The varied and often conflicting views of the managers and technical staff are reported in their own words.

Readers are asked to consider the impact of the change programmes, their mode of implementation, and their relation to more traditional approaches to work organization. The case also raises questions about corporate and organizational cultures and subcultures, the construction of meaning in organizational settings, communication and organizational conflict.

Case 1.1

Responding to reorganization at Northern Bakery

ALLAN WARMINGTON

The baking industry

The changes in the bread-baking industry in Britain over the last half century illustrate some of the developments and dilemmas of modern capitalist industry.

Prior to the Second World War even the largest cities were served mainly by localized, family-owned bakeries each serving a market of just a few miles radius. Successful bakers expanded by opening branch shops over a widening area and occasionally by taking over businesses of competitors or by appointing local agents beyond their normal delivery range. Even the largest firms rarely operated in more than one city or town.

On the other hand, the flour-milling industry was becoming ever more concentrated. By progressive financial involvement (loans and minority share-holdings) in the larger independent bakeries, the major milling groups enabled the bigger bakery firms to invest in expansion and modernization and at the same time they secured for themselves guaranteed outlets for their flour. Inevitably this led on to acquisitions and to a growing concentration of ownership in the bread-baking industry. Independent bakery firms began to give way to nation-ally organized multi-plant groups. By the mid-1960s the baking industry had become dominated by five groups, four of them having flour importing and milling, as well as baking, interests. Many plants had been taken over from former independents, but rationalization proceeded: new plants were built and others closed.

During the last 25 years or so, concentration has become even more marked. Three of the five groups have either dropped out from the bread-baking industry or been acquired by the other two. Bread baking is now dominated by just two groups, Allied Bakeries – a subsidiary of Allied British Foods – and British Bakeries – part of the RHM Group, now acquired by Tomkins plc. By the mid-1980s these two firms were producing 54 per cent of all the bread sold in Britain and perhaps 75 per cent of all the wrapped white bread. A few larger indepen-dent (or semi-independent) plant bakeries remain, notably Greggs nationwide and Warburtons of Bolton in the North and Midlands, and the independents have recently been increasing their market share, so that by 1993 the share of the two major groups had slipped to about 47 per cent.

Social and economic conditions have affected the markets for bread marked-ly and progressively since the Second World War. Bread's importance in the typical diet has been falling continuously. Tastes have been changing. Bread ceased to be a staple and, in the first phase, tended to become a convenience food – a quick filler. More recently, minority discrimination has been noticeable: a return to specialized products ('morning goods'), to small specialized bread bakers, to home baking and to 'in-shop bakeries' in supermarkets and department stores. This segment of the market tends to be relatively price insensitive. Still for the majority, bread remains the stand-by convenience filler. It is bought in the cheapest and most convenient form available (usually the standard wrapped white loaf) and competition is very much on the basis of price.

Over this period too, there has been a revolution in the kinds of outlet from which bread is bought. Up to the mid-1960s most bread was bought either at the door from retail sales staff employed by the bakery firms, or in wholly-owned bakers and confectioners shops, or in the small corner shops to be found in every neighbourhood. The supermarket revolution, and more recently the growth of 'superstores' and discount stores, have changed the whole scene. Perhaps 75 per cent of all wrapped bread is now sold in either nationally-owned multiples (supermarkets, multiple grocers or other high-street stores such as Marks & Spencer) or in cooperative stores. The fact that these stores are nationally organized enables them to negotiate very favourable discounts with the bakers. Further, with bread having a very short shelf-life, the turnover by volume is very high. Customers buy bread, if not daily then at least weekly, and bread has the function of attracting potential customers for other grocery products into the store, which thus takes advantage of 'one-stop' shopping. Superstore and supermarket margins can therefore be kept very low and the price differential between the supermarket and the corner shop is continually increasing. Thus, although bread only constitutes about 10 per cent by value of the grocery market (with morning goods and cakes forming another 5 per cent), nevertheless it has very important characteristics for the multiples. The corner shop still remains an important outlet, particularly in rural areas and small towns, but the wholly-owned bakers and confectioners shops are fast disappearing from the high streets.

Technical changes in the processes of bread baking have been occurring over the whole period in review. Developments have occurred at every stage in bread production. Plant bakeries have become increasingly capital intensive. Bread baking today is a continuous-process industry, from the feeding of flour into the mixing process, right through to the slicing and wrapping of the finished product. Automatic mixing techniques that avoid the need for fermentation, automatic dividing and weighing of the dough, automatic proving, panning, baking, depanning, conditioning, slicing and wrapping all proceed according to set programmes with minimal manual involvement. The capital costs of processing are becoming very high and to take advantage of potential efficiency plants have to be run to full capacity. So, whereas 40 years ago the typical bakery produced for perhaps 50 or 60 hours per week, and 25 years ago for 90 or 100 hours, with most lines probably only running part time, now the aim of bakery management is to achieve 100 per cent capacity utilization: that is to run every line continuously for perhaps 160 hours a week with only the minimal down time necessary for routine maintenance. As a consequence, the present tendency is to have fewer and fewer bakeries, each with higher and higher output, producing for a wider and wider area of the country. In this way unit costs of production are kept to the minimum.

Nevertheless, the baking industry, which has always worked on low margins of profitability, is now barely profitable. The two largest bakery groups both see themselves fighting for survival. The bakery divisions of both groups regularly make large losses and tend to be run as loss-making outlets for the very profitable flour-milling activities of the same groups. The independents manage to be profitable because of greater productive efficiency and greater specialization, for instance in premium bread types. Some retain their own chains of wholly-owned bakery shops.

Selling bread

In the days of wholly-owned high-street outlets and of corner shops, a bakery relied for success in the marketplace on the operation of its sales department. The sales manager (and any area managers he needed) might be assisted by a number of district or assistant sales managers, each in charge of perhaps a dozen or fifteen bakery rounds. Under them, sales supervisors were each responsible for four or five rounds. The rounds themselves were served by van salesmen, a highly motivated class of people on whose enthusiasm and selling capacity the success of the business largely depended. Salesmen were carefully selected, given continuous training, and served a probationary period with their supervisors or with other salesmen, during which they got to know the job, the characteristics of the rounds and the culture of the firm.

Having become a fully-fledged salesman with a round of his own, he was expected to monitor the area through which he drove for new opportunities, to watch the activities of competitors in that district, to maintain the best possible relationship with customers and to help, where possible, to increase sales of the company's product, and to make a success of the periodic 'promotion' of one brand or another that management decided on. Training was directed towards high motivation and high skill. The salesman was encouraged by appropriate monetary incentives, and an important part of the role of the district sales manager was to monitor, encourage and assist their salesmen in all aspects of their job. Each supervisor was expected to know the rounds and the customers of all the salesmen in his patch, and supervisors usually took over the rounds of salesmen on holiday. Both supervisors and district managers would visit important customers, look after customer complaints and follow up new opportunities of which they had become aware.

Selling is not entirely a matter of getting as much bread as possible into each outlet. Bread is perishable: quality, including freshness, is important and waste is very expensive. Control, therefore, of returns (including unsold bread taken out of the shop the following day) and of waste is very important. Salesmen could be debited personally for damaged bread or bread they had ordered but not sold. Returns were strictly accounted for and controlled.

The salesmen's jobs, therefore, were difficult. They had to judge what each outlet could take and persuade the manager or proprietor of the shop to accept the quantity, while being careful not to oversell. They had to bear in mind the dozens of varieties they were carrying and try to place as wide a variety as possible, while remembering the lines the manager was currently 'pushing'. They had to take and record orders for the following day, aggregate them and put the appropriate order into the bakery on their return. They were entirely responsible each morning for what was on their round and were supposed to check what had been loaded onto it against the manifest given to them, and also against their own order. These last two were invariably different, and they had to vary the placing in each outlet in order to try and dispose of the load they were actually carrying without creating customer dissatisfaction.

The salesman was constantly subject to assessment, target-setting, chivvying and general encouragement from the manager; but the monetary rewards were satisfactory and the average salesman was convinced that it was the bakery relied for its success on the men, not the managers. Much satisfaction was gained from that perception. If the firm was doing badly it was certainly not the salesmen's fault!

With the growing involvement of supermarkets in baking and selling bread, conditions facing the traditional bakeries underwent substantial change. By the early-1980s, the Northern Bakery's managers were seriously considering the need for a radical reorganization of its selling operation.

The Northern Bakery reorganization

The Northern Bakery belongs to one of the major national groups. It is situated on the edge of one of the metropolitan counties, on the site of what was originally a family-owned business. The plant has been rapidly expanded in the last few years and its sales area now covers about 3,000 square miles of highly populated, industrialized country and very sparsely populated northern hill country. The area stretches almost 100 miles north and perhaps 20 miles south from the bakery itself. Within this area the bakery sells to about 1,700 outlets, seventy of which are major stores. Nearly 60 per cent of its output goes to these seventy major stores, most of which are located within 30 miles of the bakery. Most of the sales to stores are sold under the bakery's own brand names but with a growing proportion of 'own-brand' goods going to certain stores, such as Sainsbury's and Marks & Spencer. There are about 150 rounds altogether and the way these have up until recently been organized into an authority structure is shown in Figure 1.

Because of declining profitability and a perception that the bakery may be losing a little ground, both to its national rival and to one or two local independents, the local management, with the cooperation and approval of regional office, have looked at the whole sales situation. Their thinking is as follows.

The relationship between individual salesmen and the bread manager of, say, an Asda superstore is very different from the traditional relationship with the manager or proprietor of a small shop. The right to enter and place bread in the shop has been negotiated not by the salesman with the manager, but by negotiators in London representing the two national organizations. The salesman will be placing bread onto a display stand wholly under the control of a professional shop manager, who is probably also selling competitors' bread and bread from an in-store bakery. Whereas the traditional corner shop might take half a dozen

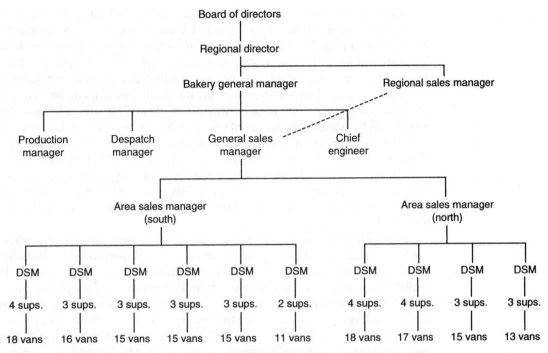

Figure 1 Northern bakery sales organization, 1982 (DSM = district sales manager)

trays of products each day, a superstore may take a whole van load or even two van loads in the course of a single day – the revolutionary 'one-drop vehicle operation'. In order to succeed in the large stores much attention must be paid to things like 'merchandising' – i.e. the attractiveness and high quality of the display, and continuous availability of the bakery's own products. In those stores which concentrate on 'own-brand' goods, the reputation of the bakery and renewal of contracts depends on assuring both the highest quality and on delivery of the demanded quantities at exactly the right time. The bakery cannot tolerate the possibility of errors when selling to Sainsbury's or Marks & Spencer. The high professionalism of major store managers must be equalled by profession-alism in sales, or sales could be drastically affected and enormous wastage could result, given the short shelf-life of wrapped bread.

Over the last few years, stress among district managers and strained relations between managers and salesmen has become evident. The district managers have become more and more involved in relationships with store managers. Both the district managers and the salesmen have complained about the managers' lack of availability to give the salesmen advice and support. Wastage has indeed been rising, controls seem to have slipped and at the same time the motivation of the salesmen seems to have decreased.

To remedy this a new sales structure is now being put into operation with the purpose of reconciling the needs of efficient distribution with high standards of customer service.

It was felt that these two aspects of the sales department function – efficiency and customer satisfaction – were quite distinct and should be kept separate in the organization of the department. The two area sales managers were to be replaced by a sales manager–distribution and a sales manager–field. The latter was to be responsible for all activities at the point of sale including activities inside the larger stores – merchandising and quality of display, contact with customers, and recognition of opportunities for expanding sales. The field staff was also to be responsible for maintaining correct stock levels in the store and for the product mix and the range which was on offer. Under the sales manager (field) were to be a number of district sales managers (DSM) who specialized in particular parts of the market. For instance, one might be in charge of a number of cooperative stores, another of the stores owned by a particular multiple, a third of a number of independents in a given area, a fourth of 'own brand' sales, and so on.

The responsibility of the sales manager (distribution) was, on the whole, control of efficiency. He was responsible for sales staff performance (including target setting for individual rounds); monitoring salesmen's activities; the availability of products in liaison with the production and despatch departments of the bakery; the administration and processing of orders; the control of returns, of vans, of trays and baskets; the administration of the salesforce and giving a general backup service. Under the SMD were to be a number of district sales managers each of whom had responsibility for between thirty and forty van sales-men and their supervisors covering a defined geographical area. These district sales managers would normally remain full time at the bakery, and any necessary liaison at the point of sale would be between the appropriate district SMF and the van salesman concerned. Nevertheless the direct line responsibility of the van salesmen was to the DSM (Control) and not to the field staff.

The new organization is summarized in Figure 2. It is important to note that, apart from the SMD and the SMF, there were very few changes of personnel in the department. All the district sales managers under the old arrangement were district sales managers under the new.

As has been mentioned, regional and national headquarters of the bakery group were interested in these changes and anxious to assess their effects as soon as possible, with the possibility in mind of extending the experiment to other bakeries facing the same problems. About three weeks after introduction, the group's internal consultation organization was asked urgently to make an assessment of the changes. After visiting the bakery they reported that it was too early to assess any trends in sales or efficiency, but all the managers concerned had expressed high satisfaction with the new structure. All the supervisors and van salesmen, however, were noncommittal, saying that so far they had seen no change in their own roles and had no reason to expect any change.

Questions for discussion

Being required to make their own assessment of the likely effects in the medium term, the consultants concluded that the control side of the structure, though

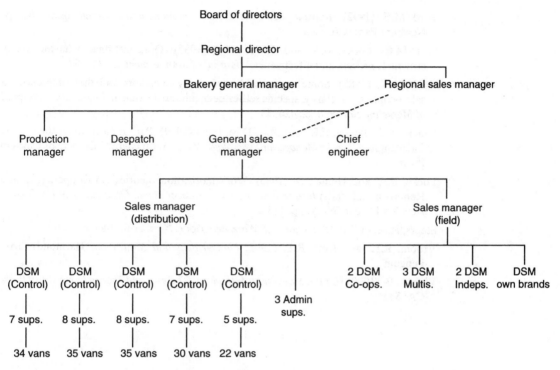

Figure 2 Northern Bakery revised sales organization, 1983

likely to have some minor problems, seemed likely to result in improved efficiencies. On the field side, they had more difficulty in coming to a conclusion and they addressed themselves to the following questions:

1 How important had high motivation among: (a) district sales managers; (b) supervisors; and (c) salesmen been to the success of the bakery in the past?
2 What were the sources of motivation in each case? How did they relate to the theories of motivation current in management literature?
3 Did the changes in structure alter the sources of motivation in any way? If so, how?
4 What would be the likely effects on the performance of the bakery sales function?

What would be your own assessment of these issues? Could any other change have produced better potential results?

Further reading

Cordery, J. and Wall, T. (1985) 'Work design and supervisory practice: a model', *Human Relations* 38: 425–40.

Ditton, J. (1977) 'Alibis and aliases: the motives of fiddling bread salesmen', *Sociology* 11: 233–55.

Ford, M.E. (1992) *Motivating Humans: Goals, Emotions and Personal Agency Beliefs*, Newbury Park, CA: Sage.

Gist, M.E., Locke, E.A. and Taylor, M.S. (1987) 'Organizational behavior: group structure, process and effectiveness', *Journal of Management* 13: 237–57.

Kohlt, A.K. (1985) 'Some unexplored supervisory behaviors and their influence on salespeople's role clarity, specific self-esteem, job satisfaction and motivation', *Journal of Marketing Research* 22: 424–33.

Leavitt, H.J., Pondy, L.R. and Boje, D.M. (eds) (1989) 'Part 1: motivation: the driving force', in *Readings in Managerial Psychology*, 4th edn, Chicago: University of Chicago Press.

Locke, E.A. and Henne, D. (1986) 'Work motivation theories', in Cooper, C.L. and Robertson, I.T. (eds) *International Review of Industrial and Organizational Psychology*, New York: John Wiley, pp. 1–35.

Steers, R.M. (1991) *Motivation and Work Behaviour*, New York: McGraw-Hill.

Vroom, R.H. and Deci, R.L. (1992) *Management and Motivation*, Harmondsworth: Penguin.

Weiner, B. (1992) *Human Motivation: Metaphors, Theories and Research*, Newbury Park, CA: Sage.

Case 1.2

Growth in NuPlast, a small family firm

NEIL CARRUTHERS

Background: pre-incorporation

The founder of NuPlast, John Wallwork, left school and went straight into his father's firm. This was an unlimited company that had been set up in 1938 as a manufacturer's agent, selling toys, fancy goods, glassware, pottery and hardware to the wholesale trade on a commission basis.

In 1960 his father died. Wallwork and his older brother attempted to run the business as co-directors, but their relationship soured and in late 1960 they split the business. John elected to take the portion of the business that covered toys, fancy goods and housewares; his brother took the rest.

Incorporation and early development

In the early part of 1961 NuPlast was incorporated as an unlimited company, and Wallwork established his base of operations in cheap, rented accommodation. When the rift had occurred with his brother, three of the existing staff went with John – two clerks and one accountant. Wallwork was a man of many parts at this stage: as the only sales executive he negotiated with suppliers and simultaneously took all of the operational decisions, including finance, often overruling decisions taken by the accountant.

Although he dominated every aspect of the business, refusing to relinquish control of any facet, his managerial style was imbued with a paternalism that demonstrated an acute sensitivity to the individual needs of his employees. Being strapped for cash, he was unable to offer competitive remuneration packages to his employees, but he shared his successes when they came. This engendered a fierce loyalty and an extremely high level of commitment and team spirit in the company.

Even though the fortunes of the firm were precarious and the corporate direction certainly unknown, this did not prevent Wallwork talking about or devising plans for the expansion of his business 'empire'. He finished the year with a sales turnover that just about covered the costs of running the business.

The next couple of years saw no great change, the critical goal of ensuring the firm's survival remaining uppermost in his mind. His belief in self-financed growth possibly hampered his ability to expand the firm more quickly, but the autonomy and flexibility suited him. This was a great period of learning for Wallwork; he had never had as much freedom, he had never supervised staff, nor had he been forced to truly suffer the consequences (good and bad) of his own actions. As a result, the business plateaued.

However, his previous financial prudence enabled him to take the first major step forward as a company; in 1963, the company purchased a large Victorian house that had been converted into offices. He didn't need all the space, so he rented the ground floor out to another company and used the spare offices upstairs as a warehouse. He recruited a sales executive to work alongside himself (splitting the region for better coverage, rather than attempting to cover a broader geographic area). This move had a steady, positive effect on the sales performance, doubling the turnover by 1966.

The first quantum leap

By the end of 1966, the survival of the firm was no longer in question. A small but loyal customer-base guaranteed that the current sales could easily be achieved. However, expanding beyond this level with the existing products was proving extremely arduous.

In 1967, Wallwork rekindled an old association of his father's. This person had pioneered the importation of plastic flowers into the UK from the Far East almost 15 years previously. Although the venture had failed then and had not been attempted subsequently, Wallwork decided to reactivate the relationship. This was a substantial risk: he had little knowledge of the mechanics of importing goods, of the product, or of the reception it would receive in the UK. Planning ahead, he negotiated sole distribution rights for the UK, getting the manufacturer to agree to import only under the brand name licensed by Wallwork.

This was a substantial coup. The market was now eager for such a product, and the sales demand quickly outstripped both the current supply of the plastic flowers, and the sales of his other products. Taking his cue from the market, Wallwork discarded his reservations and ordered a huge quantity of the flowers across the full range offered. Whilst waiting for the delivery from the Far East, he set about recruiting three more sales employees and a person to oversee the stock records.

By the early part of 1968 the sales had reached £60,000. The whole organization was manic – everyone was overworked, covered numerous unrelated tasks, and couldn't move because of the stock of plastic flowers everywhere. Wallwork was forced to rent a warehouse for the stock; this was in a separate location about 5 miles away from the office – he was unable to use the ground floor because of the lease agreement with the tenants. A supervisor, operative and stock clerk were recruited for the new warehouse.

The change caught Wallwork unawares. He had not anticipated a lower level of motivation or commitment in the new recruits and found it difficult to comprehend their seeming inability to be infected by the contagious enthusiasm of the original employees. His *laissez-faire* attitude to human resource management was beginning to falter. Staff disputes increased and their resolution took up his valuable time, time that he believed could be devoted to more 'constructive' issues, such as developing new customer accounts, collecting money from stubborn payers, and so on.

Wallwork decided to institute some procedures that had to be followed before he would become personally involved in staff-related problems. Although these rudimentary control systems were put in place to free Wallwork from the many minor problems and distractions, he had great difficulty distancing himself from them. He often became embroiled at a late stage, only to overturn the decisions that followed from the application of the formalized systems.

An emerging strategy

Flush with the success of the plastic flowers, Wallwork now had the financial resource base with which to transform his business from a caterpillar into a butterfly. As he later recalled, at this time (1969) his confidence levels were soaring and he couldn't conceive of failure. Other employees who have remained with the firm, and also a couple of long-term business associates, testify to the almost tangible radiance that seemed to exude from Wallwork in those days; here was a man on a roll.

He decided to radically alter his product portfolio. He dropped the toys, household and fancy goods in an attempt to concentrate on plastic. Whilst these products weren't the largest proportion of his income they represented a consistent portion, and dropping them instead of gradually phasing them out was a very bold move, a sign of his confidence. This strategy was effective since it gave him the spare capacity that he needed for his next venture, without increasing his overall costs, i.e. importing plastic plant pots from Hong Kong.

He started early in 1969, bringing a limited number of product lines over in small quantities. By the middle of the year it was apparent that the products were going to be 'hot'. Wasting no time, he commissioned the manufacturing agent in Hong Kong to produce pots to his own design. The initial stab had been a form of market testing, but this last move indicated his level of belief in his own abilities to succeed. He had a innovative product, a virgin market and the will to saturate it.

Sales for the year once again took a massive leap, breaking the £100,000 mark. Wallwork had to recruit three more sales employees for the UK and decided to look for possibilities in Europe. Another four people were recruited to the clerical staff. Wallwork's ability to physically oversee his empire was being radically diminished. Even though he wished to be involved in every operational aspect of the business he was unable to be so. This created tremendous feelings of frustration and a general perception that the business had now taken on a life of its own – it was no longer dependent on him for its daily operations although he was still at the helm since he continued to dictate the broader strategic direction that the firm would take.

The inadequacy of the manual control and maintenance systems became very apparent at this stage; Wallwork could not obtain the information that he felt he needed on the required timescales to make decisions. This problem was not new but it was exacerbated by his feelings of loss of control. He therefore attempted to resolve the issue of an information gap by using the services of a firm of professional accountants. They stipulated that certain informational criteria had to be met before they could fulfil their contract. This was the start of the formalization of the accounting and control systems and the momentum cascaded down into other areas such as stock records, cash accounting and even performance monitoring and remuneration levels.

Radical perceptual shift

In 1970, the demand for NuPlast's product range was significantly outstripping supply. The cash situation was positive but the business was in severe danger of overextending itself in its attempts to satisfy customer requirements. Wallwork had a difficult decision to make: should he remain at the current level until such time as he could accumulate enough profit from the business to plough back into expansion (affording a golden opportunity to potential new entrants: a ready made market that wasn't being satisfied), or should he look to expand by using external funding? The last measure was not coherent with anything that he had been brought up to believe nor with new beliefs that he had formulated as he had matured. He also saw that the threat to his autonomy was very real if a larger, commercial organization (especially a bank) were to become involved in his business.

The solution came in a fortuitous, unplanned meeting with one of his original customers from his 'fancy-goods days'. This person had sold his own business for a handsome profit and retired, but he was looking for somewhere to invest his money. He was more interested in capital accumulation than an income stream since he had been retained as a consultant by his old company. This was ideal for Wallwork; an investor who could inject £25,000 into the business but who didn't want any operational involvement in the firm.

The money was initially invested in more stock – which was immediately sold, thus generating more spare cash. Now Wallwork was able to implement his attack outside the shores of the UK. He sent two of his sales representatives to the major European trade shows. The response to his innovative products was again massive and immediate – orders began flowing through the doors faster than his administrative systems could handle.

The impetus provided by the external cash injection necessitated a radical shift in operational strategy. First, he needed to recruit a sales manager to coordinate the activities of the geographically dispersed sales employees. Second, their reward system had to become more formalized and uniformly equitable. Third, the huge expansion in the UK market meant that it was economically feasible to purchase a van for product deliveries, instead of relying on contract carriers. The above helped the business to assign responsibilities to the relevant personnel. That is, functional and specialist task responsibility was formulated and legitimized. Wallwork participated in these developments but it was the accountability which forced the participation of the relevant employees. For the first time, Wallwork could fully expect his people to know the realms of their responsibilities and take the appropriate action if their performance fell short of that prescribed.

Overall Wallwork admits that the decision to take on external finance was one of the most critical that he ever took; it acted as a catalyst for the long overdue metamorphoses in internal configurations and processes to occur and it was a springboard for the company to expand its operating arena. With the level of operations and internal stability attained, Wallwork decided to restrict his legal liability by forming NuPlast as a separate, limited company in 1972. Sales at this stage had taken a gargantuan leap up to £200,000.

The turning point: a fortuitous disaster

The years of 1973 and 1974 did not see the stupendous growth rate of 1972 continue. Wallwork had geared up for a massive explosion of the plastic products into the European market, but it did not occur. At least the demand for the plastic flowers was not sustained at a level anywhere near that which would have been predicted by the initially overwhelmingly enthusiastic response. Whilst the plastic plant pots did allow NuPlast to make headway in the European markets, the rate of growth for these did not parallel that of the UK. This left NuPlast with a huge stock holding of plastic flowers that couldn't easily be put into any of their existing or target markets – a policy for high-stock 'buffer' levels had been devised as a result of the previous stock out.

The difficulties and associated costs of accessing the US and Third World markets were perceived to outweigh the benefits, especially on such a low-margin, high-volume product. If the flowers were 'dumped' onto the domestic market there would probably be an adverse reaction from customers – demands for price reductions, etc. Wallwork decided to warehouse the plastic flowers, drip feeding the domestic market to satisfy demand. By not replacing the items sold he could minimize his overall loss (sunk cost of obsolescence). It was becoming apparent that demand in the UK for this product was also starting to plateau.

His European initiative would focus purely on plastic plant pots. This required the establishment of agency relationships in foreign territories, a new ball game for NuPlast. In the UK Wallwork was at least able to interview and screen applicants for jobs. The lack of geographic proximity and hence inability to exercise personal control over a European agent's activities should have pointed to more stringent screening techniques being used. This did not occur. Instead, the people who met and expressed an interest in the product to NuPlast's sales representatives at the European trade shows were conferred with exclusive territorial rights to their country. The tacit strategy seemed to be that if the relationship did not yield adequate returns, as defined by Wallwork (who, more often than not, had no knowledge of the market being entered), the agreement would be terminated and passed to another agent. Unsurprisingly, this haphazard approach proved to be unsuccessful.

Midway through 1975, it was apparent that turnover was going to be well below that of the previous year. This would be the first time that this situation had occurred. Wallwork didn't relish the prospect. It represented a real set-back both in financial terms and with regard to delaying the achievement of his personal objectives. A strategy analyst may have felt that the latter were still rather enigmatic, but even though Wallwork could not definitively verbalize his intentions he 'knew' where he wanted to be and could put rough timescales on this. The set-back meant that his whole plan was out of phase with reality; this was probably the first taste of real 'disaster in the wings'.

In September 1975 there was a fire in the warehouse and since most of the stock consisted of plastic-based materials, exposure to heat was ruinous. Seventy-five per cent of the existing stock was lost. This event was so catastrophic that it could have resulted in the death of the business. However, his prudent approach to ploughing back profits into the business over the years, customer loyalty, and a bridging loan from a commercial bank ensured that NuPlast was in a cash-positive situation; this would allow the firm to survive in the short term at least.

Whilst those around him saw only doom and gloom, Wallwork was already hard at work, devising operational strategies to ensure that he could quickly replace the most effective selling products. A shipment of pots was on its way to England before the disaster but hadn't arrived, so the problem was one of satisfying orders that were 'real-time', i.e. the customers that were expecting immediate delivery of their orders. Further orders to Hong Kong manufacturers would not solve this problem.

Wallwork had always thought that he would ultimately go into manufacturing the product himself at some stage in the future, and he pondered on the 'ifs and buts' of having delayed that decision – it would have been easy to deal with his current dilemma if they had had their own facilities. Meanwhile, he needed to source his product in the UK. This was not easy. Most of the injection moulders were very small operators with old machines and poor quality standards compared to Hong Kong. Jack, Wallwork's son, was brought into the business to identify new suppliers in the UK. After a number of teething problems, NuPlast was able to cover the current orders on a rolling basis; the costs were lower (no transportation) and thus the margins higher. The year that could have seen the end of the firm ended on a high note for the insurance company agreed to a quick settlement of the claim for the warehouse losses. The obsolete stock of plastic flowers had effectively been sold and NuPlast could concentrate once again on the more lucrative products.

Organizational learning

The business's concentration on plastic plant pots in both the UK and Europe allowed the growth rate to continue at a positive, steady pace, reaching £300,000 by the end of 1976. Towards the end of that year the manufacturers of the plastic flowers introduced a range of silk flowers. Wallwork once again negotiated the sole distribution rights for the product (this time extending the geographic coverage to Europe).

Although the market response was very favourable, Wallwork operated a conservative order policy for the first 18 months to ensure that they were not another fad like the plastic version. Even with this dampener in place, their contribution was significant. So, from early 1978 the silk flower range was marketed aggressively. Wallwork initiated some of his own designs and had them manufactured – these were a huge success. The company's turnover went through the half-a-million bracket for the first time, a significant watershed, according to Wallwork, since that level of organizational size in their niche sector was considered to be major. It meant that they were obtaining a much higher profile in the market and customers were approaching them rather than having to be prospected, chased and competed for.

The sales growth needed tighter coordination, especially since the number of European agents had increased tenfold. Jack was made a director with the responsibility for overseeing the sales, warehousing and distribution operations. He created a definite split between these previously entwined functions. Wallwork had perceived the stock and distribution policies to be an integral part of the overall drive for sales efficiency, necessary for ensuring that the customer receives what he or she wants quickly. Jack's action of functionalizing enabled him to identify weak points in the value chain.

His first decision was to appoint an experienced distribution manager, increase the number of company-owned distribution vehicles and set a policy for deliveries – local by company vehicles, long-haul by contractors. Next he instituted regular sales meetings at the office for the UK sales representatives, organized visits to meet European agents and set targets for each person. He also developed a more sophisticated remuneration system that ensured good performance would result in extremely good rewards, not just a premium in their sector, but competitive with most other 'professional' sales positions. Jack's lack of a history of working with the sales staff enabled him to create the necessary 'distance' in relationships to formalize his power. For example, he could take decisions concerning the poor performance of long-serving sales staff without jeopardizing his professional relationship with them, whereas his father had the personal element to consider.

The move to manufacturing

Jack's involvement at a more senior operational level allowed Wallwork to spend more time reviewing the overall direction of the business. The period around 1975 had taught him that incorporating other firms into your own value chain diluted any distinctive competitive advantage that you may have. That is, dependence on external suppliers could compromise the quality of your product and besmirch your reputation, not theirs. Wallwork's need to control as many aspects of his operating domain as possible naturally led him to the next phase of his plan, in-house manufacturing.

This was a gargantuan step in terms of capital commitment, knowledge base and the human resource aspects. The profits from the ever-increasing sales of pots and silk flowers continued to roll in. NuPlast's presence in most developed European countries was well established. Jack's time, effort and procedures ensured that the agency relationships were now highly effective and that the firm's products were on display at all the major trade shows. However, this form of growth was too major to be funded internally and Wallwork went back to the commercial bank which had given him the bridging loan in 1975. His accountants were instructed to review any information regarding governmental financial assistance to businesses.

In mid-1980, a large, modern factory was purchased. It's location was chosen for its geographic proximity to the extensive motorway network, the widespread availability of relatively unskilled blue-collar workers and the financial assistance afforded by both the central government agencies (it was located in a regional development area and attracted a grant for new businesses) and the local government (reduced rates, assistance with finding and training employees). For most of the next three months Wallwork was involved in sourcing raw material suppliers, acquiring and overseeing the installation of three second-hand injection moulding machines, recruiting a maintenance engineer and ensuring that enough people were recruited to staff the production shift. Wallwork's need to move the process along quickly meant that he took a very hands-on role in the whole 'project', devoting the majority of his working day to it and catching up on the news and existing events in the evening with his son.

The configurations of NuPlast were irreversibly changed following this decision. The total number of employees stood at around forty-five, but this would reduce in the short term because most of the current employees were loathe to travel to the new location, even though a free bus was laid on. The journey was about 12 miles and many were offered slight increases in pay for the inconvenience. Staff turnover was to prove a consistent feature in the future of the firm and, for no other reason than that she was the first to recruit any substantial numbers, the finance director was allocated the responsibility for all corporate recruitment from then on.

The size of the workforce meant that Wallwork and Jack gained minimal exposure to the production staff. The maintenance engineer was acting supervisor and liaised with both Wallwork and Jack (whose only knowledge of production was second-hand and whose views were often highly impractical). This situation proved intolerable for Jack, who didn't want to get bogged down with production problems, but it was the only way for him to coordinate the sales and warehousing functions. A general manager was recruited to oversee the warehouse and factory, but his chief role was to liaise with the directors, informing them only of major operational difficulties that would have ramifications for the wider business.

New horizons: product and market diversification

Just before NuPlast had acquired their new factory, sales stood at around £750,000. Once in the factory, their increased capability to quickly manufacture a broad range of quality products (plant pots) to satisfy the forces of customer demand resulted in the sales rising above the £1 million mark (1982).

Wallwork now felt that he could increase his market penetration by expanding his product portfolio. The substantial resource base gave him the security to increase the risks taken with regard to product changes without jeopardizing the business. He no longer looked to merely innovate incrementally within his product range, but aimed to radically widen the product offering of NuPlast, a move away from their focused, specialist niche into a more general, sectoral-based orientation. The ability to quickly and cheaply manufacture and test models which Wallwork designed, substantially bolstered his new initiative. He bought three new plastic injection moulding machines in anticipation of success.

By the end of 1983, NuPlast had developed and launched a full range of plastic garden furniture and fencing which enabled them to penetrate the multiples, national chains of DIYs, and hypermarkets. At the same time, the massive proliferation in their plant pot and silk flower ranges had allowed almost total penetration in the nationally branded stores such as Marks & Spencer, Asda, Tesco, and Woolworths. They were entering a completely different competitive arena, supplying retailers direct.

The impact on the firm's operational configurations and turnover was immense. The company experienced the fastest and largest increases in growth in its history. Sales by mid-1985 were just under £3.4 million, the workforce had increased to around seventy (covering two shifts), new warehousing facilities had to be rented to accommodate the expanded range of stock and raw materials and the distribution fleet stood at eight vehicles.

Up until now, Wallwork had been able to liaise with the various departmental managers or supervisors about every aspect of his business. Even though much of his time had been devoted to more strategic issues, such as market expansion, product portfolio management, and so on, he had continued to be involved in most of the operational aspects of his business to varying degrees. After falling ill in late 1985, Wallwork was told that he needed a heart-bypass operation. For the next four months, while he waited for the operation, his involvement in the business was extremely limited. So that he could continue to oversee his firm, he instituted a number of regular, standardized reports for each of the managers to complete.

Internal power shifts

Wallwork's anticipated prolonged period of absence forced him to relinquish control of the business to his son. In mid-1986, Jack was made managing director while Wallwork remained chairman. Jack's broader responsibility meant that he couldn't totally devote himself to any one function. So, for the first time in its history, NuPlast recruited someone straight into a directorship, a sales and marketing director. They also recruited an experienced production director who would coordinate the manufacturing, warehousing and distribution functions.

The senior management team was now more balanced than it had ever been. Jack was finding his feet in the broader context of the company and therefore had to rely on the advice of the other directors. Rather than proffer opinions which were accepted or rejected, as was the case with Wallwork, the team discussed ways of jointly overcoming difficulties in the firm. Thus the directors were more concerned with the overall performance of the company than with their functional responsibilities. Jack recognized this and restructured the directors remuneration packages, incorporating a percentage of overall profit generated into their performance reward. This further engendered a spirit of cooperation and helpfulness between the functions. Jack became the communication link with his father.

The increased communication and cooperation, coupled with the impact of the new blood, served to significantly increase the sales once again. At the beginning of 1987, just before Wallwork returned to the business on a part-time basis, turnover stood at £4 million, but the sales director's contacts in the US, Canada and a number of African and Arab countries were going to forward-order to the tune of around a £250,000. Whilst the production director was already increasing the output of his domain – he had increased the number of shifts to three, recruited more operatives for production, and increased the level of mechanization in the handling systems in the warehouse – there needed to be a further increase in machine capacity. Three more plastic injection moulding machines were purchased along with a display van. The latter could be taken to shows and be used as a walk-in showroom; this meant that the presentation of the products was improved immensely.

When Wallwork returned the team of directors was working well together. Their established communication links and understanding of their functional responsibilities (stemming from their particular skills acquired both in and before NuPlast) facilitated internal efficiency which was reflected in a highly responsive service to the customers. The company had recruited an additional eighteen staff (machine operatives, warehousing staff and a couple of new sales staff) and was marketing its products in a number of new, very lucrative territories.

Wallwork's presence seemed to intimidate the sales and marketing director and this affected the frequency and fluidity of the directors' meetings, which were often unscheduled, impromptu affairs to resolve specific issues. The coherence of the team began to dissipate. Information exchange, certainly when Wallwork was present, deteriorated. Wallwork recognized that his role in the business had changed to one of advisor to his son, but he felt exposed by the lack of information that he received. His perception of the business was becoming obsolete as the firm developed and this increased his feelings of being 'surplus to requirements'. To combat this, he attempted to enforce the completion of detailed management reports on the standard forms, set fixed meeting times for the directors and the departments, and wanted to authorize any capital expenditure over a certain threshold.

The directors began to spend more of their time fact-finding or report-filling for Wallwork than they did overseeing their own areas. They complained to Jack but wouldn't face up to Wallwork himself. Wallwork, on the other hand, didn't see that his actions were perceived as being detrimental. However, the natural momentum of the business had taken it to a turnover of £5 million by the early part of 1989. Wallwork decided to further diversify the product range, purchasing a broad range of Christmas decorations from a Japanese company for the end of the year. The business was able to gain access for their products in new, lucrative markets in the Far East (Taiwan, Korea and Japan) and the company purchased yet more warehousing space. All this served to delay the inevitable: a true power struggle at the top.

The sales director decided to leave in November 1989. His performance, when viewed objectively, had been good. However, Wallwork's personal opinion of the man was poor. This stemmed from a clash in personalities which produced a communication 'barrier'. The sales director had talked openly with Jack, but was unable to build the same rapport with Wallwork. The latter's style was to evaluate and adjudge a person as they put their argument forward whereas Jack waited until the end of the person's argument before he commented. The sales director's departure brought the power 'clash' out into the open. A replacement couldn't be found immediately and Jack had to step back into the role temporarily. This allowed Wallwork to regain the 'throne', having everyone report to him 'so Jack could focus on the tasks at hand'. The group dynamics of the directors were completely skewed and Jack, after successfully continuing the growth record – with fewer operational disruptions or problems than the company was used to experiencing – felt that this was poor reward for his performance.

The situation was partially resolved in July 1990, when a new sales director was finally recruited. Jack's 'reaccession' to his broader corporate role ended up being a relief for Wallwork, who was suffering from illness once again. His interference (and possibly interest) was reduced to a tolerable level for everyone.

The contemporary situation

NuPlast's turnover currently stands at just under £5.5 million. They have ninety-eight employees, manufacture their product range (which has only changed incrementally since 1990 – adaptation rather than radical mutation) on fourteen injection moulding machines and export to thirty-five countries. Their corporate ethos incorporates 'traditional values ... [a] commitment to quality ... [and] flexibility that ensures customer satisfaction'. Their reputation in the market is extremely good and is closely correlated to their corporate publicity – proving that they are doing what they say they will do.

The company is functionally structured, although there is increasing emphasis on allocating responsibilities according to the product type. The reporting and communication lines are often dichotomized, employees being situated in a department and therefore operationally controlled by the functional head, yet actually communicating their information to a different functional head. It would be inaccurate to say that the structure is rigid and bureaucratic but, at the same time, it is not truly fluid. Rules and procedures are in place that prevent corporate mavericks riding roughshod over the 'accepted' or institutionalized ways of doing things.

Jack has been able to push many of the routine, daily decisions down to the supervisors and managers. However, the onset of the latest recession has put a halt to the further development of this process. He hasn't increased the responsibilities of the managers or supervisors since 1991, and in some instances (following average performance) he has reduced them. He seems to have become more reliant on his father's opinion during this period (possibly falling back on his father's previous experience of similar conditions). This has reduced the corporate spirit amongst the directors somewhat but has increased their own levels of 'group think'.

Overall, external conditions are impinging significantly on decisions taken in the company. Although it is in no immediate financial danger (having established a loyal, wide, customer base), the strategy pursued is short-termist and conservative, one of operational cost-containment and internal efficiency rather than market proactivity, and is almost reminiscent of the early days when resources were restricted. Survival seems to be the underlying, tacit objective and Jack is the person who has become the man who ensures that his beliefs are followed by everyone. Contradicting him or questioning his decisions and rules is regarded as sacrilegious. He is starting to demonstrate the same traits as his father even though, on the face of it they seem to be very different types of people.

Questions for discussion

1 Was NuPlast a hostage of fortune or did Wallwork determine the corporate direction?
2 Do you think the changing situation affected Wallwork's objectives and motivations permanently or temporarily?
3 Contrast the styles of Jack and his father. Would the firm have been what it was if Wallwork had been Jack's son?
4 How could Jack's succession have been managed so as to minimize disruption to the company's activities?
5 Were all the 'problems' encountered over the years avoidable? Were they all detrimental in the long term?
6 What would you have done to ensure that you maximized the benefit to be gained from each difficult situation? What impact do you think your actions would have had on staff morale?

Further reading

Boeker, W. (1989) 'Strategic change: the effects of founding and history', *Academy of Management Journal* 32: 489–515.

Boeker, W. and Goodstein, J. (1991) 'Organizational Performance and Adaptation', *Academy of Management Journal* 34: 805–26.

Cameron, K.S. and Whetton, D.A. (1981) 'Perceptions of organizational effectiveness across organizational life cycles', *Administrative Science Quarterly* 26: 525–44.

Curran, J. and Stanworth, J. (1981) 'The social dynamics of the small manufacturing enterprise', *Journal of Management Studies* 18: 140–55.

Gibb, A. and Scott, M. (1985) 'Strategic awareness, personal commitment and the process of planning in the small business', *Journal of Management Studies* 22: 596–625.

Gibbons, P.T. (1992) 'Impacts of organizational evolution on leadership roles and behaviours', *Human Relations* 45: 1–18.

Hannan, M.T. and Freeman, J. (1984) 'Structural inertia and organizational change', in K.S. Cameron *et al.* (eds) *Readings in Organizational Decline*, MA: Ballinger Publishing.

Hrebiniak, L.G. and Joyce, W.F. (1985) 'Organizational adaptation: strategic choice and environmental determinism', *Administrative Science Quarterly* 30: 336–49.

Kimberly, J.R. (1979) 'Issues in the creation of organizations: initiation, innovation and institutionalization', *Academy of Management Journal* 22: 437–57.

McGivern, C. (1976) 'The dynamics of management succession', *Management Decision* 16: 32–44.

Miller, D. (1982) 'Evolution and revolution: a quantum view of structural change in organizations', *Journal of Management Studies* 19: 131–51.

Quinn, R.E. and Cameron, K.S. (1983) 'Organizational life cycles and shifting criteria of effectiveness: some preliminary evidence', *Management Science* 29: 33–51.

Tushman, M.L., Newman, W.H. and Romanelli, E. (1986) 'Convergence and upheaval: managing the unsteady pace of organizational evolution', in H. Mintzberg and H.B. Quinn (eds) *The Strategy Process,* Englewood Cliffs, NJ: Prentice-Hall.

Case 1.3

Managing change at Fumac Ltd

CHRISTIAN DE COCK

Fumac is a manufacturing organization located in a major industrial conurbation in the UK. It has a turnover of £200 million per year. Up until now (1995), the workforce has only slowly declined (from 3,000 to 2,500 over a 10-year period). Pay conditions have been very good and the workforce has always been very loyal to Fumac. A large proportion of the workforce has 20-plus years of service with the company and most employees live within a 10-mile radius of the plant. The organization, until recently, was used to operating in a very stable environment. Because of the specific nature of its product range, safety is a high priority issue. Safety procedures permeate every aspect of the business.

> *I joined the company 16 years ago. I worked for two large engineering companies before. It was quite different coming here, a completely different culture. It was very stable; most people thought they had a job for life.* (Tony, manufacturing manager)

Fumac had always been profitable up until 1994 (forecasts for 1995 predicted a marginal profit). The 1990–92 British recession did not have a significant impact on Fumac's profitability. However, serious problems loomed on the horizon.

Fumac's main product, accounting for 40 per cent of revenue in 1992, was expected to disappear completely from the market by the year 2000. Having operated in a virtual (national) monopoly situation until the end of the 1980s, Fumac now had to compete in an increasingly competitive international market. Until the late 1980s, 80 per cent of contracts with its customers were cost-plus (i.e. the customers paid Fumac whatever it cost the company to make the product, plus a fixed percentage). Currently 80 per cent of the contracts are subject to competitive tendering and are fixed price.

Traditionally Fumac has been very hierarchical and departmentalized within a traditional organizational structure (see Appendix I). People tended to be very territorial and to put the interest of their department before the good of the company as a whole. Strong demarcations also existed between 'staff' and 'industrials'. Perceptions varied on how much this was still the case in 1994.

In search of quality

The 'quality movement' which swept the Western world in the 1980s did not go unnoticed by Fumac's top management. The 'quality movement' originated from a growing concern by the West in the face of Japan's success in moulding ideas of quality into a coherent operating philosophy. Many companies, urged by gurus like Tom Peters to become 'obsessed with quality' and lured by the promises of consultants, jumped on the bandwagon. JIT (just-in-time), TQM (total quality management), MRP (materials requirement planning) became buzzwords in the management literature and consultant groups had golden times introducing companies to the principles of TQM. In 1988 an MRPII planning system was introduced and in 1990 Fumac finally set off on the TQM 'journey', under a very charismatic managing director.

We were lucky, perhaps, that about the same time we had appointed a director – who since moved on – who was a very charismatic leader. He was instrumental on setting the ball rolling, getting changes going. (Simon, local TQM coordinator)

The TQM programme was designed to bring about a positive change in the organizational culture, transforming it from a very bureaucratic organization into a competitive, 'lean and mean', customer-orientated organization. There had been previous initiatives on site but there was a general consensus that these had not been successful.

Fumac appointed a company-wide TQM manager and the different departments and areas within these departments were given local area TQM-coordinators. Ongoing initiatives like JIT and additional skilling (a multiskilling exercise for shop-floor workers) were integrated under the TQM umbrella. Two-day TQM awareness courses were set up where people were introduced to the principles and techniques of TQM. The courses also focused on culture, attitudes, and teamwork. By the end of 1993 2,000 employees had attended these courses.

One of the first things Fumac did was to get problem-solving teams running. Since 1990, over £8 million has been invested in TQM. A lot of things were happening initially but managers driving the initiative at the time admitted in retrospect that it was a very fragmented approach. People's understanding and interpretation of key concepts like 'right first time', 'continuous improvement', and so on varied widely.

Initially it was very fragmented, the approach. Different departments did different things, we had all sorts of consultants in. Quite a few things were started and then dropped. We were consultant mad for a while (lists about 10 consultancies). Partly because whilst it is easy to decide there is a need for change, to agree on what that change should be or how we should go about it is the difficult part. (Simon, local TQM coordinator)

Communication was acknowledged as a problem in the initial phase, and in July 1992 *TQM in Fumac* was launched, a bi-monthly newsletter that was intended to improve the communication about change initiatives. A monthly briefing session by senior managers was introduced that is still given to all employees in cascading fashion (senior managers brief middle managers and so on).

The rightsizing programme

In Summer 1993 the company introduced a 'rightsizing' programme. Rightsizing was officially introduced to match the people and the work, to get the right people in the right jobs, and was heavily influenced by the management literature on business process re-engineering (BPR emphasizes a total redesign of multi-functional processes that deliver goods or services to the customer). It involved asking fundamental questions about Fumac's activities. The main driver was the pressure to reduce costs: Fumac's two main clients were threatening to take their business elsewhere if Fumac did not radically reduce its prices.

Over the period 1994–96, the targeted cost reduction was 20 per cent. This would have to come mainly from reductions in staff (informally it was admitted that staff would probably have to come down more than 20 per cent), although a lot of confusion existed around 'the numbers'. In all the staff briefings it was emphasized that there was no fixed workforce reduction target. After analysing all the business processes on-site, managers would try to match the number of people with the workflow. At the same time, generous terms of voluntary redundancy were proposed (a newspaper article suggested 3 years' salary). The TQM manager and the local TQM coordinators became partly responsible for implementing the rightsizing exercise. Rightsizing got off to a slow start, however, and at the time of writing of the case very few tangible effects were noticeable.

> *Rightsizing was first heard about a year ago. It was rumoured before it was communicated, before anyone knew what rightsizing was. It was officially communicated at the monthly briefs we have. That was early summer, and it has been communicated ever since. Having said that, in the departments I work in I haven't actually seen it implemented. A lot of people obviously felt threatened by it, but nothing happened and we have been in that state for a year now.* (Alex, research and development (R&D) manager)

Change in the technical department: a tapestry of voices

The following part of the case will explore the issues of TQM, rightsizing, and the Fumac culture as perceived by managers and technologists in the technical department of Fumac.

Four hundred people worked in the technical department at the beginning of 1994. It consisted of four areas (see Appendix I): a product design area (PD, *c.* 30 people); the R&D area (R&D, *c.* 180 people); plant design and support (PDS, *c.* 150 people); and a laboratory doing analysis for manufacturing (lab, *c.* 40 people). In discussing people's perspectives, their first names, grade, and department will be used. Grades broadly fall into four categories: SMG (senior manager/head of department); grade 1 (higher middle management); grade 2 (middle management); grade 3 (lower management/technologists). The perspectives of the change agents – the TQM manager and local TQM coordinators – will also be presented in the tapestry of voices.

Perspectives on TQM

The following comments of the TQM manager provide a good summary of the 'official' company view of TQM:

> *It's been more evolution rather than revolution if I can use that much maligned cliché. I am sure we are like any other organization in that you think that you know what TQM is but it is only when you get further and further into it that you realize how big it is and the way it interacts with the business. TQM was seen as an umbrella initiative 4 years*

ago. The level that we are at now is that we see it as an integral part of the business process, an operating philosophy. We are at a stage where continuous improvement is genuinely recognized as a necessity. It is now also built into our strategic and business plans. TQM has come of age. We understand what it means now. We understand what we need to do to be world class. What we need to do is prioritize and focus tightly on the critical areas which are going to advance us on the world-class ladder.

Many senior managers are now personally doing their briefings, are personally leading training sessions, are walking the talk on the shop floor, try to put over the view 'we are all human beings' kind of thing.

The clues to what we needed to do have been there for a long time. For many reasons we haven't seen them or haven't done anything about it. The world is catching up with us all the time, so for all people in my position there is the frustration that what is obvious to me is not obvious to other people in the organization. We are still struggling at a management level with the significance of investing time in employees. (Richard, TQM manager, grade 1)

Clearly, some operational managers thought TQM had a significant positive impact on the business:

The philosophy and techniques of TQM have helped to overcome the inertia of this massive project [building of a new plant], we had more flexibility. We also tended to become more focused on people giving a better service, talk to other parts of the division. We had personal contracts with R&D where they promised to deliver us the goods by certain dates. And people took pride in working to achieve that. Previously they would have regarded themselves as an ivory tower. We started treating each other at the same level and got a buzz out of it. That applies across the board, people are less obstructive ... . You could label anything as TQM but on the other hand it is a continuing reminder and discipline. It helped to develop the individuals to deliver the goods. There probably would have been initiatives but the overall effect would probably not have been this good. Putting it all under one umbrella without ramming it down people's throats probably did more than what went before. (Michael, manager grade 1, PDS)

If I go back 10 years, when I was doing a similar job to what I am doing now, the attitudes have changed dramatically. The change from last year to this year I have great difficulty commenting on. There is certainly willingness from the industrial people to adapt and change their methods of working. Now we are able to do a job with whoever is available – painter, fitter, plater – and skilled to do that job. (Steve, manager grade 2, R&D)

Other people experienced TQM as a mixed blessing however:

TQM is having a gradual effect. You cannot say 'there's a step change here'. The managers are relying on TQM to make the changes for them. People are encouraged to make an input but the pressure is on them to force the changes through rather than the managers managing. It would be nice if the managers would manage. People are picked to make up their minds for them instead of doing it themselves. I hope this doesn't sound too negative, I'm not that way ... . A lot of people pay lip-service to it but they don't necessarily apply it. You can go through all your TQM theories and come up with ideas but at the end of the day, if it does not satisfy the manager he won't do it. If you want to change something that is going to cost money, you might as well forget it. (Malcolm, senior draughtsman grade 3, PDS)

It is seen as something the managers do. They disappear on courses and away days doing TQM, but in essence we have not progressed very much from that to get TQM on the shop floor. I work a lot with production people and quality assurance people and there is still very much that underlying culture of 'I won't admit when I have made a mistake or it doesn't really matter if I've made a mistake as long as I can get through my shift'. ... We should have had a stronger education programme, tried to get people buying into it at all levels, right down to the shop floor and we should have encouraged people to think about why it was the only future for Fumac; rather than doing it in a piecemeal way with certain people being taken out and given this role [of TQM coordinator]. When you talk to the guys on the shop floor, they just see it as another mechanism of spending money. They don't really see it as beneficial to them. (Eric, manager grade 2, R&D)

You'll notice that wherever you go, wherever there is a TQM coordinator, there has evolved a little empire, someone got a promotion out of it. A lot of people felt the analysts were just doing the daily routine, were not part of this and that it was a completely separate empire. There is certainly the attitude that TQM is the practical alternative to work. A lot of the meetings could just be held for TQMs sake. People who are never invited to them feel they are carrying the new culture, that they are doing the work, send out the products to the gates to make money. I have heard this, whether it was said jokingly ... People belittle TQM but the way they work is within the TQM philosophy anyway. They say: 'why call it TQM? We've always done that'. I've never come across anyone saying: 'we're not doing it because it is TQM'. Teamworking, being responsible for their own quality is seen by people as the normal way to work. There is more resistance to the periphery, having fancy graphs. Why have fancy graphs in glossy magazines? We know what is going on. (Stewart, manager grade 2, lab)

Perspectives on rightsizing

Again, as with TQM, perspectives on rightsizing varied widely, the change agents and senior managers being most enthusiastic about the initiative. Some people were confused or outright suspicious of the initiative.

I viewed rightsizing positively because it actually made us set some positive targets for reducing our cost which we did not have in TQM. That is what this company needs. Had it not been for that, we would still have been fiddling at the edges. A lot of the culture has changed but we are still vastly overmanned and inefficient. We needed that step change to complement the steady curve. It inevitably cuts across a lot of the work in TQM (getting people involved), it does not run counter to it, it just increases the rate of change. I know that people's perception is: 'you are going to use TQM and all the nice soft stuff to do us'. They won't accept the argument that rightsizing is just as much about being more efficient etc. It is just the rate at which we are going to improve that is different. (Colin, local TQM coordinator, grade 2)

I didn't feel particularly threatened. I thought there was a need for rightsizing. If you look around Fumac, there are quite a lot of people doing jobs that are not necessary. When you're working hard and doing something that needs doing (I have been here for 17 years) you get a bit frustrated when you see that others in the organization are not working at 100 per cent. When the organization said 'we are going to do something about this', I personally thought 'great!'. I suppose if you are one of the guys sitting back and taking it easy you will feel threatened. Rightsizing is needed to make the organization something you could work hard in. (Peter, manager grade 1, R&D)

Roy Evans [assistant director, technical] had a meeting with half of the design area. That was a reaction to counter what came down the grapevine. It was quite good, he seemed to be quite forthright about what he said. The meeting for the second half got cancelled and they were quite upset about it. I thought we might see some serious changes with rightsizing, but I don't know ... Are they still rightsizing? (Andy, manager grade 2, PDS)

When rightsizing came in they said 'we are doing rightsizing under TQM'. I know they are not directly opposed but the way it was announced: 20 per cent reduction of cost; and we will do it under a TQM banner: look at processes under TQM, to me that does not quite gel. It is a bit of a facade really. I think they should have held fire on hanging it so deliberately on TQM. It is not about the culture, it is about a specific need. TQM is about getting communication right, we're all together and that sort of thing. (Martin, manager grade 2, lab)

Every time you have a briefing session it's mentioned how many people are going and how many have been considered. That is as far as it goes. Why don't they call it cost-cutting or manpower reduction? Rightsizing is a wolf in sheep's clothing. Nobody sat in here and said 'next month we'll have a team in here looking at what you do, how you do it, how many people you think you need'. There's none of that. We can't see there is a plan to it. And if there is a plan it is just about manpower reduction. ... The people that have left are the guys with the knowledge, they understand all the processes. We are replacing them with contractors who know nothing about Fumac. (Malcolm, grade 3, PDS)

I just hope that by doing this rightsizing under the TQM umbrella we don't get in trouble. We could get a backlash: 'I'm doing three jobs now, there's no way to get promotion, so where does it get me?' People might think it was all a facade to look at jobs and roles to reduce numbers. I see where the perception comes from. I don't think that is the case but perhaps I am looking at it from a biased point of view in as much as my position is currently not threatened. (Tony, manager grade 2, lab)

Rightsizing came down the grapevine. Then there were a few pieces of paper put out. Then there were some meetings. Something as important as rightsizing should have been a lot more upfront. There is virtually no involvement. The idea that someone comes along and says: 'by the way, we have done this study and X jobs are going and yours is one of them' came as a terrible shock to one individual. When I saw him yesterday, one hour after he had been told he was in a state of shock. There was no support for him whatsoever. The person who sent him the bad message just said: 'Well, I think you are whining'. That was a dreadful way of treating a good employee. I would never have done that in here. While I am here no one will be treated like that. (Chris, SMG, lab)

An important issue under rightsizing was that of voluntary redundancies:

One could see the sense, the objective was quite clear. The way of going about it seemed to me as a completely wrong management approach. What it did was put people's backs up. What they actually said was that we should get rid of X number of people which equated to a cost reduction of X per cent. In that exercise there wouldn't be any restrictions on people leaving. How that made us feel was, 'no matter who you are, what you have done, how important your work is, you can leave'. That, to me, really went against the grain. I felt as though they couldn't care less whether you worked for them or not. It did put backs up in that sort of way. (Trevor, manager grade 2, PD)

In our business there has always been a division between management and staff, a them and us. It started to change when TQM came. For a year or two people thought: 'Maybe they are listening'. They are not just paying lip-service, possibly things are changing for the better. Now I get the feeling that senior managers are becoming more insular again. They are becoming more hard-nosed in business terms, possibly because they had to be, and people's perceptions are going back to the thinking that 'again it's them and us'. We are being told things again, it is discussed by them and presented as a fait accompli. *That is mainly due to the rightsizing. It is not really rightsizing but downsizing. We were told one thing and then it turned out to be something else. People feel their intelligence is insulted. You're patted on the head and then suddenly you are being struck.* (Ian, manager grade 3, PD)

Communication and culture in Fumac

This final section of quotes is meant to give an impression of the commitment of senior managers to the change initiatives, the Fumac culture, and communication (particularly in relation to TQM).

To be honest, at senior level there is a very high commitment to change. Senior management level 5 years ago would go through papers looking for mistakes so if you went to a meeting it was like one-up-manship. There was a lot of defensiveness. People used to hide things, put things under the carpet. Now all problems are brought out and it is a much easier life. I can't see any resistance from the senior managers. That comes partly from the realization that we can't carry on the business as it is. The business changes and we change with it. It is generally accepted that it is needed. (Kevin, SMG, PDS)

Senior managers still aren't seen a lot. I know he has been here but I have never seen Roy Evans [assistant director, technical] in this building. He's our ultimate boss. I've spoken to him. (Simon, manager grade 3, PDS)

Communication tends to be through glossy brochures and the monthly briefing session by a senior manager who is not necessarily totally on board who will try to convince people of its merits. By the questions that are asked, it is apparent that the guy who is doing the brief does not always necessarily agree with it himself. (Eric, manager grade 2, R&D)

TQM was wonderfully done [ironic voice]. 'We are going to become a better organization, therefore you will love TQM – whether you like it or not'. There was a video from the chief executive: 'I am determined that we are going to become a better organization; we are going to participate (slams fist on table)'. Not: 'I have the desire', or, 'we would like you to …'. The wording was awful. Whoever sanctioned that video should have been shot. It was a classic example … . It sent us a terrible message. Not, 'we think this is the right way', no vision about it, completely top down, no input, no ownership. It only survived because people are a lot better than we give them credit for. (Chris, SMG, lab)

… there is the outward image you would like to give if someone asks you at a senior level whether you agree with TQM. You are likely to say yes. Because if you say no …, it's a bit like the emperors new clothes, it's incorrect from a career point of view. (Paul, manager grade 2, PDS)

Departments tend to see themselves as not really Fumac: 'OK, we are Fumac but we have a special function'. As soon as a change initiative comes along like rightsizing they say: 'That's OK for the rest of Fumac, but it is not applicable to us because we have this special function'. A lot of departments do that. R&D might say: 'We are an outpost since we do R&D for corporate requirements; we'll listen to it and implement it where we can but we are restricted because we are above it'. A lot of people build a wall around themselves and come up with a lot of reasons why they should be regarded as something different. It has been broken down to some extent, but not enough. (Steve, manager grade 1, R&D)

The general culture in Fumac has been to get to a particular level, work out a niche and build an empire, and then fight to keep that empire. It doesn't matter how much work you have or how efficiently you are using your people; your success is measured by the number of people you have working for you, or the size of your budget, or whatever ... but not the efficiency with which you carry out the work. (Tom, manager grade 2, R&D)

Taking stock

During the autumn of 1994, the Fumac board invited a firm of consultants to review all the change efforts that had been going on over the previous five years. Their aim was twofold: they wanted to use the material in a public relations exercise, portraying Fumac as a 'quality' company to the outside world. They also wished to use the review to make new change efforts even more effective by learning from some of the mistakes that had been made in the past.

Joanna was part of a team of six consultants and her responsibility was to write a report assessing the perspectives of people in the technical department. She interviewed about fifty people over a two-month period and had access to all sorts of archival material. The Fumac board considered the performance indicators (see Appendix II) especially important. Joanna found the reflections of managers (Appendix III) recorded during informal discussions particularly revealing.

In two days time she would have to make a presentation to the members of the board. As promised to the managers and technologists who collaborated in her research, she would also make a presentation to them shortly afterwards. She wrote down a preliminary set of priorities she felt she needed to incorporate in her report, realizing that this list was far from exhaustive. It was going to be a long night ... .

Questions for discussion

1 Give an assessment of the impact of TQM and rightsizing in Fumac. How important are performance indicators?
2 Try to represent the implementation logic and outcomes of the TQM programme in a sequential manner (i.e. how do events unfold over time?). Then try to conceptualize these events (i.e. apply a theoretical framework to make sense of them).
3 How can TQM and rightsizing be related to traditional approaches to work organization such as scientific management and the human relations approach?
4 Assess Fumac's culture and subcultures. Can cultural perspectives have an impact on how change is interpreted?

Appendix I Position of technical department in Fumac's organization

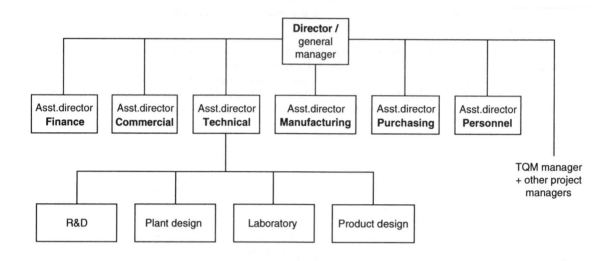

Appendix II Some key performance indicators

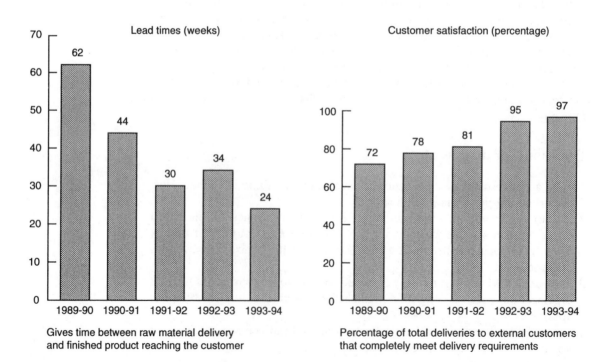

Gives time between raw material delivery and finished product reaching the customer

Percentage of total deliveries to external customers that completely meet delivery requirements

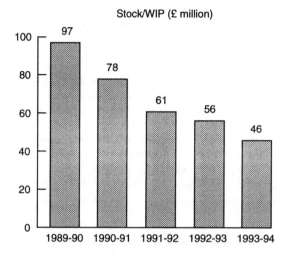

Stock/WIP (£ million)

The total value of stocks and work in progress (WIP):
indicates success in achieving cost reductions

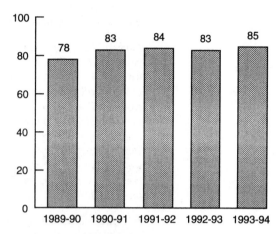

Product quality (right first time: percentage)

Proportion of products that passes first-time inspection
(as measure improves, cost of rework is reduced)

Appendix III General reflections

There are some senior managers who don't fully support it or who think like I think: 'we were already doing that'. There is a resistance, not to the TQM philosophy itself, but the formal way in which it has been introduced. Our management seems to think that if we have 1,000 teams working on 1,000 problems it is stepping forward. That has created a resistance. People have been asked to join teams and are reluctant to do so because they don't feel they are getting anywhere. It takes up a tremendous amount of time to move a small step. I agree with that in some circumstances. That very fact and the fact that there is the perception that there is a lot of fuss about nothing. They formalized it, got people's photographs everywhere; that somehow justifies the time, money, and effort it has taken to do this. I was a sturdy follower of TQM for a long time. I initiated a lot of quality improvement teams and even I now think 'why are we bothering?'. We seem to be driven into doing something. That is where the problem lies. We had a lot of similar initiatives in the past which have tried and failed. TQM has survived the longest but if someone does not change direction or add some impetus to it soon it will fall over as well. It is almost as if we are driven to make changes for the sake of making changes rather than living with the fact that people are going to make changes in their own area in their own time. Systems develop within the organization. I often feel we are trying to mend something that is not broken. That is the root of it. (Alan, manager grade 2, PDS)*

In general I don't think British industry handles it [TQM] well. There is a lot of the ingrained antagonism towards 'management', i.e. anybody above you in the organization. Other countries are perhaps a bit more team spirited ... Our management are doing things without thinking about the repercussions. If there are several avenues to go down, Fumac in general will choose the worst one nine times out of ten. That is because the managers we have got are not necessarily experienced in managing organizations. They tend to be people who have moved on through the organization. We don't have the Sir John Harvey-Jones type who can manage the change. We have got faceless people in grey suits. We had our previous managing director and while he was on-site we went some way but when we lost him it lost some of its impetus. If we had kept him we would have been further now. He was a good champion, who stood up, someone people would trust ... . (Eric, manager grade 2, R&D)

Many of the changes senior management think have taken place have taken place on paper without taking root. An example: we have got this planning system, MRPII and we use it. We haven't got the departments together enough to be able to get the best out of it. We still have got the tribal warfare: planners saying 'you can do it', people on the ground saying 'we can't' and the planners responding 'it's in the computer, you will have to do it that way and if you don't you are going to have misses'. So what happens now is that people work around the system and they cheat. I think the senior managers are still deluded and saying 'we are doing well'. What happened is that people are not working as good as they could do because they are trying to cheat the system. We measure everything we can on site. What we don't know is whether we are measuring the right things. (Chris, SMG, lab)

It is always difficult to determine why a person says that something won't work. Nobody says: 'that won't work because I might lose my empire or I might lose my job, lose some of my status or power'. People will always put forward sound business reasons, and because they are experts in that particular field it is difficult to see whether it is a genuine reason or whether the person is being defensive. By and large there is defensiveness and it has become more apparent since rightsizing has come along where jobs are disappearing and people are terrified that they will become surplus to requirements. Everyone sees that the principle of bringing these functions together is a good one, but when you get down to the detail of 'who is going to do what' clearly jobs will disappear and there has been a lot of defensiveness on all sides ... The objectivity we saw in process re-engineering as an objective methodology is being overtaken by machinations, political manoeuvring if you like. Again whether that is happening because of personal ambitions or whether they see it as the way forward and go with that rather than with the objective output of the process analysis ... My own opinion is that there are a lot more machinations at work since rightsizing came in. We went backwards in terms of attitudes at senior levels. (Colin, local TQM coordinator, grade 2)

Change requires a sustained effort and managers often lose sight of the ball. They kick the ball into play and then when it is not moving as fast as they like it they are very prone to go on and find another ball which they think might do the job better before the first game is under way. When it comes down to the nitty gritty, the continuing pressure, the recognition that you can only change culture by a continuously improving process – not in one single step – they accept it but don't really internalize it. They probably recognize what I am saying as quite true. What they seem unable to do is to put that into practical effect. They want more answers to the questions but are not always too sure what they are asking. They are all rational people, I know them all very well and I recognize they are very intelligent. But the pressures are on to see a return on what they are investing. They are investing in people now. They have introduced MRPII and JIT. It's people that are holding up further improvement. It's people that are the least predictable factor in the improvement equation. They introduce JIT and see an improvement. Great! They support it. They send people out on a team-building course and they don't come back suddenly improved. But you have nudged it a little bit on the way. The question then comes up whether the investment was worthwhile. That can only be answered in a three- or four-year down-the-line context. It is a difficult problem. I can appreciate their concern. (Mike, local TQM coordinator, grade 2)

Further reading

Barker, R. (1994) 'Relative utility of culture and climate analysis to an organizational change agent: an analysis of General Dynamics, Electronics Division', *International Journal of Organizational Analysis* 2: 68–87.

Cameron, K.S. and Quinn, R.E. (1988) 'Organizational paradox and transformation' in K.S. Cameron and R.E. Quinn (eds) *Paradox and Transformation*, Cambridge, MA: Ballinger, pp. 1–18.

Conti, R.F. and Warner, M. (1994) 'Taylorism, teams and technology in "reengineering" work-organization', *New Technology, Work, and Employment* 9: 93–102.

Hammer, M. (1990) 'Re-engineering work: don't automate, obliterate', *Harvard Business Review*, July–August: 104-112.

Isabella, L.A. (1990) 'Evolving interpretations as a change unfolds: how managers construe key organizational events', *Academy of Management Journal* 33: 7–41.

Martin, J. and Meyerson, D. (1988) 'Organizational cultures and the denial, channelling and acknowledgement of ambiguity', in L.R. Pondy, R.J. Boland and H. Thomas (eds) *Managing Ambiguity and Change*, Chichester: John Wiley, pp. 93–125.

Reger, R.K., Gustafson, L.T., Demarie, S.M. and Mullane, J.V. (1994) 'Reframing the organization: why implementing total quality is easier said than done', *Academy of Management Review* 19: 565–84.

Spencer, B. A. (1994) 'Models of organization and total quality management: a comparison and critical evaluation', *Academy of Management Review* 19: 446–71.

Sproull, L.S. and Hofmeister, K.R. (1986) 'Thinking about implementation', *Journal of Management* 12: 43–60.

Tsoukas, H. (ed.) (1994) *New Thinking in Organizational Behaviour: From Social Engineering to Reflective Action*, Oxford: Butterworth Heinemann.

Tuckman, A. (1994) 'The yellow brick road: total quality management and the restructuring of organizational culture', *Organization Studies* 15: 727–51.

Van de Ven, A.H. and Poole, M.S. (1995) 'Explaining development and change in organizations', *Academy of Management Review* 20: 510–40.

Part two

Leisure service organizations

Case 2.1

Climate and change at Chestertons Ales

Chestertons Ales group is a large organization which provides a variety of hospitality and leisure services. In response to government attempts to intensify competition in the industry, Chestertons Ales has instituted major strategic and structural changes to its operations. The case explores some of the issues arising from these changes as they affect the pub and the hotel and restaurant divisions. A firm of consultants has carried out an organizational climate survey and the results are under consideration by some of the senior managers. What are the implications of the survey results for the future management and organization of these divisions?

The case presents detailed results from the organizational climate survey as well as an account of current business issues facing the firm. Readers are invited to consider the implications of the survey results in terms of the climates and cultures of the divisions, their relation to the firm's strategy, management and organization, and the more general application of climate surveys to organizational problems.

Case 2.2

Modernizing the Royal Hotel

This case traces the transition of the Royal Hotel from its position as an independent, family-managed business to ownership and control by a large hotel group, Galaxy Hotels. Presented in narrative form, the case events are reported from the perspective of John Inskip, the regional operations director of Galaxy. Inskip instituted the acquisition of the Royal by Galaxy and introduced a series of changes to its management and operations in the expectation of significantly improving its financial performance.

The case reports the events following the acquisition of the hotel by Galaxy and their results. Readers are invited to consider whether the acquisition of the Royal had been 'a big mistake from start to finish' and, if so, why.

Case 2.1

Climate and change at Chestertons Ales

PAUL R. SPARROW

Strategic and organizational context

The Chestertons Ales group operates in the hospitality and leisure sectors. It employs over 5,600 staff, over half of whom are part-time, and has core drinks, food and accommodation products. The business focus is on wholesaling, retailing and the provision of high-quality service.

The antecedents to the events reported here can be traced back to a 1989 report by the Mergers and Monopolies Commission. In an attempt to introduce more competition to the industry, large breweries were forced to scale down their number of pubs. Many decided to concentrate on the areas of business at which they were most profitable or sought replacement sources of income. Accordingly, the Chestertons Ale group underwent a major shift in its strategic focus. It acquired a small number of pub restaurants under the brand of Chefs Platter and managed them from within its pub division. In anticipation of the expected shake-out in the industry, in 1990 it made a strategic shift away from brewing and pub management towards retailing within the leisure industry when it sold off its core brewing business to a rival brewer but retained and developed the public house estate. The organizational structure was divisionalized for the first time in the same year.

In 1992 the company sought to realign its divisional organization into what it thought was a more logical structure. A new product market/divisional structure was put in place to consolidate and support what became three separate businesses: public houses, leisure hotels, and drinks wholesaling. Two businesses – Chefs Platter pub restaurants and Town Leisure hotels – were combined within the new hotel and restaurant division in order to create a strong identity and ensure complementary development. The new division had been developed to respond to the emerging market for facilities that appealed to both business users and the local community and offered a proven format of leisure, sports, bar, restaurant and function facilities. Many of the elite managers from the pub division were put in charge of the Chefs Platter houses, a move which signalled to many that this was the division to be in. Some people in the pub division were frustrated at losing control of Chefs Platter, which they thought they had managed well enough.

By late 1995 the pub division owned 403 pubs in the Midlands, split roughly half-and-half between managed and tenanted. It employed 988 full-time and 2,326 part-time staff. The hotel and restaurant division now owned the twenty-five Chefs Platter pub restaurants, five of which had lodge accommodation, and seven Town Leisure hotels. Chefs Platters are essentially large pubs with a high percentage of food sales. Town Leisure hotels are much larger operations. The hotel and restaurant division employed 340 full-time and 1,218 part-time staff.

Chestertons Ales also owned a network of twenty wholesaling depots which had grown rapidly through acquisition to become the largest regional wholesaler of beers, wines and spirits and employed 651 full-time and twenty-eight part-time staff. There was a small headquarters staff of about eighty people.

Despite a difficult national economic environment in which there were low and declining levels of consumer expenditure, fears over unemployment and falling house prices, the strategy appeared to be paying dividends. Chestertons Ales was outperforming its regional competitors. Since the strategic restructuring, turnover had doubled to £216 million, profit had increased by 68 per cent to £31 million and earnings per share had increased by 72 per cent. By far the bulk of the profit (around 63 per cent) came from the pub division. Around 21 per cent of profit came from the drinks wholesaling division, and 16 per cent from the hotel and restaurant division. Chestertons Ales had just had another year of significant development. Its turnover was growing by 26 per cent a year and profit by 24 per cent. It was making a capital investment of £28 million. Financially, Chestertons Ales was a successful business and senior managers were looking forward to another year of progress. The mission statement (shown in Appendix I) signalled that Chestertons Ales had grand plans. It intended to acquire other chains of pubs and to expand nationally towards a base of 2,000 outlets. Maintaining rapid and effective internal growth was important.

The business intentions

Despite the overall success of the last few years, Mike Hargreaves, the managing director of the pub division, knew that his division was both the major employer and profit centre of the business and the most closely linked with the company's past traditions, when Chestertons Ales had also been a brewer. He was aware that his division operated in a market where there was a continuing annual decline in draught beer consumption of around 5 per cent. As volumes and turnover were falling many outlets struggled to remain viable. Competition for market-share led to a rationalization of licensed estates. As breweries and leisure companies repositioned their businesses they were disposing of some properties, investing in refurbishment and increasing the number of managed houses (which provided the opportunity for more financial, marketing, retail format and human resource management control and hence improved profitability).

Chestertons Ales had just disposed of thirty-eight pubs and was refurbishing ninety-five sites. For several years the hotel and restaurants division had received the lion's share of investment, but this was changing. The pub division strategy also centred around the development of high-quality licensees and staff. Chestertons Ales had increased its training activity in the division and had just won three National Innkeeping Training Awards. The objective was to continue to gain market-share by offering customers quality, service, value and choice.

Mike Hargreaves wanted to move his chain of pubs upmarket to maintain profitability. He felt the drinks industry was following the same pattern as food retailers like Safeway and Tesco, with quality becoming the byword for success. He wanted to develop a retail culture within the context of the leisure industry.

Mike had helped develop Chestertons Ales customer charter and was now thinking about customer-service training but hadn't yet actively run a programme. But Chefs Platter had just completed a customer focus culture-change programme. Clearly, the pub division could learn from the hotel and restaurant division about this. There had been some friendly rivalry between the two divisions, but Mike felt that despite relatively low investment over the last few years, his part of the business had demonstrated high returns on investment.

John Healey, the managing director of the hotel and restaurant division, also had much to be pleased about. Three years ago his division provided 10 per cent of Chestertons Ales profit, but already this had grown to 16 per cent. A year ago he had increased sales by 15 per cent and profits by 58 per cent. However, he also had his worries. The reduced level of economic activity and consumer expenditure was hitting his hotel occupancy and restaurant spending levels. Currently his sales were only increasing by 1.5 per cent and so profit was being delivered by improving gross margins and strong control of costs. He didn't want this focus on cost control to damage what had been a successful climate of growth and expansion over the last few years. He knew that many managers in the larger pub division viewed his division as being financially weaker and wanted to make sure that his strategically important but fledgling businesses did not 'die on the vine'. His objectives were to continue improving sales and profit margins, achieve a greater customer focus, develop the Chefs Platter and Town Leisure brands, and expand the number of sites and facilities. He felt that greater integration with the pub division could help him achieve this.

Examining the organizational climate

Robert Edwards, Chestertons' personnel director, was aware of this business rivalry within the firm. He put down the consultants' report and smiled ruefully to himself. The results of the study didn't surprise him really (see Appendix II for a summary of the climate survey data which formed part of the study). Robert had only been with Chestertons Ales for 20 months and had worked closely with the board during that time. He'd always felt that when he went into the pub division and then the hotel and restaurant division he had been working for two separate companies. This study into the organizational climate of the different units confirmed what he had always suspected. Of course, surveys on peoples' attitudes, values and behaviour rarely gave you good news, but this report needed thinking about.

Chestertons Ales had once more decided to adjust and restructure its operations in line with the new realities of the business (see Appendix III). The decision had been made by the board, but had been proposed by the managing director of the pub division. In December 1995 Chestertons Ales announced to its staff that it was going to form a new catering unit within the pub division (which was itself being renamed PubCo) by moving the Chefs Platter pub restaurants into PubCo. On 1 March 1996 the new structure would become operational.

There were a number of strategic synergies between the two businesses, especially as PubCo was now upgrading many of its traditional pubs and adding catering operations to them. However, running a pub restaurant business was significantly different to running a pub and although the two units were being brought together under a single structure, the intention was to avoid diluting the operational focus of each business and maintain the existing separate operating logics (and brand names). Chesterton Ales wanted gradually to make the managed pubs in PubCo more like the Chefs Platter restaurants by seeking out best practice in both the pub estate and Chefs Platter houses and then introducing it to both. It was therefore important that the high standards of the Chefs Platter business be maintained. Consequently the whole management structure of Chefs Platter was being moved over to headquarters, along with some elements of PubCo.

Some common managerial functions such as marketing support were being centralized. Two regional Chefs Platter operations managers would then report to the central operations director of PubCo. A newly appointed manager was going to look after Chefs Platter and also take responsibility for some of those pubs in PubCo that had a large catering element. There was no sense in managers in the hotel and restaurant division handing over the jewel in their crown. They had jointly come to the decision that Chefs Platter was now established and should be moved in with the core of the business. However, Chefs Platter managers felt that their operation had a more modern management approach, was more retail-orientated and customer focused. They didn't want the proposed integration to dilute these perceived advantages, but generally welcomed the opportunity for career advancement that the new structure afforded. However, the new structure did mean the effective merger of Chefs Platter with PubCo and this brought issues of cultural and strategic compatibility to the fore. It also signalled the return of many houses to PubCo that had been lost to them when Chefs Platter had been moved into the hotel and restaurants division nearly four years previously.

Robert Edwards and Mike Hargreaves had commissioned an organizational climate survey and study in the period between the announcement of the planned structure and the actual commencement of operations. Clearly the shift in strategy would demand changes in the beliefs, values, attitudes and behaviour of the staff. The acquisitions in the wholesaling business had led to a clash of cultures and resulted in a difficult implementation process, and they both knew that there were some obvious cultural differences between PubCo and Chefs Platter operations. Robert and Mike had commissioned the study because they wanted to gain some insights into how the new organization structure might work. How did the two units operate in practice? How did the cultures of PubCo and Chefs Platter differ and how did they interact? What sort of operating logic and cultural issues would the new structure need to deal with? How close would they be to developing a shared retail culture?

As Robert looked at the data from the climate survey he reminded himself what it meant. The Business and Organizational Climate Index (BOCI) instrument consisted of seventeen scales, each assessed by eight questions, ranked on a four-point format (from zero to three). Each dimension of climate was therefore measured on a twenty-four-point scale. The seventeen scales were wide-ranging in scope, covering: orientation to information technology, sociability, open mindedness, industriousness, questioning authority, interpersonal aggression, leaders' psychological distance, rules orientation, cultural orientation, readiness to innovate, orientation to the wider community, intellectual orientation, quality orientation, future orientation, scientific and technical orientation, administrative efficiency, and customer orientation.

The consultants had told him that the advantage of using the BOCI was that it was so constructed that it could be completed by all job levels and functions within an organization and was usable across organizations, thus making inter-organizational comparisons possible. However, they had also warned him that a drawback of using the questionnaire was that the norms that could be identified were only those included in the instrument. The consultants had gathered data for both the PubCo and Chefs Platter operations using a representative selection of staff. Because each climate dimension was measured on a twenty-four-point scale, it was possible to see relatively how high or low Chestertons scored against other organizations and how each division scored against others. The data he was looking at represented the average score across employees in each division.

The consultants had also provided data from a cross-section of 100 other UK firms, which helped Richard assess the climate in Chestertons in relation to that found in other organizations. Some of the data showed that all UK companies tended to score the same – for example the level of leaders, psychological distance was on average low across all UK organizations – as one would expect given the national culture. However, in other areas there seemed to be some significant differences between Chestertons and other UK organizations.

He knew too that the consultants had also interviewed a lot of staff to build up a picture of the underlying culture of the organization. Reading the report it became clear that the consultants felt that each business operated on different logics. The old pub division had not been subjected to as much change as Chefs Platter in recent years. Most of the pub managers had been with the business since before 1990. They were typically male and worked with one or two full-time staff and several part-time people in the smaller pubs, which were still seen as 'ale houses'. Managers ruled pubs with a firm hand, but morale was fairly high. Managers were employed for their local knowledge and their ability to 'keep the doors open'. They depended more on their operations managers to develop the premises. Most staff and customers identified with the quality of what they still saw as their main product – Chestertons Ales.

Some larger pubs also had restaurants and employed around thirty people. The lines of demarcation were quite blurred, but the management style and atmosphere differed between the two areas of the pub, being more autocratic and frenetic in the bar but relaxed and consensual in the restaurant area. Generally, though, managers in the pub division had a narrower business outlook than the Chefs Platter restaurants and control was achieved through monthly financial analyses, although EPOS technology meant that daily inventories and sales figures could be reviewed by managers. Pub managers saw this as an intrusion and lack of trust on behalf of the company. As some of the better managers had moved out of the pub division those who remained were stretched. Area managers typically looked after twenty-five pubs each, compared to an industry norm of around fifteen to twenty. Office staff in headquarters had quietly nicknamed the two divisions as GlamCo and GlumCo!

In contrast Chefs Platter restaurants were controlled through weekly financial analyses. They had a strong focus on information analysis. As a complex business, unlike the pubs, Chefs Platter managers made considerable use of EPOS technology. They also needed to analyse staffing patterns across several operations. A typical outlet employed forty people and had its own management structure. Two or three deputy managers each ran their own units in which the majority of staff were part-time covering long opening hours. The climate and culture in Chefs Platter was still in a state of flux. As a new business it had spent the last three years shaping itself. The management style had emphasized quality and customer service. In excess of 50 per cent of new managers had been brought in and there had been several changes to the management structure over the last few years. Nevertheless, some strong features seemed to pervade the Chefs Platter business.

Control was effected by the selection of key individuals with similar values. Managers were highly committed to their work and saw themselves as part of a larger organization through their considerable contacts with each other, internal competitions between 'houses' and a pent-up demand for career development. Managers were expected to be pragmatic and creative. They were given considerable autonomy in the running of their houses as long as they pursued those standardized aspects related to the brand image. Any attempt to introduce bureaucratic controls to ensure standardization was always resisted. They were on individual incentive plans. Manager of the Month awards were made on the basis of a 'mystery diner' method where, unknown to staff, 'customers' made assessments of the houses' level of customer service. Managers lived to work. They were seen as open, honest, trustworthy and professionally respected. As a consequence authority could be devolved to those individuals who could be trusted and empowered to get on with the job.

The effectiveness of the operation relied upon a high level of trust and empathy. Most staff identified strongly with the particular 'house' they worked in. The leadership style of the managers was important in engendering this feeling of participation. Relations between house staff were friendly and informal, but governed by a strong sense of professionalism which was built into a clear set of rules. Individual success was measured strongly against performance targets. 'Houses' were run like entrepreneurial ventures. Although there were controls on decision-making there was a willingness to experiment and innovate. Decisions were implemented quickly and carefully evaluated. The climate was one of tough, competitive organization: a fair day's work for a fair day's pay. Those employees who didn't like it left the 'house' but those who remained valued the apparent fairness of the management style. Managers assumed, overall correctly, that the staff viewed work as a means to live. Those who were interested in information would ask for it, but most had little interest in the greater affairs of Chestertons Ales. They were wrapped up in their house teams and received little exposure to interhouse attempts at integration. They were more inclined to conform to their managers' view of how to run the house than to any central ideas of a Chefs Platter brand image. The customer-focus training programme was just one of the many 'pet projects' of those at headquarters that had reduced in significance over time. Generally, Chefs Platter staff felt that they matched the highest levels of professionalism within the restaurant sector and acted as a role model for the more antiquated PubCo.

The next step

This afternoon Robert has a meeting with Mike to discuss the results of the climate study. Although Mike had been happy to commission the climate survey he hadn't seen the results. Robert knew that he needed to summarize the situation, tease out the implications of the study and make some recommendations about the new organizational structure pretty quickly. Mike would be keen to listen, but it was clear that he had set his store out on the back of the new organization structure.

As the time for the meeting approached, Robert's head was filled with questions? Did the findings of the consultants and the survey matter? Would the way the organization structure worked be influenced by the prevailing organizational climate in the two units? Was there a way round this situation that would still meet the strategic imperatives of the business?

Questions for discussion

1 Why did the senior managers want to integrate Chefs Platter within the PubCo structure? How would this latest change in structure facilitate the strategic development of Chestertons Ales?
2 Using material from the BOCI study and the consultants report, how would you characterize the organizational climate of Chefs Platter and PubCo? What were the main differences in organizational climate and culture between the two?
3 Does the current organizational climate in both Chefs Platter or PubCo fit in with the chosen strategy? To what extent do their climates hinder or help the implementation of change?
4 Would you expect the new merged structure to be successful? Would it be affected by the different organizational climates and if so, in what way?
5 What recommendations concerning potential changes and improvements to the new structure and management practice would you make?
6 How else might an analysis of organizational climate be used to assist organizational development? What other applications for climate surveys can you see?

Appendix I Mission statement and customer charter

- **Mission statement for Chestertons Ales**
  To make each of our pubs the preferred choice in the local market which it serves.
- **Customer Charter**
  We must all play our part in fulfilling the commitment made in our customer charter.

Quality. We will always strive to ensure that you, our customers, are served in comfortable well-appointed and clean surroundings.

Service. We will always offer a warm welcome with friendly and efficient staff aiming to please you at all times.

Value. We will always strive to give you value through the quality of our products, standards of service and customer care.

Choice. We will always offer you the widest possible range of leading products and, where possible, will continue to broaden this range to suit all our customers tastes and requirements.

Appendix II The Business and Organizational Climate Index (BOCI) survey results

A team of consultants had been called in to analyse the organization climate within PubCo and Chefs Platter. They had administered a structured survey called the Business and Organizational Climate Index (BOCI) to 150 employees in the pubs, restaurants and headquarters and interviewed around forty managers. The data collected from the survey provided a quantitative basis for measuring the principal parameters of organizational climate (see definitions of each scale below). The table below provides the average scores on each of seventeen scales for Chefs Platter, PubCo and a control group of 100 typical UK companies. Each score is on a scale from zero to twenty-four.

	Chefs Platter	PubCo	All UK
Leaders' psychological distance	11.6	9.2*	9.6

e.g. • it is necessary to be polite to stay out of trouble
- senior personnel rarely refer to one another by first names
- there is a recognized group of leaders who receive special privileges

Questioning authority	13.5	11.8*	11.6

e.g. • criticism of policies and practices is encouraged
- people here are not likely to accept management ineptitude without complaint or protest
- people delight in challenging official policies
- when people disagree with a decision they work to get it changed

Orientation to customer service	19.1	16.4*	16.6

e.g. • senior managers put a lot of stress on satisfying the customer
- a lot of training and education emphasizes the importance of the customer
- the customers always come first in this organization
- people here would never put costs before customers anytime

Orientation to quality	19.6	18.3	18.1

e.g. • our workforce feels highly responsible for the quality of their work
- customer complaints about quality are treated very seriously here
- our suppliers are taken to task if they don't provide us with high quality service

Open-mindedness   16.1   13.3*   13.3
e.g. • errors and failures are talked about freely so others may learn from them
     • no one needs to be afraid of expressing extreme or unpopular views
     • criticism is not taken as a personal affront
     • one of the values most stressed here is open-mindedness

Orientation to IT   12.5   13.5   12.9
e.g. • most managers are quite at home with computers here
     • top management are very positive about using new technology to improve
       effectiveness
     • people who push the use of computers are likely to get to the top
     • people who don't use computers are regarded with derision

Future orientation   15.0   14.3   14.5
e.g. • the ability to plan ahead is highly valued
     • people are encouraged to take a long-term view
     • senior management is often occupied with consideration of basic goals
       and purposes
     • failure to plan ahead is regarded as a serious error here

Scientific and technical orientation   10.8   10.7   11.7
e.g. • senior personnel are considered as experts in their own fields
     • this organization is research conscious
     • a discussion about the latest scientific inventions would not be uncommon
       here
     • many people in the organization have a background in science

Intellectual orientation   12.9   13.0   12.9
e.g. • people spend a great deal of time thinking about complex problems
     • most people here are stimulated by intellectual activities or problems
     • careful reasoning and clear logic are valued here
     • most people here are well-read

Managing culture   16.2   15.2   14.4
e.g. • senior management work hard to encourage people to believe in the
       organization
     • a lot of effort is put into helping you learn about the company's values
     • this organization has a strong sense of identity
     • a lot of effort goes into selecting the people who will fit into the culture

Industriousness   18.5   15.4*   16.6
e.g. • people here put a lot of energy into what they do
     • there is so much to be done here that people are always busy
     • day-to-day activities require a sustained effort
     • everyone here takes their work seriously

Sociability   14.6   15.2   12.0
e.g. • everyone here has a strong sense of being part of a team
     • there is a lot of group spirit

- people spend a great deal of time together socially
- social events get a lot of enthusiasm and support

Interpersonal aggression   9.8   10.0   10.7
e.g. • people here are always trying to manipulate activities to their own advantage
   - if something goes wrong, almost anyone is likely to get blamed
   - a lot of people in this place walk round with a chip on their shoulder
   - personal rivalries are quite common

Rules orientation   17.0   13.0*   15.8
e.g. • people are expected to report violations of rules and regulations
   - people quickly learn what is to be done and not done here
   - formal rules and regulations have a very important place here
   - it is expected there will be no deviation from established practice, no matter what

Administrative efficiency   15.6   12.0*   13.5
e.g. • work is well organized and progresses systematically
   - most activities here are planned carefully
   - there is no wasted time here, everything is planned right to the minute
   - there is a specific place for everything and everyone

Readiness to innovate   15.0   13.9   12.9
e.g. • policy changes occur quickly here after careful deliberation
   - new ideas are always being tried out here
   - unusual or exciting plans are encouraged here
   - programmes here are quickly changed to meet new conditions

Orientation to wider community   14.7   13.9   13.4
e.g. • the activities of charitable and social agencies are strongly supported
   - social issues are often discussed here
   - the organizations' activities are often featured in the newspapers
   - service to the wider community is regarded as a major responsibility

Note: Those scores marked (*) for PubCo are statistically significantly different from Chefs Platter at the $p < 0.05$ level.

Appendix III Product market structure at Chestertons Ales, 1992

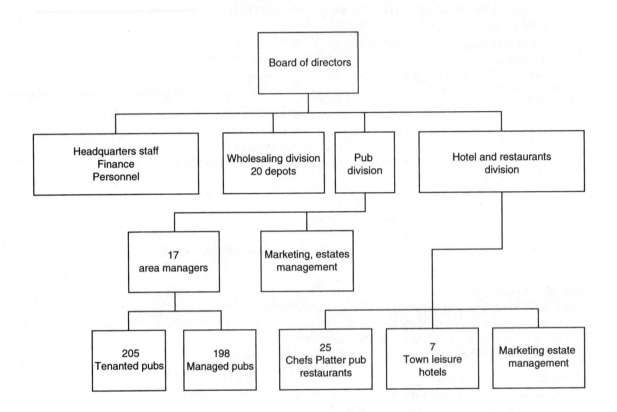

Appendix IV Proposed product market structure, 1996

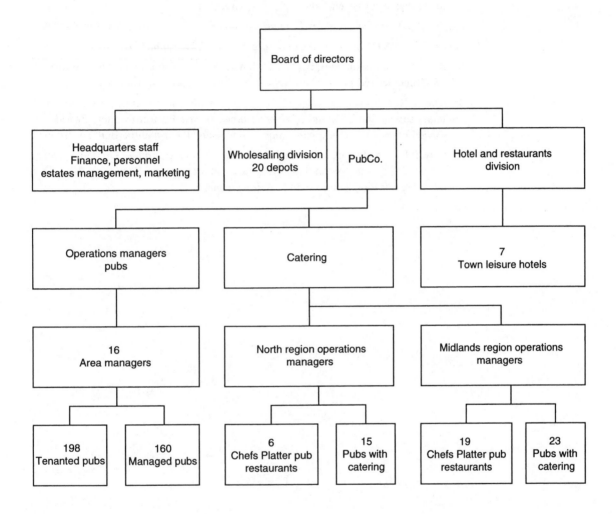

Further reading

Daft, R.L. (1989) *Organization Theory and Design*, St Paul, MN: West Publishing, pp. 188–94 (on bureaucracy, size and the life-cycle of the organization), pp. 230–3 and 320–8 (on control systems and type of organization).

Ott, S. (1989) *The Organizational Culture Perspective*, Pacific Grove, CA: Brooks/Cole.

Payne, R.L. (1991) 'Taking stock of corporate culture', *Personnel Management* 23: 26–9.

Reichers, A.E. and Schneider, B. (1990) 'Climate and culture: an evolution of constructs', in B. Schneider (ed.) *Organizational Climate and Culture*, Oxford: Jossey-Bass.

Sparrow, P.R. and Gaston, K. (1996) 'Generic climate maps: a strategic application of climate survey data', *Journal of Organizational Behaviour*, forthcoming. Provides an overview of the nature of organizational climate and the use of the BOCI instrument.

Sparrow, P.R. and Hiltrop, J.M. (1994) *European HRM in Transition*, London: Prentice-Hall, pp. 267–9 (on structural change as a social process), pp. 216–9 and 220–37 (on what is organizational culture and can it be managed?).

Case 2.2

Modernizing the Royal Hotel

GRAHAM BARLOW

John Inskip gazed out over the estuary towards the golf links on the far shore. Though it was October and the evenings were drawing in rapidly, tonight the sunset was magnificent. It bathed the flotilla of yachts and small fishing vessels riding at anchor in a blaze of golden light, while the higher sky was a galaxy of pastel colours, ranging from pink to pale green. 'A galaxy of colour', Inskip mused wryly to himself, thinking that the wheel had come full circle. He turned, looking towards the Royal Hotel standing serenely behind him in the iridescent light. He reflected that it was in this spot that he had stood almost exactly two years before.

The Royal had a particular significance for Inskip. As a boy, he had entered the hotel briefly on two occasions and the experience not only created his impression of the hotel as the epitome of high living, but also had led him to make a career in the hotel industry, latterly with Galaxy Hotels. Galaxy Hotels had 'branded' their 'pubs' (a term Galaxy's managers used when referring to their hotels among themselves), grouping them into three categories: **inns** (mostly traditional inns, usually with about two dozen bedrooms, often housed in an extension); **family**, (usually seaside or commercial hotels which had received 'the Galaxy treatment' to improve their facilities and enhance their appearance); and **leisure** (fundamentally, more upmarket hotels which could sustain higher rates on account of their position or facilities, and to which a Galaxy leisure centre might have been added). Within Galaxy, there had been talk that Paul Fisher, Galaxy's chairman, had been considering introducing a further brand, 'prestige', to which some of Galaxy's better leisure hotels might be allocated. But nothing had come of this yet due, it was said, to the opposition of Chris Edmonds, Galaxy's chief executive.

Reorganization was a way of life at Galaxy. Three years ago, branded hotels, formerly organized on a divisional basis (inns division, family division, leisure division) instead had been grouped together by location. This meant that most of Galaxy's divisional managers had become regional managers, responsible for a mix of all three types of hotel in their region, instead of hotels of a single brand as before.

Inskip didn't mind the reorganization: it had been good for him. He had entered the hotel trade when he left school and after a range of jobs and experience, twelve years ago joined Galaxy as an assistant manager. He quickly learned that achieving good financial results was a key to success: 'success is a good balance sheet', he was fond of telling subordinates, and this certainly had driven his career with Galaxy. He had progressed rapidly: assistant, deputy, manager, general manager, remaining in each position for a couple of years, or less. Then he had become manager of a group of hotels within the family division. With the latest reorganization, he had become a regional manager and had taken charge of a group of inns and family hotels in and around Westerpool. Six-months later, he had been made operations director for the same region. His responsibilities effectively were the same, but within Galaxy his new title indicated that his views in shaping policy could carry greater weight than those of a regional manager.

As well as new opportunities, Inskip's appointment to Westerpool had triggered memories, for he had spent his boyhood in that historic city, now a substantial centre of commerce and population. As a boy, he had visited Hamilton when he could, for it offered much which appealed to him. Some fifteen miles south of Westerpool, it was one of several fishing villages along the coast. But Hamilton also was the seat of the Cavendish family, the Earls of Hamilton, and the presence of their Templecourt estate consolidated Hamilton's reputation as a sought-after residential area. Hamilton's further reputation as a select resort had been consolidated by the Royal Hotel.

Standing in its own grounds, the Royal Hotel with its elegant stone-faced frontage was quite as imposing as Templecourt house. Though the hill behind Hamilton village gradually had become built up with high quality housing, and Hamilton's yacht and tennis clubs approached the hotel's front drive, develop-ment had encroached no further than this. The hotel continued to look out over the estuary, while the hill behind it was now part of Hamilton's golf club.

Beyond the belt of fir trees around the landward perimeter of the hotel's grounds, the rocky headland remained beautiful and apparently remote; and as it had been designated an area of outstanding natural beauty, it was likely to remain so. Beyond that, Hamilton was surrounded by green belts. Though several of the former warehouses at the harbour had been converted into expensive flats with accompanying boutiques and restaurants, the village itself retained its traditional appearance of unpretentious, well-cared-for charm (tenaciously cultivated by members of the Old Hamilton Society and other influential voluntary groups); and Hamilton remained the most sought-after residential area to the south of the Westerpool conurbation.

The Royal had a reputation far beyond Hamilton as a rather special hotel. It had been owned by the Somerville family for generations. Recently, however, Inskip had heard that Jane Somerville, who currently guided the hotel's affairs, was suffering increasingly from arthritis. Lacking suitable heirs to take over the business, she wished to sell up. If the rumour had any substance, this might be an unique opportunity for Inskip to acquire the Royal for his patch; he hadn't a pub at the prestige end of the range. Though it was many years since he had seen the hotel, Inskip had always associated the Royal with an air of faded elegance. If it was more run-down by now, it could be a good buy, ripe for improvement. Hence, on a fine evening early in October, he made a discreet visit to the hotel to look it over.

He parked by the yacht club, which looked smarter than he remembered; indeed, the whole of Hamilton looked well-kept and upmarket. Otherwise, nothing seemed to have changed. In the warm light of the autumn sunset the hotel looked unchanged, too, with its immaculate flower-beds and its name carried only on well-styled but relatively inconspicuous signs by the driveway. At the least, his pubs would have larger, smarter Galaxy signs, Inskip thought.

Within the hotel, Inskip's memories flooded back. He had entered a large lounge; around him were armchairs, sofas, tables, some with lamps, many with vases of fresh flowers, and people sitting, talking, reading. The hotel seemed little different, comfortable rather than smart. Inskip was reminded of his boyhood sense of uncertainty, for then there had been no signs to direct him; and none were to be seen now. Across the lounge, a broad hall concealed the reception desk and stairs and lift to the upper floors. Inskip walked towards it then paused, uncertain whether to have dinner (the hotel's restaurant had a very good reputation) or just a drink. Really, he only wanted a quick look round.

'Can I help you, sir?' A neatly dressed girl looked at him pleasantly, enquiringly.

'I was thinking of having dinner.'

'Yes, sir.' She indicated the hallway facing him. 'The dining room is through to your left'.

Surveying the dining room, Inskip was impressed immediately: it was good. Though large, it was lit to convey an atmosphere of intimacy, and so designed that most diners could enjoy the view out over the estuary. In the gathering dusk, lights had begun to twinkle on the small boats riding at anchor, complementing the candlelit tables. Though the room was full, it did not appear crowded; despite a steady hum of conversation, it felt quiet and well ordered; though all its staff were young, they appeared purposeful and well trained. Among them, Inskip noticed an older man whom he took to be Gerry Baskerville, the Royal's general manager. Baskerville, too, had a good reputation. He was swift, jocularly friendly towards guests with whom he was familiar, business-like towards others, and he missed nothing.

Inskip's observations were interrupted by the *maitre d'hotel*. A table could be ready for him in about half an hour; meanwhile, could he get Inskip a drink? Inskip declined (he'd seen what he needed of the dining room but took a menu with him to study), preferring to continue looking around the hotel. He glanced into the rooms along the corridor opposite the dining room (drawing rooms, library, and others – including one marked 'private'), working his way towards the rear of the hotel. There he found another stairway. The opportunity of a quick look upstairs was too good to be missed.

'Can I help you, sir?' He turned quickly. A young man regarded him enquiringly.

'I was looking for the bar'.

'Yes, sir, the Shell Bar's on the right near the dining room.' He indicated the way. 'Upstairs there's only residential accommodation'.

Inskip duly visited the Shell Bar. A well-proportioned room bearing a nautilus shell motif, it was an elegantly furnished cocktail bar. Inskip noted that it had fewer than a dozen customers and decided to continue looking around the hotel. As he stepped back into the corridor, he saw the same young man walking towards him, so he made for the washroom. This was spotless, and empty apart from a middle-aged man dressed in old corduroy trousers and a crumpled tweed jacket with the elbows worn through, who was about to leave. Outside, Inskip noticed that the wearer of the battered jacket walked towards the rear of the hotel, then disappeared into an unmarked door off the corridor. Curious (for the man's appearance contrasted oddly with other guests he had seen), Inskip followed.

Opening the door, he found himself stepping into what appeared to be another bar, much smaller, simply furnished, oak panelled, and quite full. Inskip threaded his way to a dispense hatch in the wall and glanced about him. Every seat appeared to be taken. Then a bell tinkled as a door opened in the panelling at the far end of the room. A large man stepped inside. Greeted familiarly by those present, he picked his way towards the hatch and stood beside it, as he did so nodding to Inskip, opposite him. A wizened little man suddenly appeared at the hatch and addressed the newcomer.

'Evening, Mr Ford. A drop out of the brook, I take it?' he said, producing a filled glass. Then the barman caught sight of Inskip and shot him an appraising glance. 'I'm very sorry sir, I didn't see you there.' He looked quickly around the room, shaking his head. 'It's so full in here.' He shook his head again. 'I think you'll find more room in the Shell Bar, sir: it's just through that door to your right, sir. I'll see that you're served there immediately. Thank you very much, sir.' He vanished as abruptly as he had appeared.

Inskip was taken aback. He decided to forego a drink, for other ideas were forming in his mind. A keynote of his earlier success had been his ability to drive a hotel's profits upward and a tested formula for doing so had been to increase bar sales. The Royal seemed to present a wide open door to such opportunity. The cocktail bar looked good, but clearly was underutilized. As to this bar, it was far too small and service was hopelessly inadequate. Yet there were underutilized rooms nearby – the library, for example – which would convert easily into a bar which could be a real money-spinner. He glanced round the bar again. He noticed that space had been found for Mr Ford, the newcomer, now sitting with a group in the far corner beneath a ship's bell (part of an amateurish attempt at vaguely nautical theming which relieved the time-stained panelling of the walls, Inskip judged). 'Yes,' he thought to himself, 'there's definitely growth opportunity here.'

Outside, the corridor was deserted. Inskip swiftly made for the stairs and climbed to the first floor. He had half expected the upper floors to look careworn, but the corridor facing him, silent, well lit and carpeted, certainly did not. Seeking a quick glimpse within, he tried the handles of a couple of doors, but they were locked. He walked on down the corridor looking about him, the royal blue carpet muffling his feet. An elderly woman with blue-rinsed hair matching the colour of the carpet suddenly appeared and walked towards him. She stopped. 'Good evening, sir. Can I help you?' Her words were polite but her tone was menacing and her gaze piercing.

'I was just looking over the hotel.'

'Yes, sir, quite. You aren't staying in the hotel are you, sir?' Inskip agreed that he was not. 'The upper floors have residential accommodation only, sir. But visitors are welcome on the ground floor.' Her manner betrayed no hint of welcome: she maintained her steely gaze. 'Mr Johnson will show you down, sir.' Inskip suddenly realized that an elderly manservant had been standing behind him; now the man stepped forward. 'If you'll kindly follow me, sir, I'll show you the way.' Inskip duly did so. Turning at the lift to glance back down the corridor, he saw the gaze of the blue-rinsed virago fixed unswervingly on him. He decided that if Galaxy was to acquire the hotel, one of the first things he would do would be to institute some staff changes.

Outside, Inskip noticed that the hotel's car park, concealed on the landward side of the hotel, was now floodlit. While he was here, it might be useful to get some idea of its size. He found it large and surprisingly full, with a sprinkling of Rolls and other exotic models. Walking between the cars, he noticed that some ten per cent bore overseas plates, among them a Mercedes coupé with a German registration, a model that he had long coveted. He looked over it approvingly, stooping to peer inside in an attempt to read its mileage, but its interior was too dark for him to do so, and its door was locked. Then he became aware of a movement behind him. Turning, he found a huge man who had materialized out of the night. Dressed in a raincoat buttoned up to his neck, the giant eyed him narrowly. ' 'Oppit,' he said, gesturing with his thumb. Inskip chose to ignore the remark. 'I was just admiring this car.' 'Oh, you were, were you? Well, I've been watching you. And you'd better admire cars somewhere else. Go on, 'oppit.'

At that moment, with a light footstep a man appeared and unlocked the passenger door. 'Good evening, Tommy.' 'Evening, Mr Marschner.' Inskip felt it necessary to speak. 'I was admiring your car', he said. The newcomer pocketed something from the car's glove compartment, then locked the car door, darting a quick glance from Inskip to the giant. He smiled. 'I'm glad you like it', he said. Calling over his shoulder, 'Good night, Tommy', he turned to walk back to the hotel; Inskip fell into step beside him. Out of earshot, Marschner chuckled. 'Tommy can be bit intimidating', he said. 'He virtually lives outside the place. But he's very good at his job.'

'Is he?', Inskip replied, shortly. 'His customer relations skills could be improved; and he's not the only one.' Inskip mentioned his brush with the blue-rinsed woman upstairs. Marschner chuckled again. 'Ah, Betty', he said. 'She can be a bit of a dragon, but she's very good with children and **very** good at her job.' He chuckled again. 'The first time she stayed with us in Freiburg she had the whole house looking as if it was ready for an admiral's inspection when we got back.' He continued explanatorily, 'We asked her to house-sit in Germany for us a couple of years ago. We thought it would be a break for her and a help for us. She was very good. She came again last year, too, but each time she'd only stay for a week. She had to get back to her beloved Royal, she said.'

'You seem to know the hotel well', Inskip said conversationally. Marschner shrugged. 'We've been coming here for years now. We just meant to stay at Hamilton once, to play golf you know. But we kept coming back. The place grows on you. It has everything for us: countryside, beaches, sailing, fishing, riding, tennis; all good clubs, good stuff for the children as they grew up. And there's Westerpool if you need it. But there are good shops in the village. More of them than you'd expect, especially down by the harbour now. And there are discos for the children. Safe you know; no drugs, violence, no stuff like that. The children came to know local children, we came to know local families. The whole thing grows on you, you see', he smiled.

'Local families use the hotel, too?'

'Of course, it has a very good restaurant. Good value, too.'

Marschner turned to enter the hotel. 'Now, please excuse me. I must go inside. Goodnight.'

During the next few weeks, Inskip looked into acquiring the Royal. It was for sale, and negotiations had been opened. Inskip had reviewed the hotel's balance sheets and operating data with Galaxy's financial analysts. They told him all he needed to know, showing that the hotel was a sound business and could be a good proposition at the right price. However, there were other bidders in the field, among them rumoured to be Harry Ross, an independent hotelier. Inskip had not been able to confirm this, but had been left in no doubt that the Somervilles were not interested in selling at Galaxy's bid price, which had been turned down flat.

Inskip had assumed that the Royal's room sales would be seasonal, with occupancy rates possibly averaging around 50 per cent. He was surprised to find these nearer to 80 per cent. He saw little immediate prospect of increasing revenue streams significantly either from room sales or from the restaurant, both of which clearly performed well. Also, the hotel enjoyed a good function trade. An extension at the rear of the building housed a large ballroom and banqueting suite with provisional bookings stretching two years ahead. Further significant potential here was questionable, certainly in the short term. However, Inskip noted that functions accounted for nearly 50 per cent of the hotel's liquor trade. In his view, the Royal's bar sales were derisory. This touched on Inskip's formula for success. Driving up revenue from bar sales had proved a sure-fire recipe for enhancing his hotels' profit performance before, and he saw every reason to believe he could pull it off again at the Royal. This could tie in with a second stratagem.

Currently, the Royal did not possess a leisure centre, a facility which Inskip considered essential for any up-to-date prestige hotel. However, at the rear of the site there were two adjoining well-proportioned stable blocks which had been converted to provide staff accommodation. At the Royal, most staff, young or old, often lived in, either in the converted stable blocks, the hotel itself or, in the cases of the hotel's general manager and head chef, in nearby houses which the hotel owned. In the Galaxy group, staff live out. If the Royal's staff did so, this would free the stable blocks for conversion to a characterful leisure centre.

These, then, were the essentials of Inskip's ideas for the Royal. First, provide a large up-to-date bar by converting existing underutilized public rooms (the 'library' and drawing rooms opposite the restaurant; there was plenty of alternative space in the front lounge), thus creating a major new revenue (and profit) stream. Second, build an up-to-date leisure centre. This would underpin a rise in room rates and, if developed as a leisure club, also could provide another useful revenue stream. Not only would Inskip have added a prestigious hotel (plus leisure centre) to Galaxy's portfolio, he also would have jacked up its profitability at the same time. He aimed to achieve both in two years or thereabouts. Whether increases in profitability could be sustained after that was another matter. With any luck, he'd have moved on by then and it would be somebody else's problem.

There were two flies in the ointment, however. First, the Somervilles' adamant refusal to lower their asking price; second, Chris Edmonds, Galaxy's blunt speaking chief executive, was cool about the deal. Though Edmonds considered the asking price expensive, he claimed this was not the primary reason for his objection, but that the hotel didn't fit well with Galaxy's core business and, moreover, could be complex to run. Inskip had disagreed on the latter point. He had a clear formula for running a hotel and knew from experience that things became complicated only if people were allowed to depart from it; he said as much to Edmonds. Edmonds merely had responded with a terse 'I see', and closed the conversation. As Inskip left the room, Edmonds added dismissively, without looking up from his desk, 'you've more to learn than you think'.

There was little love lost between the two men (though for his part, Inskip was careful not to show this). However, Inskip had been stung by Edmonds' parting shot. He considered Edmonds uncouth, and he much preferred Paul Fisher, Galaxy's suavely elegant chairman. It was Fisher, Inskip suspected, who had backed his promotion. Indeed, it was partly Fisher's interest in the possibility of introducing a 'prestige' brand that had caused Inskip to look into the Royal in the first place. After his brush with Edmonds, Inskip resolved to go for the hotel, and to enlist Fisher's support in doing so. In two years' time, when his strategy for the Royal had paid off, it could be Inskip who was addressing Edmonds dismissively.

Inskip went over his ideas in some detail with Galaxy's bar design consultants and the company's architects. The latter confirmed that converting existing public rooms to a bar, if that was what Inskip wanted, would not involve major structural alterations. He also had discussed the acquisition with Mike Nichols, Galaxy's finance director, who confirmed that the Royal was a good business, though the cost of servicing the acquisition price would be substantial. Inskip believed that he could achieve this, at least in the short term, and pressed his case with Fisher accordingly. Fisher was sympathetic; but after a further meeting with Nichols, modified his position. The new building involved in creating a leisure centre could be an expensive proposition for a lower rate of return than Inskip's proposed bar conversion. Consequently, Fisher felt that work on the leisure centre should wait until Inskip's new profit generators came on stream sufficiently to justify it.

The implications of delaying building the leisure centre coupled with Nichol's reservations about the Royal's return on investment at Galaxy's revised bid price, had begun to cause Inskip considerable misgivings. Both hazarded his strategy for demonstrating conspicuous success within two years and then handing the hotel on. He resolved to back-pedal in the course of the subsequent discussions he anticipated having with Fisher and Edmonds about the acquisition. Shortly afterwards, he found himself summoned to Fisher's office.

'Well, John, I've discussed the Royal with Michael [Nichols, finance director] and, of course, with Chris. They have some reservations about the hotel, of course, especially at the Somerville price but I know you're keen on it so I've decided to give you a go. I'm afraid your leisure centre will have to be put on the back burner, just for the present of course. But I'm sure you'll soon make a go of things sufficiently to sort that out, too.'

Disconcerted, Inskip subsequently had called at Edmonds' office. He had expected opposition from Edmonds and had intended to back down in face of it. Instead, Edmonds was noncommittal. Looking up briefly from his desk, he dismissed the topic (and Inskip with it) commenting cryptically, 'Harry Ross knows what he's doing'.

Inskip put aside his new-found misgivings about the Royal and decided instead to concentrate on making his plans an outstanding success. The news that Galaxy would be acquiring the hotel produced a ripple of change at the Royal. Though Inskip would have liked to keep him, Gerry Baskerville was firm about wishing to move on as soon as the hotel was handed over. But, Inskip reasoned, Baskerville's departure could also bring advantages. To begin with, it offered an incoming manager a clear run, and Inskip already had a suitable successor in mind, Donald Saundby. Saundby had won a reputation within Galaxy as an up-and-coming young man with go-ahead ideas; the Royal would be his first appointment as a general manager. He was keen to add to his success, and that was just what Inskip wanted.

All the Royal's over-age staff had elected to retire when Galaxy took over, and many other staff had chosen to move on (with the exception of Tommy, the outdoor man). Saundby could begin by updating some of the Royal's staffing policies, among them the practice of employing two shifts of part-time chambermaids, principally to service guests' rooms both morning and evening. Inskip regarded the latter practice as antediluvian and unnecessary. (In Galaxy, all guests' rooms normally were serviced by midday. Thereafter, they would not be serviced again until the following morning.) Similarly, employing waiters to provide room service to residential floors in the evening (among them, the ancient Mr Johnson, now retiring, who had escorted Inskip to the lift) was archaic: he would not be replaced. There were other possible windfall gains, too. Baskerville's departure would free his attractive house for disposal.

Saundby was enthusiastic about Inskip's plans for the hotel. He saw the new bar as a major profit generator and, with Inskip and Galaxy's consulting architects, had been involved in its design. Quality furnishings were to be used throughout, and a Victorian theme had been selected, Saundby suggesting the 'Golden Age' as an appropriate name. Inskip agreed: it seemed to betoken the bar's financial success. The architects saw no structural obstacles to the conversion, though they expressed reservations, especially about Inskip's decision to create a new entrance to the bar directly from the car park on the landward side of the hotel.

Inskip's other pubs increasingly needed his attention. For several weeks he saw little of the Royal, though he kept in touch with progress and with the development of Saundby's new team. Saundby had recruited a keen young bar manager with a reputation for boosting trade, who was likely to be just what was needed for the Golden Age. Tommy, the outdoor man whose customer relations skills Inskip had found wanting, had been sacked during Saundby's first week, while Clairette, the head chef, had also chosen to move on. His departure was not without advantages, for his house, too, could be sold.

Early in April, the renovations were finished. Inskip promptly arranged to visit the Royal, but pressure of diary commitments obliged him to postpone. However, driving back to Westerpool that evening, he decided to call at the hotel in case Saundby still might be there. He noted with satisfaction the five new flagpoles along the driveway and the illuminated Galaxy signs on the side of the hotel and above its entrance. Once inside, clear Galaxy direction signs enabled customers to find their way.

Inskip was especially pleased with the Golden Age bar. Formerly, guests entering the hotel had looked across the lounge towards a picture-hung wall beyond reception. Now the wall had been taken down and the new bar, glittering invitingly, could be glimpsed from the hotel's front entrance. A new entrance to the bar led directly from the car park, while surrounding partition walls had been broken through at various points to enable ready access to the bar from other parts of the hotel. Inskip noted with satisfaction that already it was modestly busy. Then he walked through to look at the Shell Bar and the adjacent small, panelled bar, which had been redecorated and converted into a reading room. Both were empty.

At reception he enquired after Saundby, but the general manager had left. 'Had he an appointment with you?' the receptionist enquired.

'We'd arranged to meet earlier today, but I had to postpone. I was passing and called on the chance that he was still here.'

'I see, sir. Would you like to speak to Mr Stanhope instead? He's the duty manager.' The receptionist indicated a young man who was about to walk past them, cradling a ship's bell. She called to him. 'Mr Stanhope! This is Mr Inskip, the regional director.'

Stanhope was a young assistant manager recently recruited to Saundby's team. Inskip hadn't met him until now, and the young man plainly was disconcerted to be introduced in such circumstances. He looked about him hastily for somewhere to put the bell down. 'No, don't bother,' Inskip said. 'Just let Mr Saundby know that I called and that I'll give him a ring in the morning. You're new, aren't you?', he added conversationally. 'How are you finding things?'

'Very well, sir, thank you.'

Inskip turned to leave. As he did so, he nodded towards the bell the young man was cradling awkwardly. 'What's the trophy?'

'A ship's bell, sir. It came from Freddie's Bar'.

'Freddie's Bar?'

'Yes, sir. It's the reading room now, sir. Mr Saundby told me to get rid of the junk from it, but I particularly liked this. Mr Saundby said I could keep it', he added hastily.

'Sure', Inskip replied easily. He recognized the bell now, and as Stanhope shifted it in his arms, Inskip could read the lettering on it, 'HMS Hamilton'. 'I didn't know there was an HMS Hamilton. What was it? D'you know?'

'A destroyer, sir, in the last war. The first HMS Hamilton was sunk. The Somervilles organized the fund-raising for this one. There was a plaque about it in the library. They did a lot of fund raising, for charities, the lifeboat institute, and so on. They seem to have kept Hamilton pretty well provided with new lifeboats – there were photographs of them in Freddie's Bar. But most of the pictures were of the destroyers. The bell came from the last one, when she was decommissioned.'

'I see. And the rest of the stuff's gone, you say?'

'Yes, sir, Mr Saundby told me to get rid of it.'

Inskip dismissed the sudden thought of theming which had come to him. The war was over a long time ago; people didn't care about it now. Then another thought struck him. 'Freddie's Bar,' he queried, 'I hadn't heard that one before. How d' you know it was called Freddie's Bar?'

'They told me in the village, sir. They said it was the best club in Westerpool: I expect they meant in Hamilton. But I don't think it was a proper club, sir, just an informal thing.'

'I see. Well, goodnight. I look forward to seeing more of you.'

'Yes, sir. Goodnight.'

The hotel's July performance review figures showed that its overall profit performance had remained much as the year before. The Golden Age bar was making a greater contribution to revenues, but it was early days yet and Saundby expected its performance to build steadily. Results should be better by September.

The hotel's July and August monthly returns indicated that Golden Age revenue had increased, but apparently at the expense of the restaurant and Shell Bar: the September–October performance review confirmed this. Room occupancy rates were down. While this had been reflected in the restaurant's business, the biggest loss of trade by far had come from a falling away of non-residential customers. Moreover, the workload of the restaurant and kitchens had been influenced by a sharp drop in midday and afternoon functions. Hitherto, the hotel's library and drawing rooms, all conveniently situated opposite the dining room, also had been used for smaller, private functions, usually during the day. Now, all three had gone to make room for the Golden Age bar. Alternative accommodation could be provided in the larger-scale banqueting suite, but when customers had been offered this most had declined. Banqueting and larger function bookings had thinned somewhat, too, chiefly on account of cancelled provisional bookings. However, business traditionally peaked during the autumn and winter and Saundby expected to make good these losses.

Inskip scrutinized the following sets of monthly returns intently. Though the performance of the Golden Age bar had built steadily to December, room occupancy rates had fallen dramatically over the same period. The restaurant's business had also slumped, though latterly it had picked up somewhat. Anticipating hard questioning, Saundby came to the January review well prepared. He had sought an independent review and had commissioned a project group of business studies students from Westerpool University to carry out an attitude survey among customers of the Golden Age bar. Undertaken on weekdays and at the weekend, this confirmed that the hotel was on the right track, Saundby had concluded. Golden Age customers had been well (over 80 per cent) satisfied by the bar and its facilities. A number of good suggestions they made already had been incorporated. Saundby also had acted to counteract the slump in the restaurant's business by introducing a cut-price standard Christmas menu. As a result, trade had picked up appreciably: the Golden Age bar had been the source of a good number of bookings.

As to the hotel's performance in other areas, Saundby already had plans to deal with these. He expected occupancy rates to rise again with the summer, but meanwhile planned to boost room sales by introducing cut-price breaks. Break accommodation would be let only according to room availability. (Saundby didn't add that it also might give him a better chance of selling rooms on the floor above the Golden Age bar. Despite some soundproofing, guests in rooms above it had complained forcefully about noise.)

Finally, functions. Function business had been disappointing during the autumn. As prospects hadn't been looking too good for the spring, Saundby had sounded out contacts of his and already could have two large sales conferences lined up for early March. If the Royal really decided to go for conference business, it could turn round all the adverse trends, for every residential conference not only could use the function suite, but also would need bedrooms and the restaurant. They'd probably also want a couple of smaller lecture and syndicate rooms; and Saundby had thought of that, too. As Inskip's plans for a leisure centre seemed unlikely to be realized immediately, Saundby offered a practical, temporary alternative: modify the stable blocks' ground-floor rooms to form a conference suite (a simple, relatively inexpensive job) and redecorate the former staff bedrooms above to provide additional single bedrooms. The Clairette's house had just been sold; Saundby could get the whole job done for what the house had fetched. That would include a new conference parking area on the site of the seed-beds and the old greenhouses. Many of the plants in these had been dead or dying; hence, he'd had the gardening contractors clear them out. Now, the greenhouses fulfilled no useful purpose: they were just standing empty, were dilapidated and would cost a fortune to repair. But the site they occupied would be ideal for conference car parking.

Inskip questioned Saundby closely about his proposals. As far as he knew, the Royal had not before actively sought business from conferences. But something needed to be done, and quickly, to improve the performance figures. After agreeing funding with Nichols, he gave Saundby the go-ahead for his proposals.

The January and February performance figures (often a lean time in a hotel's calendar) were disastrous. Functions had been few, while the restaurant's business and room sales were at rock bottom: there had been few takers for three-day breaks in mid-February, despite an attractive price. Even business in the Golden Age had fallen back. However, the April review figures offered a glimmer of hope. The conference suite conversion in the stable blocks had been completed on time and the sales conferences (albeit only two- and three-day affairs) had boosted business substantially. Trade in the Golden Age had leapt and during the conferences the restaurant had been busy. (In February, the number of staff in the kitchen brigade had been reduced and a simpler, lower-cost menu structure had been introduced which had stood up well for the March conferences.) And in March, with the conferences, room occupancy levels had leapt too. The only snag was that the conference rate included food and accommodation, effectively discounting the price of both. As a result, the hotel's overall profit performance was well down on past figures and, as Inskip was uncomfortably aware, it was currently producing a hopelessly inadequate return on investment, let alone the golden profit stream he had anticipated. He felt uneasy about Saundby's conference strategy, but as far as he could see he was locked into it, at any rate until Saundby got the profits up. He agreed that Saundby should pursue conference business vigorously, but also other residential business, especially during the summer. He instructed: 'Look up the past regulars, the good spenders, and mail-shot them – all.'

Over the summer, Inskip's other hotels kept him busy. Their profit performance had tended to plateau (in two cases, to dip), and the Royal already had taken up too much of his time. Its monthly performance figures had become erratic, jumping upwards when conference guests were staying, falling back again when they left. Overall profit performance remained poor, as Inskip was uncomfortably aware. At the end of August, he had a call from Stanhope, telephoning him to say goodbye. The young assistant had handed in his notice at the beginning of the month, apparently after a number of disagreements with Saundby. He didn't elaborate on these, but added that he didn't believe the Royal was suitable for the type of conference business it was getting. 'Really, it wasn't designed for that sort of volume business. And plenty of other places, competitors, are. They were built especially to cater for it.'

The September–October performance review promised to be a searching one for all concerned. Inskip called at the Royal intending to spell out to Saundby the difficulties facing them and to discuss how the review should best be approached. Entering the hotel's lounge, he was disconcerted to find piles of luggage filling the whole of the right side of the room. More luggage, in smaller heaps, was piled up on the left. The lounge looked more like a left luggage office than a prestige hotel. His mounting anxiety exploded when he saw Saundby. 'What the devil's all that luggage doing in the lounge?' he demanded. Saundby replied matter-of-factly, 'September's a good month for conferences. We've a big one going out today and another coming in. The first lot haven't gone yet and some of the second already have arrived. Their rooms are still being serviced. We should have the second lot's luggage gone by lunchtime.'

There was something uncharacteristically dismissive in Saundby's manner. Inskip changed the subject to the coming performance review and Stanhope's replacement. Saundby dealt with all Inskip's questions, but in an unusually muted way, appearing preoccupied. Inskip pondered this as he left. He wondered apprehensively if the figures he had received told the whole story. He resolved to carefully go over them again and to have a thoroughly searching review at the end of the month.

Returning to his car, he noticed a familiar Mercedes coupé with German plates. On impulse, he went back to the hotel. 'Have you a Mr Marschner staying with you? I think he's German.' The receptionist checked. 'Yes, sir, we had, but he left today. Actually, I have him down as Swiss, sir, with an address in Germany.' As the car was still in the car park, Inskip reasoned that Marschner still might be about the hotel. Scanning the lounge, he noticed Marschner sitting reading a newspaper, partially obscured by one of the piles of luggage. Inskip approached. 'Haven't we met before?' Marschner lowered the newspaper and looked up blankly; then, with sudden recognition, 'Ah, yes, I remember. You liked my car'. He chuckled. 'And Tommy didn't much like you.' 'Quite', Inskip replied shortly. Noting the disapproval in Inskip's tone, Marschner protested, 'He was only doing his job, you know, and he did it very well. He was a great asset, really. But it's all gone now, just a car park. A real tragedy.'

'I'm sorry, I'm not with you. What has gone?'

'His greenhouses. All the flowers. Look what's there now', Marschner gestured dismissively. 'Just lawns. Stuff like that. And a car park.' Inskip looked puzzled, so Marschner went on, 'Tommy was always outside. He could look frightening when he wanted, but really he was quite shy. A gentle giant. And he loved flowers. His orchids were known for miles around. One of his greenhouses was full of them. He was big with the horticultural society in Hamilton. A very, er ...' Marschner sought the right word, '... snob affair; no, not snob: you know, well-connected people ... **prestigious!**', Marschner smiled triumphantly. 'It was **the feather in the cap** to be someone in it. And Tommy was someone in it. His orchids always were the best. Sometimes his other flowers, too. People came for miles to see him in his greenhouse. Lord Cavendish used to come. He was keen on orchids, and Tommy sometimes went over to Templecourt. It was quite the feather in the cap when Tommy showed you his collection in his greenhouse. A bit like Freddie's Bar.'

'Freddie was into orchids?'

'No, no, nothing like that. It's just that it was also the feather in the cap to be invited by Freddie.'

'How d' you mean, **invited**?', Inskip asked.

'Freddie was a barman of the old school, you know, always very brisk, very dapper. He had an eye like an eagle and a memory like an encyclopaedia.' Marschner paused, adding with a chuckle, 'when he chose to remember. He was the steward in the Shell Room, you know. He liked to introduce guests to one another, if he thought they'd get on together. When he got to know you, if he approved of you – that was very important – he might invite you into his own bar round the back. At first always to meet someone.'

Marschner smiled reflectively. 'He introduced me to Paddy Hennig. **Mr** Hennig, **Mr** Marschner, of course: Freddie always addressed people very properly; but in his bar among the customers it was always first names only. I don't know why Hennig was called Paddy; actually, he was German, you know, a former prisoner of war. He stayed on and married a local girl. Then he started up his company, Clarendon Foods. You've heard of them?' Inskip said that he had. Clarendon was a major national manufacturer of processed frozen foods.

'Well Clarendon started in Westerpool, you know, and Paddy was its chairman. A good man, he did a lot for charity. Most of them did, in Freddie's Bar. A lot of them were pretty big, too: chairmen, directors, lawyers and so on. Though you'd never guess it to look at them.'

Marschner eyed Inskip. 'You know how, in the dining room, it always used to be jacket and tie for guests at dinner in the evenings, you know, a touch of formality?', Inskip said that he did. 'Well, in Freddie's Bar it was just the opposite. You dressed down, old clothes, casual clothes, that sort of stuff. People who wore fine suits during the day, in the evenings could drop into Freddie's Bar looking like tramps. And the proper way to come in was up the back stairs, by the kitchens.'

Marschner warmed to his theme. 'Really, Freddie's Bar was a sort of club. Not that it was only men there; there were women, some wives, some not. Hilary Mackie used to go there. She's one of Westerpool's MPs, you know; and John Watson, another MP. Did you know that one of your Government ministers lives in Hamilton? Sometimes the chief constable would be there – but I'm not sure that Freddie really approved of him. Mind you, it wasn't only rich people there, you know, but all sorts, especially if they did work for charities, or were members of the lifeboat crew and stuff like that. As long as Freddie approved of them.'

'What if Freddie didn't approve of them?'

Marschner twinkled. 'Oh, he had his ways. Usually he'd suggest that they used the Shell Bar instead. Nicely, you know.'

'And if they didn't choose to go to the other bar?'

Marschner chuckled. 'He was a real character, full of tricks. He'd vanish into his hatch for a long time. He'd forget to bring the drinks, he'd bring the wrong drinks. He'd be confused. He'd be hard of hearing.' Marschner laughed. 'I remember one man bellowing with Freddie cupping his ear and shaking his head as if he couldn't hear until the customer gave up and went out again.' Then Marschner's smile of happy recollection changed. 'But that's all gone now. Instead you have ... this.' He gestured with disgust towards the piles of luggage.

'I think it's to do with a conference. I expect it'll be gone soon.'

'Ach, that's only part of it. It has ruined the restaurant. Once the restaurant was so good, the food, the service, so elegant. Last night, the conference came in altogether, all happy, perhaps because it is nearly over; all noisy, laughing, shouting, carrying beer, dressed anyhow. It changes the whole atmosphere. I don't blame people. If they've been sitting all day, they want to laugh, to stamp, to make noise. But the noise can be terrible, especially from that ...', he paused, gesturing in the direction of the Golden Age bar, again seeking the right word, '... that **circus!** And in spite of the air conditioning, the smoke from it still gets everywhere. But the noise is worse. When the bar is really crowded, like last night, the noise is terrible. I couldn't stay in my room, it was so bad.'

'Your room was near the bar?'

'Right above it. I'd heard that the Royal had gone down, but when they sent me the brochure about summer breaks, I thought I'd give one a try when I was over. But one night has been enough. The hotel has gone to the dogs. A real pity. It used to be so good.'

A smartly dressed woman arrived and Marschner stood up. 'Hello, Hans. I'm sorry I'm late. I had to collect Sarah.' Inskip excused himself.

Inskip left the hotel thoughtfully. Marschner had raised a host of issues which he hadn't really considered. He'd have to rethink the agenda for the October performance review.

Two days later, Inskip received a phone call from Saundby. Saundby wished to resign as the Royal's general manager. If Inskip agreed, he'd like to go as soon as possible, preferably immediately after the October review. Inskip was taken aback, but in view of what Marschner had told him, he was not altogether surprised. The Royal's performance wouldn't help Saundby's career prospects with Galaxy (it wouldn't help Inskip's either). Nevertheless, Inskip had not expected that Saundby would choose to leave Galaxy altogether, and ask to do so quite so precipitately. He decided that the October review would include a particularly searching audit and inventory check.

Stanhope's successor had not yet been appointed; if Inskip allowed Saundby to go as he asked, that could add to the difficulties. On the other hand, experience had taught him that it rarely paid to try to retain staff once they wished to go. After speaking to Philip Wright, Galaxy's personnel director, Inskip agreed provisionally to Saundby's request, subject to a satisfactory October review. For Saundby, this meant that the audit and inventory check should reveal no hitherto unknown deficiencies. For Inskip, the review's implications were more disturbing. Fundamentally, Inskip was uncertain as to what to do next. Though results were bad by any criterion, he wasn't sure that he could succeed in changing course in the short term.

The audit and inventory check took place during the first week in October. Both were satisfactory as far as they related to Saundby, and immediately afterwards he left the company. The following week, Inskip was summoned to Galaxy's head office by Chris Edmonds. He spent the rest of the day going over the Royal's figures in detail and trying to think of ways ahead for the Royal which Fisher, if not Edmonds, would be likely to approve. Arriving at head office, he was surprised to be shown not to Edmonds' office but directly to that of Paul Fisher. He found Edmonds waiting for him in the anteroom. 'Morning, John. Fisher wants to see you.' Though Edmonds was known for plain speaking, this greeting was unceremonious even for him. Walking to the chairman's door, Edmonds announced, 'He's here now.' Fisher, immaculately dressed, was sitting behind his huge desk. Another man, whom Inskip didn't recognize, was sitting to Fisher's left in front of it. Fisher was less ceremonious even than Edmonds.

'What's been going on at the Royal, John?'

Inskip was taken aback. He began uncertainly, 'I know that the performance figures haven't been good, but ...'

'It's not the performance figures I'm concerned about just now, though God knows they're bad enough. What else has been going on?'

Inskip gaped. 'Going on, sir? What do you mean?'

'We've been contacted by Westerpool police', Fisher said. Looking towards the figure seated opposite him, he went on, 'you'd better tell him, Superintendent.'

Fisher turned to Inskip. 'This is Superintendent Maxwell of Westerpool police. After the police got in touch with us, I asked if he kindly could come to see me personally to discuss the matter and he's been kind enough to do so.' He looked back towards Maxwell.

'You've been having a bit of call-girl activity at the Royal this summer,' Maxwell said. 'Good class of girl, known to us of course, but no trouble really. Bit of fun for some of the conference guests. But of course the word gets out about that sort of thing, and some of the locals are a bit hot under the collar about it. We had a look, kept the place under observation. Things have changed lately. They tend to, you know. A different class of girl, now; drug dealing might be involved, too. I think the press has got wind of it. Nothing's been published yet, but if there has to be a prosecution, it would blow the whole thing wide open.' Maxwell looked back at Fisher.

'Thank you, Superintendent.' Fisher glared at Inskip. 'Galaxy built its reputation as a good, clean, family hotel brand. That's our image. What d' you think publicity about something like this would do for it?'

Inskip gulped. His mouth was dry and words wouldn't come.

'All right', Fisher said. He gestured dismissively towards the door. Edmonds rose and left the room. Inskip followed.

Back in his office, Edmonds turned to Inskip without ceremony. 'As Saundby's gone, we're putting a new man into the Royal. Though whether we keep the place is another matter. I think not. We shouldn't have bought it in the first place.' Looking hard at Inskip, he continued, 'we'll be putting a new operations director in, too: sorry, John. But some of the Priory pubs in the north east need sorting out. You know, which of them are worth keeping as family pubs and which we should sell on. I want you to get up there and get on with it. It'll be a step down for you, but it's a job that needs doing and you should be able to handle it. As to this damned Royal Hotel of yours, I can't help thinking it's been nothing but a big mistake from start to finish.'

Inskip looked out over the estuary. Behind him, the Royal hotel stood, golden in the blazing light of the Autumn sunset.

'A big mistake from start to finish.'

Inskip turned Edmonds' accusation over yet again in his mind; and yet again he asked himself the question: where had he gone wrong?

Note

The 'Royal Hotel' exists, though some of the events in this case did not occur there. However, they are authentic and derive chiefly from the author's field research within the hotel industry.

Further reading

Goffman, E. (1971) *Relations in Public*, Harmondsworth: Penguin.

Hall, E.T. (1959) *The Silent Language*, New York: Doubleday.

Hall, E.T. (1966) *The Hidden Dimension*, London: Bodley Head.

Kaplan, R.S. and Norton, D.P. (1992) 'The balanced scorecard – measures that drive performance', *Harvard Business Review* 70: 71–9.

Kaplan, R.S. and Norton, D.P. (1993) 'Putting the balanced scorecard to work', *Harvard Business Review* 71: 135–47.

Mars, G. and Nicod, M. (1984) *The World of Waiters*, London, Allen & Unwin.

Mars, G., Mitchell, P. and Bryant, D. (1979) *Manpower Problems in the Hotel and Catering Industry*, Farnborough: Saxon House.

Orwell, G. (1989) *Down and Out in Paris and London*, Harmondsworth: Penguin.

Pettigrew, A. M. (1987) 'Context and action in the transformations of the firm', *Journal of Management Studies* 24: 649–70.

Pettigrew, A.M. and Whipp, R. (1993) *Managing Change for Competitive Success*, Oxford: Blackwell.

Van Maanen, J. (1979) 'The fact of fiction in organizational ethnography', *Administrative Science Quarterly* 24: 539–50.

Van Maanen, J. (1988) *Tales of the Field*, London: University of Chicago Press.

Whyte, W.F. (1948) *Human Relations in the Restaurant Industry*, New York: John Wiley.

Part three

Financial service organizations

Case 3.1

The rise and fall of Hamlet Insurance Company

This case describes the development of an insurance company from its beginnings in the mid-1960s to the late 1980s. A subsidiary of Denmark plc, Hamlet became a focus of concern to Denmark's senior managers who advocated a radical restructuring of its business. The case examines the problematic relations between Hamlet and its parent company as they developed in the 1970s and 1980s, paying particular attention to Hamlet's salesforce and the new pressures exerted upon them following the passing of the Financial Services Act. These difficulties culminated in the dismissal of Hamlet's chief executive.

Readers are asked to consider the role of Hamlet's chief executive in the reported events, the causes of conflict between insurance sales and bank branch staff, the process whereby Hamlet's strategy developed, and the quality of service it gave its customers. Issues raised by the case include: organizational leadership, conflict, strategy and structure, external regulation, employee motivation, organizational culture and the management of change.

Case 3.2

Culture and control at International Commodity Traders

International Commodity Traders is a commodity trading house located in the City of London. The case describes the traditional organization of the firm and the changes which have been implemented within it in recent years in response to environmental changes (markets, technology, and so on) and in the face of a severe financial crisis provoked by a 'rogue' trader.

The case focuses on organization, management and interpersonal relationships within one division of the firm, the coffee and cocoa division. The work of each of the division's sections is described together with the current problems facing the division. Long-standing collaborative relationships are being placed under increasing strain with deleterious effects on the division's performance.

The case invites readers to consider the changing culture of the organization, the nature and management of its activities, and possible ways of managing its current problems. Issues of ownership and control, recruitment and training, power and leadership, organizational culture, motivation, conflict, strategy and structure, technological change and the changing structure of financial markets are raised by the case.

Case 3.3

Project Spectrum – implementing re-engineering in a bank

Project Spectrum was an IT programme intended to improve risk management and credit control in a large bank. This case examines the progress of this project in three of the bank's UK groups: Corporate Banking Group, Financial Institutions Group and City Corporate Group. The problems associated with the implementation of the project are examined. Views of the members of these groups concerning the project are reported in their own words.

The case asks readers to consider the factors influencing the take-up of the project by the various groups, paying particular attention to organizational culture and politics. Issues of conflict, departmental perspectives, change management, communication and group relations are also raised by the case.

Case 3.1

The rise and fall of Hamlet Insurance Company

GLENN MORGAN

Introduction

In the late 1980s, the headquarters of Hamlet Insurance Company was located in a small town in the south of England. It was the dominant employer in the town and throughout the 1980s, its expansion had resulted in sets of ever more glamorous and expensive office facilities being built across the town, culminating in Ramsey House with its Chinese pagoda-style roof, leafy courtyard and balconies, surrounded by duck ponds, fountains and well-manicured lawns.

Hamlet was the insurance subsidiary of a major UK financial services group, Denmark plc. Denmark's main business area was retail banking, though as well as its insurance interests, it also had separate business units concerned with credit cards and car finance. Founded in 1966, Hamlet was by the late 1980s seen as one of the most successful insurance companies in the UK. However, its future appeared uncertain as a number of senior executives in the group headquarters and the bank questioned whether it was necessary for Hamlet to continue in its present form. Instead, they suggested the company could be shrunk significantly, its salesforce reduced and restructured, its head-office management reduced and its range of businesses cut down. The case describes the development of the company from its origins to its position in the late 1980s.

The origins and development of Hamlet, 1966–72

In 1966, Denmark was a very traditional banking organization. However in an attempt to adapt to changing market conditions, it had agreed to set up a new company to sell unit trusts to its bank customers. During the 1960s unit trusts had become increasingly popular as a way of protecting money against inflation. Real rates of interests on bank accounts were in effect negative during some of the periods of high inflation which characterized the 1960s and particularly the 1970s. By placing money in equity-based collective investments such as unit trusts, customers were able to achieve real growth in their wealth.

The task of launching the unit trust company was entrusted to a young bank manager from one of Denmark's branches in the south of England. Clive Clifford appeared to be one of the few people in Denmark who had an interest in marketing and this led senior managers to believe that he might be capable of launching the new company and its products. For some months, Clive Clifford and his secretary were to be the only employees of the new company, burrowing away in the heart of the City developing plans for the launch of a major new unit trust. Although unit trusts had been around since the 1930s and their advantages as a form of saving, particularly in periods of high inflation were well known, they continued to be seen as something for the elite and not the mass of the population. Clive Clifford was convinced that this situation could be changed. Customers of Denmark's bank branches were predominantly from the lower–middle and working class but many of them had either savings or surplus income which could fund the purchase of unit trusts. He therefore set out to develop a promotion campaign which emphasized that unit trusts were for anybody and everybody. The campaign centred on a cartoon figure called 'Harry' who was a character designed to appeal to the average citizen in the UK – a tactic repeated later in the British Gas 'Sid' campaign prior to privatization.

The unit trust fund was launched in January 1968 and a record amount of funds for the industry at that time was brought in over the first ten days of its existence. In the background, however, there were already problems emerging. Unit trusts are traditionally sold in two ways. The first is the press and publicity blitz which occurs when the fund is first opened. Companies spend a massive amount on advertising and launch. Some of their costs are met by the immediate response of clients to press adverts. So-called 'off-the-page' sales (i.e. where the customer purchases by filling in and returning a reply slip out of a newspaper) tend to decline after a few weeks. After this point, there needs to be active selling of the product. In Hamlet, the plan was that this selling would be carried out in Denmark's bank branches.

From the start, it was obvious that this would be problematic. Some of Denmark's branch managers refused to sell the unit trust believing that equity-based investment was not a suitable savings vehicle for their type of customers. Over the first couple of years some of their fears were borne out in that there was a depressed stock market and a growing international oil crisis which depressed returns to the units. Most of the branches were willing to sell the unit trusts but had little idea what a unit trust was and how it might serve their customers. Banks had traditionally had a very limited product range – money transmission services (cheque books and current accounts), savings accounts, and loans. Managers learnt how to assess risks on loans and sell them to their customers. They had little detailed knowledge of unit trusts or the equity markets on which they were based. Ordinary branch staff were even more in the dark and therefore cautious about positively recommending Hamlet's unit trust. By the end of 1970, sales had fallen to just fifteen per week, from a branch network of 1,500 even though the bank as a whole received commission directly from Hamlet for every policy which was sold!

The growth and development of Hamlet, 1970–88

By 1970, Hamlet was in the doldrums. It had achieved one of the most successful unit trust launches of the period but had found it difficult to continue its growth. The management made two decisions which would rectify this. First, they linked their unit trusts to life insurance policies. Life insurance premiums had for many years had a privileged tax position in order to encourage people to save. During the 1960s, the industry had been shaken up by the arrival of a number of new companies such as Abbey Life and Hambros (later Allied Dunbar). These companies had developed what were termed unit-linked life policies, where the client bought both life insurance and units in a unit trust fund, managed by the company. Unit-linked policies, unlike the traditional with-profits endowment policies sold by companies like Standard Life and Norwich Union, allowed the client to see the exact value of their savings as reflected on a day-to-day basis in the value of the fund publicized in the financial press. Hamlet management decided therefore to link their unit trust sales to life insurance. This opened a bigger market where questions of security and tax relief (derived from the life insurance part of the contract) could be linked to questions of growth in the equity markets (the unit trust element of the contract).

Hamlet also learnt from the other new companies that the best way to sell these products was by having a dedicated salesforce. However, they also decided that unlike other salesforces which were developing at this time in life insurance, the sales people would sell their products through the bank branches and not by the practice of 'cold-calling' i.e. visiting or phoning people on the off-chance that they can be persuaded to buy life insurance. Hamlet therefore needed the cooperation of the bank branches. However, this did not come easily. Selling unit trusts was bad enough to many managers. The thought that their branch would now be invaded by a salesman (most of Hamlet's salesforce were men, until the late 1980s) was absolutely abhorrent to Denmark's old fashioned managers and they refused to allow it.

Hamlet had to be content with access to just seven geographical areas in the first instance. Seven salesmen were employed, known in company legend as the 'magnificent seven'. Each of them was allocated an area, often containing more than one branch of the bank, and their job was to sell Hamlet's unit-linked policies to the bank's customers in that area. The impact of these specialist sales people was immediate. In 1971, the year before the salesforce came into being, Hamlet paid only £21,000 in commissions to the bank; in 1972, when the salesforce started, the figure went up to £146,500. As the salesforce grew, so did the amount of commission paid to the banks, up to £1,250,000 by 1978 and £20.1 million in 1985. By 1985, there were over half a million policies in force and the salesforce was approaching 300.

In the light of these achievements, branch managers gradually softened their attitudes and by 1982, the Hamlet salesforce had access to the whole of the bank network.

In these years, Hamlet was driven entirely by the requirement to sell policies. There was very little strategy to what they did; indeed, they had no corporate planning function until 1985 and then the senior management position in the department was allocated to an accountant who left after four months! The Hamlet sales people had a few simple products in their bag (literally, in that they had to carry round huge rate books with details of premiums for people of all ages) and their job was to get out and sell them.

Who were the sales people?

As the salesforce grew, Hamlet divided the branch network into seven large geographical divisions and within these divisions, there were a number of areas.

Each area had a manager who recruited and controlled a team of about ten to twelve people. Managers had a great deal of autonomy in those days about whom they recruited. One thing was sure; lack of knowledge about insurance and financial services was no barrier to entry. Indeed, often, managers thought it was better to get people who were good at selling since they could always be taught about insurance, whereas selling required a special sort of personality or 'bottle' as it was often called. 'Bottle' and 'nerve' were key characteristics because selling life insurance was a difficult occupation. Few customers went out to buy life insurance; few knew what a unit-linked policy was; few wanted to talk about the benefits it would bring their spouse after their own death – nobody liked the idea of their spouse being the merry (and rich) widow or widower. There were substantial barriers and hostilities to overcome if anybody was going to be persuaded to buy. Often these barriers were not overcome, so a salesperson had to be able to cope with rejection on a regular basis.

Salesforce rewards

Why put yourself through this? The first answer was money. Hamlet's salesforce was remunerated on a commission only basis. Although there was a short period after initial recruitment when the company would support a salesperson with an advance on expected earnings after three months, the salesperson's monthly earnings was determined solely by commission on products and premiums. In the words of management, this made the salesforce 'hungry'; no sales, no money. On the other hand, the commission system was very generous (particularly given the relative ease of finding customers through the bank branches). In the mid- to late-1980s, there were Hamlet sales people earning over £100,000 per year, probably twice that of the most senior managers in Hamlet's head office and perhaps three times that of the bank managers of the branches in which they were located. Even 'average' performers could achieve earnings of £30–40,000 per year whilst there were a range of other benefits on top of this. Sales people were supplied with cars, a non-contributory pension plan and, after six months, access to a subsidized mortgage scheme.

Each year, the company would take all its sales people who had achieved their targets (approximately 75 per cent of the salesforce) for its annual sales confer-ence, normally to a glamorous European destination such as Marbella or Berlin where prizes would be awarded for best performance and senior executives would unveil new plans and products. Usually such events were 'compered' by television personalities to add to the show-business glamour and glitz of the occasion. High performers could also win entry to two other clubs – the Chairman's Club for the top fifty of each quarter and the top fifty of the year. In one year, the quarterly trips (for salesperson and partner) included a long weekend in Interlaken, a Rhine cruise, and a visit to the United States. The end-of-year trip was to the USA for six to seven days. The top ten performers for the year were invited to become members of the International Club; amongst the destinations for this group were India and a Caribbean cruise. On a smaller scale, regional and area managers would also offer prizes to the best performers amongst the salesforce.

Salesforce and management control

Rewards for working for Hamlet were potentially high, yet there was an expected turnover of 25 per cent per year amongst the salesforce and in difficult years this figure went up to around 60 per cent. The 'loneliness' of selling as an occupation is part of the explanation but these pressures were also exacerbated by the management control system. Each salesperson had to achieve a certain number of sales per month if the company as a whole was to achieve its overall target. This basic target was simply derived from dividing the amount of sales required by the number of sales people. However, each salesperson was also given their own individual target. This was agreed between the area sales manager and the salesperson.

Sales managers used the personal target to stretch the salesperson and make them work harder year on year. They also adjusted it to the nature of the area which was being worked. The leafy suburbs were deemed to offer easier pickings than inner-city estates. If the salesperson failed to reach either of these targets in a month, the manager would want to know why. In some cases, managers broke the overall target down into the number of sales which had to be achieved in a week, or in a day or even in an hour.

Failure to achieve targets led to incessant pressure from managers, whose earnings in turn were primarily determined by the number of sales made by the area team. Performing consistently under target was a cause for dismissal though managers were unlikely to use this formal method, preferring to make life so uncomfortable for the poor performer by harassment that they left of their own accord.

Relations with the bank branch

The work of the sales people began in the bank branch. Each seller would be allocated a branch (or in the case of small branches, a number of them). They would be expected to get their customers from the clients of the branch. Three methods were used to 'trawl the customer base', as it was known in the company.

First, and most importantly, there was the referral system. A person walked into the branch, for example, with a redundancy cheque to pay in. The bank cashier would be expected to note that this made them a potential customer for an investment sale and to ask the customer if he or she wanted to 'see our investment specialist, Joe Bloggs, who is available now'. The Hamlet sales representative would ideally have a small office in the branch where an interview could be conducted and personal financial details discussed. Few sales were made straight off like this; normally the salesperson would arrange to visit the potential client at home in the evening to go through the sales process in more detail. Bank cashiers were told that they had to make a certain number of referrals each day.

Second, sales people would sometimes become a bit impatient and would 'hover' behind the tills watching customers as they came in. Until the late 1980s, they might even look at the details of the customer's account to help them to decide whether to try and get an interview. (This practice became unacceptable following discussions with the Data Protection authorities in 1988 since, in theory at least, the salesperson was not employed by the bank and therefore not entitled to see information on bank clients.) If they wanted an interview, they would ask the cashier to refer the customer over with an innocuous phrase such as 'our Mr Smith would like to see you.'

Third, the bank manager would send out so-called inertia letters to customers telling them for example that 'our representative Ms Jones will be in your area on Monday and will call on you at 7.00 pm'. Unless the customer opted out, the Hamlet representative would call on them. This was the least preferred method of selling as it was almost a 'cold call' and therefore representatives only resorted to it in emergencies.

In all cases, the identity of the sales person was submerged in to that of the bank branch structure. It was generally accepted that customers felt more positively about banks than about insurance companies. However, the legal distinction between the two companies remained and in some areas, such as that associated with Data Protection, this could affect the way sales were conducted.

The system depended on the ability of the salesperson to get on with bank branch staff and the manager. However, there were a number of barriers to this. The sales people were paid significantly more than the cashiers and the branch managers and yet they depended on them for leads. Cashiers would only cooperate if the manager pressed them to do so. However, managers often resented the 'young upstart sales person' who was earning so much more money. The cashiers were often women who felt an affinity with their customers and were not certain that they should be purchasing these 'new fangled, risky' products. Finally, branch managers were sometimes in conflict with the sales people. For example, up until 1988 (when the Financial Services Act came into operation and prohibited this), managers could sell the insurance products of other companies and receive a personal commission for doing so. In other words, a customer might indicate in conversation with the manager that he or she wanted to purchase a life insurance policy. The manager might decide that rather than referring the customer to the Hamlet salesperson, he (the manager – mostly men!) would sell the customer a policy from the Prudential or some other insurance company. This would have the advantage that the manager would personally pocket a commission, but it could also be justified on the grounds that a Prudential policy was better value than a Hamlet policy! Few bank employees felt that Hamlet products were really good value to their customers. So long as the branch was meeting its overall target for selling Hamlet products, until 1988 there was nothing to stop the manager selling in this way on their own account. Of course, Hamlet sales people would be outraged and would complain to their area managers who in turn would take it up with area managers in the bank. However, throughout the management structure of the bank, there was a feeling of resentment against the insurance company and such complaints were not treated sympathetically until the corporate and regulatory environments began to change.

The sales people faced a series of problems if they were going to be successful. In the first place they had to sell life insurance (which few people wanted). Then they had to meet the targets of the company and their managers. Finally, they had to create good relationships with bank staff even though they were very different in terms of rewards and expectations. Not surprisingly, not everybody could balance these competing pressures even though the potential rewards were great. Thus turnover amongst the sales people was high in the first year. In particularly bad years, it could reach almost 100 per cent. Few people lasted more than 6–7 years before either leaving the company or moving into sales management.

Salesforce and customers

The whole system was predicated on a particular relationship with customers. Generally speaking, people were ignorant of what they were buying. In fact, it was generally believed to be better for a sale if people did not even understand that they were buying an insurance policy because this would make them nervous. Instead, they should be sold to their greed – 'buy this and you too can benefit from growth in the stock market' – whilst the potential downside should be concealed. There was one huge downside which was what is termed the surrender value of the policy. If the customer invested £1,000 in a policy in the first year and then decided that they did not want to continue with it, they would find that the amount that they would actually receive on surrender would be only about £100. This was because the company designed products which enabled it to pay large commissions to its salesforce by diverting much of the first two years' premiums into commission and expenses. Even at the peak of the stock market in the 1980s, the value of a policy only began to surpass the amount the client had actually put in after about four years. Most clients were unaware of this and very shocked if it ever came to their attention.

Unfortunately, it did come to their attention because almost 20 per cent of policies were discontinued within a year of the contract being taken out, whilst by the end of the second year, the figure hovered between 30–40 per cent. Why did so many people surrender their policies? The answer was that the salesperson who was pressured by managers to achieve targets, pressured the customer into signing. After a while, many customers had second thoughts because they could not afford it or decided they had other priorities. When they realized the surrender value, they were outraged, often taking their complaints to the bank branch or sometimes to the press. This in turn created further tension with branch employees who felt that 'their' customers had been badly treated by the insurance company. By the time complaints came to light, the salesperson had often taken the commission and might have moved to another area or even another company.

Hamlet's corporate headquarters and organization

In spite of these problems, Hamlet's growth from the mid-1970s to 1988 was phenomenal. By 1987, it had over £2.2 billion of funds under management and was making a contribution to the profits of Denmark of £49.8 million. Business was increasing in these boom years of the Thatcher economy at astounding rates; in 1987, sales measured by premium increased by 52 per cent for life with pensions regular premium policies, 66 per cent for single premium life and 77 per cent for unit trusts.

In the head office, Clive Clifford became increasingly ambitious for his company. A key decision in the mid-1980s was to employ a major international consultancy group to analyse and advise on the company's future. Although it was part of a wider group, Hamlet began to see itself as separate and more dynamic than the rest of Denmark. By this time, Denmark itself had reorganized as its businesses had spread into credit cards as well as other miscellaneous areas. It had structured itself as a multidivisional company with a corporate head-quarters and four main operating divisions based on insurance (Hamlet), the bank, its credit card operations and its other businesses (see Figure 1).

However, Hamlet increasingly saw itself as an insurance company competing with other major insurers such as the Prudential. It began to plan its strategy in new terms, assuming an independence and autonomy from the parent company.

One major move which it undertook was to expand into general insurance. It developed its own house contents, property and motor insurance. The adminis-tration of this business soon became so large that Hamlet purchased a new site in south Wales to act as the centre for all its general insurance. The company also developed what it termed an 'external' salesforce. This salesforce was not to be linked to particular bank branches. Instead, it was to operate in a way very similar to cold-calling salesforces, though it would be given lists of names from other parts of Denmark's business to provide a start. The external salesforce was developed partly in response to antagonism within the bank to Hamlet's activi-ties. Its aim was to give the company more autonomy from the bank in the future.

Finally, there was an attempt to introduce more planning into the whole organization. A corporate planning function was set up in 1985 which gradually began to put in place information systems. The planners saw as one of their key roles the need to move the company from being reactive to sales growth to anticipating and directing this sales growth. Administrative systems were on the

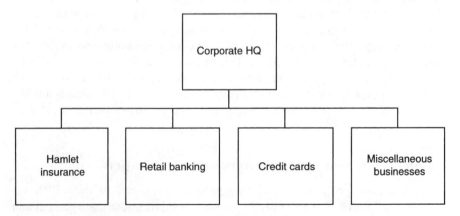

Figure 1 Denmark's corporate structure in the mid-1980s

point of being overwhelmed by the amount of new business coming in and therefore there was a need to ensure appropriate support in the form of clerical labour and IT. There was also perceived to be a need to develop products more rapidly. Marketing specialists were brought in to the company. They began to develop new products which in turn made administrative and selling tasks more complex. A further area of development was Europe. Hamlet decided that it was going to act like many other large insurance companies at the time and expand into Europe. It therefore identified opportunities and eventually went into a joint venture with two European companies to establish a new 'bancassurance' operation in Italy.

By 1987/88, Hamlet was becoming a full-range insurance company. It had expanded its head office by taking on many more clerical workers, professionals from marketing and managers to control the whole process of growth. This was almost entirely paid for from the profits made by selling through bank branches. Yet there was increasing ill-feeling within the branches, and the bank more generally, that it was the bank and its customers who were paying for this expansion. Hamlet's senior management sensed this unease but their response was to diversify away from their dependence on the bank rather than resolve these problems at their root.

Nemesis: Hamlet 1988–92

In 1986, the Financial Services Act had been passed. This Act had developed out of a series of debates concerning investor protection which had begun in the 1970s with a number of scandals in the Lloyds insurance market and amongst small fund management groups. However, following reports by the consumer law professor, Jim Gower, the issue of investor protection had become defined more widely to include the life insurance and investment industry. The Act created a system of self-regulatory bodies which were to enforce, under government supervision, a set of key principles. In particular, companies selling life insurance now had to show that their sales people had taken care to ensure that they knew the customer (i.e. had information about the client's present and future financial position and expectations) and had, in the light of this information, given best advice (i.e. had sold the most suitable product and level of premiums from amongst those they were authorized to sell). Companies were responsible for the actions of their sales people in this respect and therefore had to ensure that they were properly trained, managed and controlled. If the self-regulatory bodies on their periodic visits to the company discovered that these rules were being flouted, the company could be fined or, in the extreme, stopped from collecting new business.

Essential to this model was that sales people identify who exactly they represent. This was associated with what was known as the polarization principle – sales people were either employees of one insurance company, authorized to sell only the products of that company, or they were independent financial advisers (in which case they were not tied to any one particular company and were expected to provide clients with advice from the whole of the market).

This latter point had an immediate impact on Hamlet and its relations with the bank. Up to 1988, the bank had been in effect selling Hamlet products **and** those of other companies. It could no longer continue to do so. It had to decide whether it was going to tie completely with Hamlet or go it alone in some way, either by opting for the status of an independent financial adviser (as the NatWest Bank and many building societies did at this time) or by tying with another insurance company (for example, Abbey National tied with Friends Provident). For Hamlet this was a desperate battle which it could not afford to lose. Although it had pretensions to be an independent insurer, the threat of losing its base inside the bank branches was a potential disaster. It therefore pressed managers at the group headquarters to ensure that the bank became tied to Hamlet. Eventually this was achieved though not without a significant amount of argument and bad feeling. In return, however, the bank extracted some concessions from Hamlet.

Up to this time, bank staff had not sold any of Hamlet's life insurance or pensions policies. These were sold only by the Hamlet salesforce. However, it was accepted that if the bank was now tied to Hamlet and its managers and staff could not sell the products of other companies, they ought at least to be able to sell those of Hamlet. Thus the bank created the position of financial services consultant from amongst its own staff and instructed and trained people to sell Hamlet life insurance products. From the accounting point of view, sales made by the bank's own employees generated more income for the bank than did sales made by the Hamlet salesforce. Whilst it might be argued from a group point of view that this did not matter (since it was in effect only a question about within which accounts the same money appeared) from the point of view of power and prestige in the companies concerned this was an important issue. Therefore, bank management, in particular, began to plan for increased sales by their own employees. However, this could not be achieved without affecting the sales of Hamlet sales people. During 1988, therefore, a war began to develop in the bank branches over who was to do the selling. Hamlet sales representatives competed with the bank's own financial services consultants over the same customers. The result in many branches was that bank employees made the easy sales turning over the more difficult ones to Hamlet sales people. This had an immediate impact on the earning powers of the Hamlet sales people and it was at this point that the turnover of Hamlet's salesforce rose dramatically to around 60 per cent in the year as sales people became sick of the conflict and looked for jobs elsewhere (easy enough at a time when insurance companies and banks were expanding their salesforces dramatically).

Senior management at Hamlet argued that the result of this competition was detrimental to the group as a whole. It was resulting in a loss of business through loss of trained staff and declining morale. Furthermore, the bank's consultants were not experienced sellers; therefore they were not generating as much business with customers as would the Hamlet salesforce. For nearly a year, these arguments went on between the bank, Hamlet and the parent company. Eventually, the group headquarters forced the two sides into an agreement based on what they termed the specialization principle. It was agreed that the bank's consultants would sell general insurance, term insurance and endowments associated with mortgages. All other business which included life insurance savings products, pensions and unit trusts would be sold by Hamlet. Bank staff would be targeted to provide leads to Hamlet sales staff in these areas. The specialization agreement was greeted with relief and some triumph by Hamlet senior management and its salesforce. It appeared that two major threats to the company's core business (polarization and bank selling) had been overcome and now Hamlet could continue to develop on a more sure footing.

The senior management at Hamlet were now confident that they had overcome their major difficulties and were back on course for further growth and the realization of their goal of becoming a fully fledged insurance company. It was decided to commission a further consultancy report to examine how the company should move towards this goal. Once again, a high profile international group of consultants were employed and their recommendations accepted by management. The consultants argued that it was necessary to give the separate business lines (life and pensions, general insurance, unit trust and broking) which had developed since the previous consultancy report recommending diversification and expansion, more autonomy and responsibility through creating divisional profit centres. Until this point, the structure was based on functions – sales, marketing, finance, administration. Under the new system, a series of separate divisions based on the business areas were set up – the life and pensions company, the unit trust company, the general insurance company, and the insurance broking company (see Figure 2).

Marketing, IT, and administration were all devolved to the division, whilst a few corporate level functions remained around planning and business development. The idea that lay behind this was that a divisional structure identified clearly where accountability lay for the business lines. The profitability of the life and pensions part of the business was now clearly identifiable as the chief executive of the company had to manage his budget for all aspects of the business. Individuals within the company found their job titles changed overnight as they were transferred out of Hamlet to its operating companies.

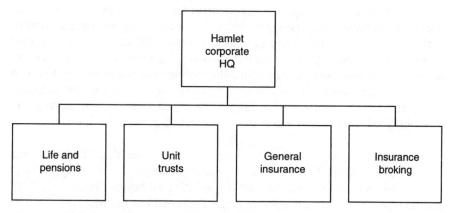

Figure 2 Hamlet's multi-divisional structure, 1988–9

This model was predicated on the belief that Hamlet had four distinct business areas which operated separately and could be accounted for separately. However, it rapidly became clear that this was not the case. The life and pensions company was by far the biggest of the four divisions. The salesforce was allocated to it which was a problem for the unit trust company. The unit trust company wished to sell its products through the salesforce which was controlled by the other company. In theory, there would have to be an internal pricing mechanism allowing for a transfer between the two companies, but how would this be determined? Other issues soon started to arise – who owned the Hamlet brand? How could consistency be created? This was even more important in that the brand itself did not really belong to Hamlet but more to the bank. Meanwhile marketing in each company was aggressively pursuing its own plans for the expansion of its own area of business. On the administration side, where IT support was critical, issues arose over the ownership of the existing system and future system development. Meanwhile, the bank was in a state of bemusement at the whole affair. They were now having to talk to four marketing directors, four administration directors, etc., whereas previously there had only been one.

Within a year, the confusion and aggravation was so great that Clive Clifford decided that he had to take the company back to a functional structure. In effect, the divisional structure was based on the illusion that Hamlet had many distinct businesses which would grow rapidly once loosed from the constraints of the functional structure. However, the chaos that resulted from the change reinforced the growing feeling within the bank and the group that Hamlet senior management were overreaching themselves.

During most of the 1980s, the Denmark group had been content to let Hamlet and the bank evolve their relationships without much direct input. For a time, the group had concentrated on diversification and acquisitions at the expense of focusing on its core businesses. However, these acquisitions had turned out to be expensive failures and there was increasing shareholder pressure to improve performance. In 1988, a new chief executive had been appointed and gradually old-style managers in the bank and the group either left or were removed from positions of power. As the new management became established, they began to focus their strategy onto their longest standing and largest business – that of the bank. The bank possessed a nationally known and respected brand name. It had millions of customers with a high level of loyalty. The task became one of maximizing the profitability potential of the bank customers by providing a full range of financial services products. The group was no longer interested in diversification or expansion for its own sake. Every activity had to be justified by how far it met the objectives of serving the bank customer base.

For Hamlet, the effects of this strategy gradually made themselves felt over the course of 1990–91. On the negative side, expansionist plans such as the move into Europe no longer appeared such a good idea. Although the group did not actually stop the venture, it ensured that it remained low key and isolated. The planned expansion of the external salesforce did not materialize. When it was first launched in 1988, it was expected that it would match the size of the internal salesforce within a few years; instead it soon began to languish as business was difficult to generate and in 1992 it was closed.

Most important of all, however, was the gradual integration of the banking and insurance which occurred under the hegemony of bank management. First of all, the group reorganized so that Hamlet and the bank became part of one division of retail and insurance banking (see Figure 3).

This placed Hamlet management directly underneath a senior manager responsible for both banking and insurance business. Within this division, the mission was clearly identified as the provision of high-quality personal financial services to the bank customer base. Most of the new senior management of this division were either from the retail banking side of the business or recruited from outside into retail banking, rather than insurance. This clashed directly with the view of Hamlet senior management that they were in charge of an insurance company in competition with other insurers, and not simply a subordinate part of a bank. In effect, the new structure subordinated them exactly to the bank and its managers. This gradually became clearly apparent.

This clash was symbolized in the person of Clive Clifford. He had been with Hamlet from the start. He had led with enthusiasm and according to some employees 'charisma'. He had encouraged an informal atmosphere in the company and tried to meet and get to know as many of the staff, both in head office and in the salesforce, as he could. He often made the effort to go out to the local pubs with the new sales trainees who came to the company's training centre at head office and he would be closely involved in the sales conventions. The company produced a monthly newspaper for employees as well as a more substantial quarterly magazine. In the newspaper in particular, photographs of Clive Clifford presenting prizes to employees or attending various local and national events sponsored by Hamlet were common. Everybody in the company felt as if they knew Clive in some way. He was considered approachable, human and, best of all, successful.

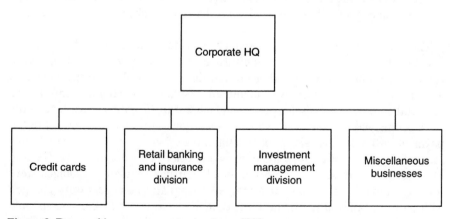

Figure 3 Denmark's new corporate structure, 1990

It was with dismay, therefore, that word suddenly broke in early 1991 in the head office of Hamlet that Clive had met with the chief executive of the new retail banking and insurance division and been told in no uncertain terms that he was no longer wanted. In the space of a couple of minutes, Clive was ousted from his position at the centre of Hamlet. Still only in his early fifties, Clive was offered generous early-retirement terms on condition that he left the company rapidly and with no fuss.

Not surprisingly, morale amongst the employees of Hamlet plummeted but this was only the start. The next moves involved far more change. The group announced that in order to facilitate cooperation between the bank and Hamlet, the two senior management teams would be integrated on one site. This site was in fact to be the new building into which the bank's head office had been recently moved. For employees of Hamlet this would mean a move from a small quiet town in the south of England to a central urban location a hundred miles away. Before this, however, there was to be a rationalization of the management structure. There were currently at least two of everything, one in the bank and one in Hamlet – two marketing departments, two finance departments, two IT systems departments, two planning departments. The goal of the rationalization was first of all to reduce the number of posts overall and then to slot people into these posts, with those who did not wish to move or who failed to find a slot being offered redundancy terms. For Hamlet employees used to working in conditions of growth in the informal atmosphere of their head office, there was now fear and foreboding about what the future would bring. The chief executive of the division who had so unceremoniously ousted Clive Clifford was seen as a 'hatchet man' who had no emotional attachment to the traditions of Hamlet. Senior bank managers were perceived as hostile and glad to see Hamlet people brought down a peg or two. The result of this was that some of the key people in Clive Clifford's Hamlet either refused to make the move or were left out in the cold.

The move of the senior management out of its original headquarters impacted on many of the secretarial and clerical staff in the company. Although insurance administration and systems remained and with this many clerical tasks, the number of better-paying and more prestigious tasks of secretarial work to the range of senior managers in Hamlet was reduced as the numbers of these executives fell.

The impact on sales staff was affected by broader changes in the bank branch system. These were gradually being turned into retail environments in which there were a range of services delivered by different people. The specialization agreement held but there was increased emphasis on communication and cooperation between the sales people and bank staff. The distinctive style of the sales people was toned down. Whilst commissions still remained central to the payment system for the sales people, a lot of the other incentives were gradually reduced. So sales conventions and prizes were scaled down dramatically. The role of sales managers also became redefined. Further regulatory changes were forcing standards of training and competence up and managers were charged with more responsibility for the professional development of the sales people and not just driving them on towards targets. These changes brought the bank and sales management closer in their concern for the long-term well-being of the customer and reduced the chances of overenthusiastic selling leading to the permanent loss of a dissatisfied customer.

By 1992, Hamlet's pretensions to be a separate insurance company had been effectively destroyed. There was no independent and autonomous senior management team which could develop its own plans and then try to argue them out with the bank and the group. The group had established an integrated management team which had as its goal the provision of high-quality products to the existing customer base. In the process, many of the old ways of doing things had been lost, as had many of the old employees. A new, more formalized management system had been set up.

Questions for discussion

1 In a subsequent publication, Clive Clifford suggested that the business will succeed which, amongst other things:

- has the necessary degree of self autonomy to succeed
- appoints a leader and then lets him lead
- is free from excessive internal controls
- treats its staff as people
- has fun.

    Are these the lessons of the rise and fall of Hamlet?
2 What, if anything, did Clive Clifford do wrong in his years in charge of Hamlet and was head office right to remove him?
3 Was it inevitable that there would be a clash between the insurance sales people and bank branch staff? How significant was the gendered division of labour within the bank and Hamlet to this?
4 How was strategy developed in Hamlet and what impact did this have on organization structure? What role did the head office take in this? Was it correct to act in the way it did?
5 How well did Hamlet serve their customers? Was regulation of selling practices in the form of the Financial Services Act unnecessary?

Further reading

Campbell, A. and Goold, M. (1994) 'Adding value from corporate headquarters', in B. De Wit and R. Meyer (eds) *Strategy: Process, Content and Context, An International Perspective*, New York: West Publishing.

Collinson, D., Collinson, M. and Knights, D. (1990) *Managing to Discriminate*, London: Routledge.

Crompton, R. and Sanderson, K. (1990) *Gendered Jobs and Social Change*, London: Routledge.

De Wit, B. and Meyer, R. (eds) (1994) *Strategy: Process, Content and Context, An International Perspective*, New York: West Publishing.

Knights, D. and Morgan, G. (1990) 'Management control in salesforces', *Work, Employment and Society* 3/4: 369–89.

Knights, D. and Morgan, G. (1991a) 'Selling oneself: subjectivity and the labour process in the sale of life insurance', in C. Smith, D. Knights and H. Willmott (eds) *White Collar Work*, London: Macmillan.

Knights, D. and Morgan, G. (1991b) 'Corporate strategy, organizations and the subject', *Organization Studies* 12: 251–73.

Mintzberg, H. and Waters, J. (1994) 'Of strategies, deliberate and emergent', in B. De Wit and R. Meyer (eds) *Strategy: Process, Content and Context, An International Perspective*, New York: West Publishing.

Morgan, G. (1994) 'Problems of integration and differentiation in the management of "bancassurance" ', *The Service Industries Journal* 14: 153–69.

Morgan, G. and Knights, D. (1991a) 'Gendering jobs: corporate strategy, managerial control and the dynamics of job segregation', *Work, Employment and Society* 5: 181–200.

Morgan, G. and Knights, D. (1991b) 'Constructing consumer protection: the case of the life insurance industry', in R. Burrows and C. Marsh (eds) *Consumption and Class*, London: Macmillan.

O'Reilly, J. (1992) 'The societal construction of labour flexibility: employment strategies in retail banking in Britain and France', in R. Whitley (ed.) *European Business Systems*, London: Sage.

Whittington, R. (1993) *What is Strategy and Does it Matter?*, London: Routledge.

Case 3.2

Culture and control at International Commodity Traders

ALAN B. THOMAS AND WALTER SKOLY

The City of London is world-renowned as one of the oldest and most influential centres of international finance. Although its position has been eroded by the growing prominence of competing centres in New York and the Far East, it remains a key part of an increasingly global financial network through the activities of the Stock Exchange, the merchant banks, insurance companies and other institutions such as commodity trading houses.

Commodity trading involves dealing in the futures markets where 'hard' commodities, such as metals, and 'soft' commodities, such as sugar and spices, are bought and sold. Sometimes trading involves no more than dealing in contracts with no involvement by the trader in the physical movement of the goods themselves, but some firms go beyond this to offer a comprehensive service capable of obtaining and delivering commodities to customer requirements on a worldwide basis. Although there were once many firms in the City which specialized in these activities, today there are less than a dozen, of which International Commodity Traders (ICT) is one of the oldest and best established.

ICT has a long history dating back to 1820 when Samuel and James Riveaux founded Riveaux Brothers as a coffee trading company. Over the years the company drew in new partners from the Weck, Jeyes and Dean families and by the outbreak of the Second World War the last connection with the Riveaux family had been severed. More recently, as the company has expanded, ownership has been further diversified but a sense of 'family tradition' remains strong.

The company now operates from modern offices in the City of London with branch offices located around the world. The range of 'soft' commodities handled by the company has expanded to include sugar, cocoa and spices and the firm has recently been reorganized on a divisional basis. The coffee and cocoa business forms one division with separate divisions for sugar, spices, fund management and brokerage services. In 1970 the firm employed fifty people, mainly at its London office, but now has nearly 2,000 employees worldwide. The late 1970s in particular was a period of phenomenal growth with many new offices established at various locations in many countries.

The company's coffee and cocoa division has 280 employees, ninety of whom are located at the London office. This divisional centre collates information from a network of offices and agents in numerous locations in Central America, Africa and the Far East. In the last few years the operations of the division have become a matter of increasing concern to senior members of the firm.

The changing environment of the coffee and cocoa division

For much of the firm's history the coffee and cocoa markets had been well understood by the traders and developments were largely predictable. Knowledge of crop performance and supply and demand equations enabled some measure of control to be exerted over day-to-day activities and the various trading parties were well acquainted with each other. Trading took place on a club basis where norms were well established and values mutually shared. Communications were relatively slow by modern standards and financial security was provided by a stable banking system which extended significant lines of credit to companies involved in the markets.

Today's conditions differ markedly from those of the past. Markets, regulatory authorities, economic conditions, human and financial resources have all become sources of concern. The cocoa market is now regarded as exceptionally volatile, international efforts to produce workable production agreements having largely failed. The coffee market is more stable but still subject to considerable uncertainty with frequent disputes among producer countries concerning output and prices. The risky nature of these markets means that although substantial profits can be realized by astute trading the possibility of spectacular losses is ever present. The ghost of the Hunt brothers' loss of over $1 billion dollars in the silver market in 1980 still haunts the minds of many traders.

The old pattern of stable trading relationships has been weakened as the variety of stakeholders has multiplied with the continuing fragmentation of markets and market participants. Where once there were a handful of respected buyers and sellers there are now a multitude of unknown players. The swift evolution of conditions in East Europe and the shifting patterns of economic activity have also created new difficulties. Dollar devaluation, a fall in commodity prices and the consequent impoverishment of buying and producing countries has had deleterious effects on market activities. Previously credit-worthy buyers have seen their buying power eroded as central governments have been unable to meet import bills. The debt crisis of the last ten years has weakened the banking system and left the world financial system sensitive to the risks inherent in commodity trading activities. In addition, modern telecommunication networks have tended to increase the volatility of markets and have contributed to the growth of competitive pressures.

With its long tradition of successful operations, ICT at first found it difficult to recognize that conditions were changing fast. But a few years ago it suffered a potentially catastrophic financial loss. Although this could be seen as simply an inevitable and isolated event in an inherently risky business, it seemed to some to stand as a warning sign that the firm needed to undergo a process of self-examination if it was to continue to prosper.

Structural developments

From its founding until the early 1950s the company was a small, family-owned business. Entrepreneurial activity centred upon the dominant family member of the day who managed the company in a traditional paternalistic manner. The organization placed great faith in its members, and trading teams were made up of a few individuals who were committed both financially and emotionally to the firm. As the firm acquired new partners, drawn from wealthy families, this paternalistic tradition continued, but the rapid growth of the company in the 1970s placed this tradition under increasing strain.

Following its financial crisis, ICT was reconstituted legally as a private company in which the former partners held the majority of the shares. In addition to these key members, a few hand-picked individuals were also permitted to buy shares. Other employees received generous salaries and profit shares and in general a close-knit, family environment stressing loyalty and life-long service was the keynote of the company's way of working. Members socialized outside the office and shared the fruits of their mutual success together.

Today the company has nearly a hundred shareholders. All shareholders are required to be working members of the company and must relinquish their shares on retirement or in the event of resignation. Shares cannot be freely bought and sold and must be maintained unless exceptional circumstances dictate otherwise. Members who own shares have most or all of their personal resources invested in the firm so that, in the event of a collapse, personal losses would be substantial. Divisional employees are thus dependent on the performance of all the firm's divisions to realize their expectations of return on their shareholdings. Unlike some of ICTs US-owned competitors, who hire and fire according to trading conditions, the overlap of employee and shareholder interests emphasizes continuity.

The exercise of influence over the company's internal affairs has traditionally stemmed from the activities of a few powerful individuals who have sometimes combined with others to form ruling coalitions. One long-serving member of the company described its management structure as 'a feudal system governed by a kind of enlightened autocracy' in which employees could be seen to be grouped together into 'estates' arranged in a hierarchy of prestige and power. A sketch of the structure when seen in these terms is shown in Figure 1.

Prior to the period of expansion, traders had operated in a variety of markets applying their general trading skills to a variety of commodities. As the firm grew, however, trading activities tended to become more specialized. Partly in response to this, a formal divisional structure was created in the late 1980s with each division acting as an operating company dealing with a specific group of commodities.

At the divisional level the controlling group is the divisional board of directors which consists of the group chairman, divisional managing director, divisional finance director, the senior traders for coffee and cocoa, and the divisional financial controller. The board is charged with the responsibility for guiding strategy and formulating policy to achieve set goals and it carries out these tasks as it thinks fit. Recently the board has established a 'mission statement' for the coffee and cocoa division which states that:

> The division aims to achieve a competitive advantage over its competitors, and to seek a reasonable margin of return on its activities, through its control of costs and credit, its relationships with its customers, its technical expertise, its knowledge of market characteristics throughout the world, and its ability to manage risk.

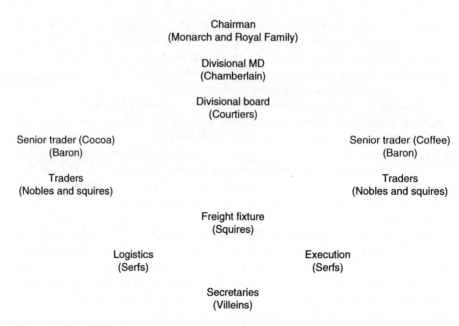

Figure 1 The division's status structure

Overall coordination of the division's activities is the responsibility of the managing director. His task is to guide the long-range planning process, monitor progress in achieving strategic objectives and provide day-to-day decisions on the shape and direction of trading policy. The post has been established only recently. Previously, there had been no formal management structure and the nomination of directors had been little more than a confirmation of emergent political influence and trading success, with the structure of the ruling hierarchy being defined largely in terms of internal recognition. Even now there is a sense of unease at the introduction of 'managers'.

At the higher levels of the division, leader status is achieved through peer-group acceptance of an individual's perceived personal standing and authority. Such acknowledged leaders are expected to act as representatives of their supporting group within the organization as a whole, and continuing support is dependent on their ability to meet their group's expectations. Traditionally, the possession and display of 'heroic' attributes have been crucial to the achievement of leader status, particularly those attributes most closely associated with success in the trading task.

The organization of coffee and cocoa trading

A sketch of the formal organization of the coffee and cocoa division is given in Figure 2. The central task is trading but for this to take place successfully there must be close coordination with other divisional units. The main tasks of the divisional units are described below.

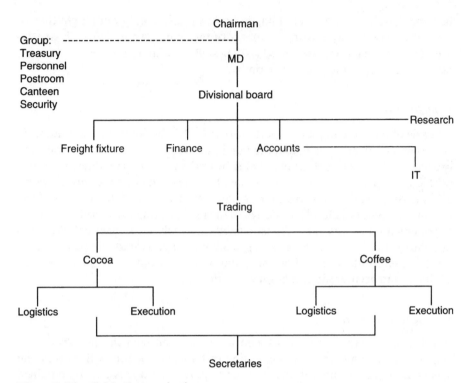

Figure 2 The division's organization

Trading sections

These sections are involved in the negotiation of purchase and sales contracts with buyers and sellers across the world. Contracts are negotiated in a range of world currencies and involve committing the company to significant market, credit and country exposures. There are ten traders at the London office and they have to assess risk, fix prices, match purchase and sales commitments, manage price exposure, take out insurance, arrange freight, obtain banking cover, manage currency transactions and obtain credit approval where necessary.

The trader's role is to seize and exploit business opportunities as they arise using a bundle of specialist skills and knowledge that must be acquired through experience. The trader's role is ill-defined and each trader is expected to define the job into existence. New traders are expected to pick up the skills of the job by exposure to activity at the trading desks, watching experienced traders and working out for themselves how to trade successfully. There is no formal training and this reflects the individualistic, sink-or-swim philosophy of the successful traders. Newcomers undergo a gradual process of acceptance and assimilation into one of the prevailing power groups on the basis of demonstrated ability to trade effectively. Successful 'apprentices', who must find their own masters, are incorporated into these groups and may, in time, be offered the opportunity to become shareholders. Shareholding is, however, less a matter of a right than of a privilege granted by existing members of the share-owning elite. Those who are unable to acquire the required trading skills or who do not display the right attitudes are encouraged to move on.

Logistics section

The role of the three logistics experts is to bring the division's commodities from the point of delivery specified in the purchase contracts to the point of delivery specified in sales contracts as negotiated by traders. The commodities are transported by ship, train, barge or truck from factories and ports around the world and the coordination of these movements is crucial to the effectiveness of the distribution process. Good knowledge of the range of transport modes available together with the costs and risks associated with each one is essential. Precision and the avoidance of errors are at a premium for a good trade on paper can be rendered unprofitable by suboptimization of delivery options. Communication of timely and accurate information is essential.

Execution section

ICT has six execution specialists who are concerned with the preparation of shipping documents and the negotiation of those documents with buyers and sellers to obtain payment. Each contract requires that documents be obtained from suppliers for presentation to buyers. All forms of communication are used (fax, telex, telephone) and every piece of information given or received must be completely accurate. Documents are negotiated either through the banking system or directly with clients.

The work requires great precision and is performed within rigid time constraints. Delay and error cost money. A good contract can be rendered uneconomic by poor documentary handling. The effectiveness of the execution department is of critical importance to the company's ongoing profitability as well as to the image it projects into the marketplace.

Freight fixture section

Two specialists manage the arrangements for sea freight between the point of sale and the point of delivery. This is a highly specialized function requiring many years of experience of the freight market. One of the freight specialists negotiates freight with owners and owner's brokers. The other deals with the payment of freight charges and the resolution of disputes with suppliers, owners and receivers. The performance of the section is crucial to the realization of contract potential.

Accounts section

The preparation of management and financial accounts is managed by ten people at the London office. The role of the accounts section is to provide accurate and timely management accounts to support the trading function. Good financial accounting is vital in a volatile environment where performance can fluctuate widely.

The diversity of trading activities makes for a complex accounting system, and the central profit-and-loss account is subdivided into many sub-accounts for which individual traders are responsible. The section is overseen by a financial controller who reports to the finance director. Individual members of the section are assigned to geographical areas of trading activity so that each trader can respond directly to a responsible member of the section. Good communication between the trading desks and the accounts section is essential.

Research section

This section is responsible for the identification and analysis of business opportunities both for the division and for third parties to whom it sells its know-how. Although it is located within the division, its activities are largely independent of the day-to-day trading function and its orientation is to broad issues over longer timescales. The six members of the section possess a diverse range of specialist skills ranging from naval architecture and agronomy to econometrics and statistics, and there are no specific job descriptions other than to develop opportunities as they arise.

The attributes required for successful performance by members of some of these sections are shown in Appendix I.

Figure 3 shows the principal flows of activity surrounding trading. Typically a trader will make a contract with a client for the delivery of a specified quantity of a commodity to a particular location on a given date at an agreed price. The trader will then secure the deal on the futures market. Logistics and freight fixture will then be notified of the contract. Nearer the time of delivery the execution section will arrange for the physical movement of the goods and the contract will be fed into the accounts section. Business thus originates in the trading section but in the course of trading each section initiates some part of the trading process. The chief actors emerge from the trading, logistics and execution sections while marginal players come from the support sections – accountants, treasury and IT specialists. This web of interaction is supported by the non-technical units such as messengers, canteen and cleaning staff. Within these webs individuals assume specialist responsibility for decisions related to the work in hand.

The time-spans associated with the processing of contracts are not uniform and are frequently dictated by market conditions and the wishes of buyers and sellers. Some contracts may be written for five years while others involve just a few days of concentrated attention. Workflows are thus unpredictable and no strict rules for practice can be promulgated to govern their regulation. Activities are centred around powerholders who, through the influence they wield and the resources they control, create pockets of patronage that vie with other groups for survival.

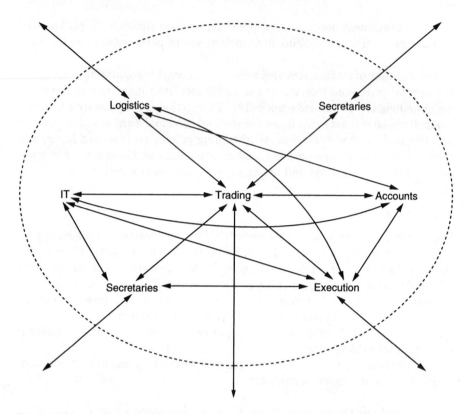

Figure 3 The trading workflow

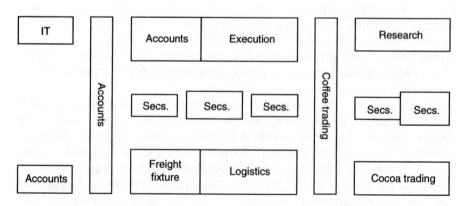

Figure 4 Floor plan

Section members occupy desks in a large open-plan office area (see Figure 4). All the division's day-to-day activities are carried out within this area. The trading desks are distinguished by the array of computer screens, telephones, and large ceiling-hung monitors displaying financial data. There is a small separate lounge where visitors can be received, and a boardroom where the walls are adorned with photographic head-and-shoulders portraits of the founding partners and their successors. The managing director has no office of his own and, like other members of the division with senior managerial responsibilities, occupies one of the trading desks where he works like any other trader. The physical structure of the area gives an open, egalitarian impression and everyone is on first-name terms.

Verbally transmitted information is the basis for many of the decision-making processes. Written information largely serves to provide the justification for decisions already taken. Physical location on the office floor tends to reflect patterns of influence, and powerholders use it as a stage from which to address members of their own and rival groups. Differences in dress codes and attitudes are readily visible to all.

The average age of traders is around 35 years, partly a reflection of the recent rapid expansion of the firm. Tending to see themselves as 'young lions' they bring considerable energy and ambition to their work. They are overwhelmingly male. Formal recruitment to trading positions is rare. Although an 'experiment' with graduate recruitment had been made, it was regarded as having been a disastrous mistake. Occasionally, new traders have been recruited on the basis of 'cold calls' by outsiders, but access to trading opportunities is normally given only to the relatives, friends or associates of existing traders.

In the administrative functions members are older, around 45 years on average, and are more conservative in their outlook. Recruitment is more formalized and more attention is given to explicit on-the-job training. For some of the more technical functions, such as accounts and IT, appropriate specialist qualifications are generally required. A small but significant number of women are employed in the non-trading sections, especially in the accounts section.

In general, new members of the division are recruited into the coffee or cocoa 'clubs' and learn to adopt their particular beliefs and values. Typically, they do so by informal means during sorties to the City's watering holes and during business trips abroad.

Belief in the 'infallibility' of the trader is a well-established part of company lore. During its period of rapid growth, young traders had entered the company and risked everything to invest in the business. Their exploits and the 'fabulous wealth' they created for themselves and the company became the stuff of legend and sustained the cult of the heroic trader which persists to this day. The mystique of trading has helped to reinforce the traders' position at the centre of the daily workflow where they act as leaders, coordinating the activities of the supporting sections in order to successfully execute the contracts they have initiated.

The effectiveness of the trading activity is heavily dependent on the ability of the organization to muster the requisite variety of competences, to resolve the challenges that emerge from the environment, and to learn from the experience gained through this interactive process. The depth of skill available in the sectional resource pools is critical to successful trading.

Current issues

The grave financial loss experienced by the firm had sent shock-waves throughout ICT. During its long history it had its share of ups and downs but nothing that could be considered life-threatening. Major losses, liquidations, collapses and crashes were not unknown in the City but these had largely passed ICT by. But following its close encounter with disaster the company vaguely sensed that it was facing some kind of deep-seated crisis. Old certainties seemed suddenly to have evaporated and assumptions that had served the organization well for so long were now put into question. In particular, those outside the owning elite felt a deep sense of unease and a loss of confidence in the men at the top.

Although the company had been able to surmount its immediate financial problems because of the healthy state of its reserves, a sense of panic gripped its members. How could the disaster, perpetrated, as the senior members saw it, by the excessive ambitions and irresponsible activities of a single trader, have been allowed to happen? And what could be done to prevent its happening again?

One response was to institute new forms of control. The traditional culture of trust and cooperation that had been the guiding ethos of the company began to be eroded by harder and more rigid attempts at organizational control. Divisionalization was seen as one way of rationalizing the firm's activities yet this, together with the loss of confidence in the old ethic, had produced a situation in which a fragmented collection of differentiated working groups found themselves without a clear sense of their identity and mission. A general anxiety swept the company which prompted individuals to focus on personal goals with little concern for the good of the company as a whole.

This tendency was reinforced by the company's approach to the allocation of rewards. Monetary bonuses were tied to individual achievements although the basis upon which those achievements were assessed was felt by some to be rather arbitrary and gave rise to a sense of resentment on the part of those who felt their contributions were not adequately recognized. Traders were believed by many to benefit disproportionately from the bonus system. Although details of individuals' incomes were not formally disclosed they were a frequent topic of conversation and speculation at gatherings away from the office. Similarly, shareholders came to be viewed with mixed feelings by those who had not been offered the chance of acquiring an equity stake in the firm, the identities of the haves and the have-nots being common knowledge among all but the most junior members.

There was also a tendency to engage in 'empire-building'. It was widely believed, for example, that one trader was indulging in profitable but highly risky working practices largely in order to build his personal sphere of influence and enhance his bonus. Furthermore, other traders had begun to copy his style.

Similarly, the head of the logistics section had begun to treat his control of crucial information as a way of enhancing his personal power.

Another worrying development was the emergence of a growing divergence between the coffee and cocoa sides of the division's activities. Although these aspects of the business did require traders to possess somewhat different skills, so that traders in one commodity never traded in the other, in the past relationships had typically been cordial and cooperative. Now, occupying separate areas of the trading floor, the coffee and cocoa traders began to see themselves as in fierce competition for the services of the supporting sections. How much support they actually received tended to depend on the personal influence of individual traders and the popularity of their activities in the eyes of the support groups.

The efforts of the senior cadre to establish more formal control over the division's activities by, for example, emphasizing formal reporting and responsibility networks, met with incomprehension and scepticism on the part of the traders. A requirement that credit limits be sanctioned by higher authority was felt to be especially irksome, inhibiting the traders' ability to trade as and when they thought fit. A series of confrontations with finance ensued which fostered a climate of mistrust and an unwillingness to share information. Poor communications have increased errors in the decision-making process.

Relations between the traders and the execution section have also become strained. Execution requires accurate and timely information from traders but this has become less readily supplied. Members of the execution section began to resent the way in which they felt they were being used by the trading sections, but thought that they lacked the status to confront the traders about their activities. Instead they devised 'traps' as a way of disciplining what they saw as the 'wayward' trader. As one of the execution specialists remarked, 'There was a time when we knew what information traders would need almost before they did, but now I don't tell them anything unless I'm asked.'

Within the sections relationships have also deteriorated, especially within execution and logistics. There is a feeling of defensiveness and a fear of encroachment by others on the territories that have been marked out by individuals in their relations with traders. Although these territories are partly defined by the differences in the specialist knowledge and expertise which section members develop through their association with particular traders, there is also a barely-acknowledged awareness that they have in part been manufactured as a means of self-defence.

A large proportion of managerial time is now spent dealing with conflicts and disputes. This is not only distracting the firms' members from their central trading tasks but is also further disrupting the increasingly fragile personal relationships between key actors. There is a feeling among some of the members that the firm has somehow lost its sense of identity and with it the deeply-embedded sense of community that had, since its inception, been the hallmark of ICT. Others seem less concerned by these developments and believe that they have more than enough to do simply doing business. As one said, 'Times are changing in the City but so long as we have the freedom to trade we'll win through just as we have always done'.

Questions for discussion

1 How would you describe the culture of the organization? Has this changed in recent years and, if so, why and with what effects?
2 How is the work of the organization organized and managed?
3 How would you account for the problems being experienced and what interventions would you suggest that might help to ameliorate them?

Appendix I Required skills

Trading
- numeracy
- ability to build social relationships
- ability to think forwards
- ability to make decisions on the basis of incomplete information
- energy
- courage to take calculated risks
- negotiation skills
- team skills
- foreign-language skills
- ability to think strategically.

Logistics
- attention to detail
- strategic thinking
- ability to make decisions from a range of imperfect options
- ability to handle trading decisions and turn them into profit
- foresight
- negotiation skills
- foreign-language skills
- ability to shoulder responsibility for decisions taken.

Execution
- accuracy and precision
- negotiating skills
- ability to think forwards
- ability to assess priorities
- foreign-language skills
- ability to operate under pressure.

Freight fixture
- attention to detail
- negotiation skills
- risk assessment (reliability/solvency of owners)
- ability to optimize outcomes from a range of options.

Further reading

Clarke, W.M. (1991) *How the City of London Works: An Introduction to its Financial Markets*, London: Waterlow.

Daft, R.L. (1995) 'Manufacturing, service, and advanced information technologies', in *Organization Theory and Design*, St. Paul, MN: West Publishing.

Durham, K. (1992) *The New City*, Basingstoke: Macmillan.

Handy, C. (1993) 'On the cultures of organizations', in *Understanding Organizations*, Harmondsworth: Penguin.

Kahn, H. and Cooper, C.L. (1993) *Stress in the Dealing Room: High Performers Under Pressure*, London: Routledge.

Mintzberg, H. (1983) *Structure in Fives*, Englewood Cliffs, NJ: Prentice-Hall.

Ott, J.S. (1989) *The Organizational Culture Perspective*, Pacific Grove, CA: Brooks/Cole.

Pfeffer, J. (1992) 'Understanding power in organizations', *California Management Review* 34: 29–50.

Schein, E.H. (1984) 'Coming to a new awareness of organizational culture', *Sloan Management Review*, Winter: 3–16.

Webb, G.H. (1987) *The Bigger Bang*, London: Waterlow.

Case 3.3

Project Spectrum: implementing re-engineering in a bank

CHRISTIAN DE COCK

The implementation of project Spectrum took place in the mid-1990s against the backdrop of an organization (financial institution) which was perceived by most employees as very hierarchical, cost-conscious, and not necessarily very vision oriented. The initial research for the project looked at the value that could come out of re-engineering the business with emphasis on large corporate areas (non-high-street banking). Concretely this meant putting new IT into place for effective risk management and more effective structuring of credit proposals **across** different business areas. Spectrum was thus conceived of as a system which sought to handle information in a different way **and** which would provide a catalyst for change.

> *We spend more time talking about the cost of things than the quality of the loan sometimes. We have to juxtapose that against what works best for this type of project: a flatter organizational structure, more decentralized control, more empowerment for the staff, a lot more vision, and less emphasis on short-term cost issues.* (Mike, senior project team member)

A formal business case, based upon the initial research, was developed by the end of 1992. This included a financial analysis (detailed costing elements), a strategic analysis, technology blueprints (selection of technology components that would be used), and re-engineering blueprints (fundamental challenge to rigidities in organization). The Spectrum applications and business information store were intended to support a number of activities that span the business process, including: customer information management, credit applications handling, risk management, deal structuring, and customer service. Each business function would use Spectrum services to create or refer to the information needed. In using the Spectrum applications, managers and analysts would directly input information to a general database while working on credit proposals, etc. This would constitute a significant break from traditional working practices where deals were worked out on paper and subsequently inputted by clerical staff.

Time was spent with both directors and managers of four business areas to see whether the need for the project was genuine and that a sound financial and business need existed. Spectrum was the first decentralized project with the business areas paying for all the components of the effort. This process of building business support at several levels took roughly a year and the project team got the necessary agreements from three business areas that led to developing the specific implementation approach. These areas were Corporate Banking Group (CBG), Financial Institutions Group (FIG), and the New York division. The City Corporate Group (CCG) originally decided not to join the project. In what follows the case will explicitly focus on perspectives from the UK groups: CBG, FIG, and CCG (see Appendix I). The founder business case was finally approved in April 1993 and the system was intended to be implemented fully (including training of users) by April 1995.

In October 1993 joint application development teams were set up but these were quickly abandoned (according to the project team because no senior representatives from the business areas showed up) and instead the project team started showing people information on VDU screens of what they could expect and on which they could comment. This was the start of a long and protracted bargaining process on the requirements and preconditions for rolling out the Spectrum system. Disenchantment started to grow on both sides.

In June 1994 a new project director took over. Although the implementation should have been well under way by then negotiations on preconditions still continued to be painfully slow. Initial comments from the business areas indicated that the project had oversold itself and that the project team were just not listening to people in the business. The project team retorted that people in the business areas had underestimated the amount of time they had to invest themselves to make Spectrum a success, and just wanted to automate what they already had. Each business area was asked to delegate a business representative to liaise with the project team and 'sell' the system internally.

In November 1994 CCG joined the project and immediately made most progress of the four UK areas involved. New York was also reported to have 'gone live' although interpretations of what 'going live' involved differed widely among the different stakeholders. The most defensive areas seemed to be FIG and CBG.

In March 1995 a third-party review was published, evaluating the state of the project. Interpretations of what was actually recommended in the report and lessons learnt from what had happened again varied widely between the various stakeholders. Nevertheless, there seemed to be a general agreement that 'assumed understanding' had been a major problem in the project (an understanding that was never really there). Several important issues (e.g. who would take responsibility for training the employees in the different business areas) remained unresolved.

In what follows, the various perspectives of the key stakeholders (summer 1995) will be put forward.

View of people in the Corporate Banking Group (CBG)

The issue of trust was perceived as the main stumbling block by both managers and business analysts. Honesty about the implementation process was one issue that emerged clearly as open for improvement. Concerns were raised about the fact that recommendations from the third-party review were not being followed through. Ownership has not been returned to the business areas: 'our power and influence is zero at the moment'. There was a perceived lack of urgency on behalf of the project team and the credibility of Spectrum in CBG had suffered because of the delays and unfulfilled promises.

Although everyone had initially been very positive about the project, there now existed a high degree of scepticism about the eventual benefits. A list of preconditions had been drawn up. These would have to be fulfilled before the system could be introduced in CBG. People believed that 'the world had moved on' since the original business case had been written. Consequently there was a growing sense of apathy towards the project in its current format.

On technical difficulties/slowness in making progress

We as a business area – as long ago as the middle of last year – sat down and drew up a list of what has become known loosely as our list of preconditions for implementing Spectrum. We have stuck to those preconditions since then, very consistently. Therefore it is very disappointing to see that 9 months down the line we still have that same list of preconditions and we have exactly the same outstanding problems as 9 months ago. A lot of time and effort has gone into it, but in practical terms we have not really got anywhere. So the credibility amongst the people in this division has obviously suffered. The name Spectrum is regarded as a bit of a joke ... . (Graham, business representative)

Once we go live we will have lost our hold on the project to deliver improvements, that's the feeling ... (Martin, director).

On relations with project team

The project personnel appear very defensive. It is late, it is probably over budget – I can't really comment on that – it hasn't delivered what has been promised. So the project has not covered itself in glory, it has to be said. We as users have become more demanding and said 'no! 80 per cent is not good enough, we need it much better than what you are proposing.' That has produced the defensive reaction from the project side. (Graham, business representative)

What could have been better is the public relations the project have put out. They promised many things without delivering, and you lose confidence very quickly that way. If something could be done it would certainly be on that front. The project has lost so much credibility. Someone should have been realistic, 'look you will get exactly what you want but it is going to cost lots of money and take lots of time, now go away until 1996'. They then would get it working and come back with a fully working package. (Philip, analyst)

It is good to say that New York are live and using the system. It makes us in London think 'Oh my goodness, shouldn't we be there'. But the reality of life ... It makes one very disappointed, not that we are lied to, but ideas are being developed to lead us to think that we are behind. (Eric, manager)

On changing perspectives

At the very start it was all very exciting. Having worked in the bank for many years, you very quickly build up that frustration that there is information there but you have difficulty using it, grabbing it ... But those very early suggestions of what could be achieved got lost because of the need to concentrate on what the project team called 'core values'. It looks like all the effort has gone into the practicalities of gathering information without thinking about 'what do we do with it now?'. So all added benefits disappeared, of time, budget, or whatever. If you would graph it, from being very high at the beginning it has sloped quite steeply because we have been let down, been disappointed, things not having been delivered or don't work as you want them to work ... . (Martin, director)

View of people in Financial Institutions Group (FIG)

The general perception of FIG was that expectations were set too high by the project team at the start of the project. This had created a certain amount of disillusionment. The project had thus gone from a stage of being welcomed by the business in its conceptual form to one where the delivery had proved disappointing. Different managers were using the system to different degrees and for different purposes. The system was 'live' but not to the point of everyone using the system to its fullest potential in their particular job requirements.

The business area as a whole had put a relatively liberal interpretation on the implementation process. The view was: 'we've spent a lot of money on this, we know it is not perfect, but let's at least try and use it because we will only improve it technically by getting some proper user input'. At operational levels there was some doubt about the actual commitment of senior managers to Spectrum. People believed the project was not really business led, that the system had been driven by software requirements rather than user requirements. Functionality seemed to have been sacrificed in order to stick to time scales and budgets.

On technical difficulties/slowness in making progress

I think it is a good system but it should have taken off a lot quicker than it has done. It has had a lot of faults. If they had been solved in the beginning ... To start a lot of people were really excited and it sounded really good, but because it has taken so long people got disinterested, 'what's wrong with the system we have already got?' that sort of mentality. (John, business representative)

On senior management support

My perception is that there is very strong vocal support for Spectrum in terms of 'this is the way we have got to go, we have got to support this type of technology'. But when it actually gets down to the practicalities of it, people do not give the impression of being fully supportive. They do not seem to be 100 per cent behind the project, either in saying 'this project is going to succeed come what may' or saying 'we have to decide whether this project is the way we want to go, therefore we have to 'test' it to destruction (find out what the good points are, what the bad points are and make a decision)'. (Steve, manager)

On focus of project

It appears that the systems has been driven by the programmers or the software requirements rather than by the user requirements. There are a lot of things in the system which do not make sense, which are not user friendly, which are not – to my mind – logical. There are a lot of annoying little things, not major system problems. It does the job you want it to do but it does not necessarily do it in a way which is particularly easy. If, to my mind, you want broader acceptance you shouldn't have these little quirks. (Michelle, analyst)

On trade-off: time and budget versus functionality

My personal view is that we should never have got to the stage of ten users on Spectrum at the point that we did. There was a certain amount of pressure from Spectrum so that they could go back and say: 'right we have got X numbers of users'. This business of going 'live'. Right, we are all live. Rubbish, we are not all live in terms of everyone using the system to its fullest potential in their particular job requirements. To my mind it should have been a more targeted, more responsive, and more phased approach. The emphasis of the project was on cost. Budgets were being set, they met these budgets, well fine ... If cost is your primary target you are not going to get what the business area wants. (Steve, manager).

On managing expectations

There is a fundamental problem in terms of expectations. Expectations have been mishandled in that the business areas had been told 'right this box will land on your desk and you will be able to do XYZ from day one'. There was probably an immense amount of pressure on the project team to get something out that was working as quickly as possible and provide a broad spectrum of functions as early as possible without necessarily going down the route of trying to make sure that each of those systems worked the way we wanted it to work; and without necessarily saying to the business areas 'look you take this from day one without it being the answer to all your evils; there is going to be a tremendous amount of effort required and two-way communication'. (Tom, director)

View of people in the City Corporate Group (CCG)

There existed a clear difference in perception and enthusiasm about Spectrum between people at the practical, user end (analysts/managers) and people who had to evaluate Spectrum in the wider context of CCG's activities (managers/directors). Users were enthusiastic although they had had to face many implementation problems. Their biggest complaint was that they didn't have enough terminals and their biggest worry was that their business area was going to pull out of the project. More senior people were very wary about the bigger picture; there was a certain amount of 'Spectrum fatigue' because of delays and disappointments with the system.

The system was perceived to be working but most people agreed that it was not really 'live' (in the sense of a real live environment) yet (a paper copy is supplied for everything that is done on the system). Senior directors have not been driving Spectrum as hard as they could (they are perceived to be neutral or negative by the analysts) because of the many ambiguities and uncertainties at corporate level. These vibes are picked up by people at ground level and inevitably Spectrum has gone down the list of priorities. People knew the implementation of the project was travelling fastest in CCG, were proud of it, but believed they could do a lot more if they would get unequivocal support and guidance from senior levels. 'The fact that CCG are doing a 15 per cent job is only looking good because the others are doing a 7.5 per cent job. Perhaps we should all be working at 95 per cent to make this a success.'

On assumed understanding

That theme, 'assumed understanding', if I could talk long enough, it would pop up all day long. I don't know whether it is a problem with Spectrum or a problem with the people that are on it from the business side ... People who go along to a Project Review Group meeting have piles of work to do. Spectrum used to generate loads of reports, massive amounts of paper coming out of Spectrum, long tedious meetings. And you get tired, you have got other things to do. You are not a techie anyway. I miss things. I think I understand what something says but actually I completely misunderstood. So we do have these difficulties ... They don't understand our business properly these guys. Maybe they can't. I don't know what the problem is. They do have some bankers in there. But if they understand our business then, for some reasons which suit themselves, they are limiting the way that understanding affects what they do. (Stewart, director)

On implementation problems/uncertainties

When it started off we were in the starry-eyed optimist haze and so were they [the project team] actually: we are going to re-engineer the credit process and that is only the start. Then they gradually knocked aside all these exciting ideas that we had and basically it has been pulled back to the point where they are not trying to re-engineer anything any more. They are just looking for a particular way of processing credit applications. It is a different system: it is more expensive and it does less. Having said that, when we started we didn't know what was achievable. What we have got now is reality. There is an awful lot of disappointment, frustration and anger, and what I call 'Spectrum fatigue'. We are a year beyond where we thought we were going to be. We are still working away at it and the uncertainty has been dragging on for months ... If we had never started this, we wouldn't go into it now. The problem is that we have got so much sunk costs, so much sunk time. And we have got the pilot going downstairs where the people are very enthusiastic ... . (Stewart, director)

On speed of implementation

At the ground level, the corporate teams, it's been travelling very fast, because we had the system on our desks, we had daily use of them. We are encouraged to use them where possible. Higher up in the risk structure, I don't think the emphasis has been there to get the people onto the system. They're a lot slower. (Mark, senior analyst)

On other business areas

CBG have a level of influence which to my mind is out of all proportion to their contribution to this. They are holding hostages. Their involvement in this is crucial and they are holding back. They are saying 'we are not going in until we get exactly what we want out of this'. We on the other hand have said 'the only way to get this thing to work is to get in there and use it and prove that it works' . (Tony, manager)

View of the Spectrum project team members

Project team members felt that the project did not bear any blame for the 'time and budgets' versus 'functionality' controversy. They were given a budget by senior business people and delivered the functionality they could within the budget and time scales set to them. They ascribed the problem to a lack of communication between different levels within the business units.

The members of the team agreed that the involvement of the business should be greater but the perception of what 'leading' meant differed from that of people in the business. For the project team, this involved assigning more staff to the project, putting in a lot of hard work from the business side. The project team made demands on the business areas in order to fulfil the targets set to them by the steering committee (made up by the heads of the different business areas and very senior managers).

The team shared the fear of people in the business areas that Spectrum would not be a re-engineering tool but just another credit processing tool. However, the potential remained, but success wholly depended on the people who were actually driving the implementation. In many instances it was still a case of 'that's how I do my work and this team are not listening to me'. Relations with the business areas were perceived to vary quite strongly. This had mainly to do with the attitude of the managers responsible for the implementation process.

On senior management involvement

Management in the business areas – although it wasn't always the same person who is there now – agreed they wanted to implement Spectrum and committed their business area and the group to spend a certain amount of money to make that happen. But they didn't have the necessary focus or the attitude toward managing resources to see that through. So although they sit on the steering committee and approved the project they don't actually encourage implementation of the project. It is as if they hired a group of fifty people and then gave them nothing to do, spent the resources and then didn't make any effort to make sure there was a return on that resource which I think is very irresponsible. It manifests itself in different ways: the amount of attention they pay to the project, the type of people within the business areas they give us to resource the project. Benign neglect ... In some business areas there is some direction: 'we will implement it providing the project does XYZ'. In others there is no sense of direction at all. People don't know whether they are supposed to be using it, whether management wants them to or not, or doesn't care ... . (Christine, business analyst)

On managing expectations

Certainly the first release of the software looked too much like just another credit risk tool. They hadn't properly understood that bankers now were going to input the data instead of a team of credit clerks. Although that always had been emphasized in the business case they never understood what it really meant. The problem was that Spectrum oversold itself, promised too much in the early days. It was talking about automated information feeds as if by magic you were going to have all the information on a customer available in a repository that you could instantly access. In some way we were promising magic to occur but you can only reap those benefits if you dome some hard work yourself to make sure that that repository of information is there. (Tom, technical implementation manager)

Should the project be more business led?

I agree with the target. My perception is that they think it is up to IT to give them the lead on a plate so that they can turn up to a meeting once a month and have all the information presented to them in the form they want without any hard work on their part. We want to give them the information as necessary but we want them to put in five, ten times the effort that they put in now to do it. They don't wish to apply manpower to it. Leading it is not a case of sitting on a committee and pronouncing. It is being involved on a day-to-day basis and we would welcome that. But they are not willing to step forward in that role, they don't see that as the business involvement role. That's the gap. We all agree that it should be business led but we all have different perceptions of how you lead in the business. (Richard, systems development manager)

Their own management is dictating to us what we should or shouldn't be doing ... when we are tactical and try to plan in advance they get antagonistic 'here they go making unreasonable demands again'. The steering committee is filtering too much through the project and not feeding it directly to the business areas ... And there are, of course, the political Exocets that are in people's interest to fire off once in a while. (Simon, project director)

On slowness of implementation

The implementation has been slowed down because business areas have been slow to implement. They will probably say that we have been slow to deliver, so I can see this argument going both ways; but at some point someone in management needed to make a decision 'you must all use it from now' or 'you must show me your plan to start using it from now' as opposed to constant reasons people provide as to why they can't use it. (Christine, business analyst).

On joint application development teams

The base assumption was that people coming to it from the business side actually were senior people who understand where they've been in the business and where they want to go. What actually happened quite early on was that we ended up with a series of junior people at these sessions who weren't obviously briefed at all in terms of how they might look at the business flow and the future flows and how inefficiencies could be driven out. We ended up with a number of embarrassing sessions where we felt we were telling them what we thought their bosses ought to have been telling them. We actually changed the development methodology at that point and we went much more for showing people screens of the applications they needed, saying this is what we think it's going to look like. Tell us if it's wrong, tell us what you think we should be doing; we think you should be thinking of changing your business in these areas. To me, on the development side, that was the point from which all disenchantment grew. In other words the idea was that we were telling people what they had to do and we weren't listening, because what we were hearing was: 'we want exactly what we've got today. So if you can replicate what we've got in GCIS [which is the existing system] then we're happy'. (Duncan, senior development manager, head of development team)

On re-engineering the business process

It's still a case of 'that's how I do it and this team aren't listening to me'. The challenge is to get under the skin and say 'look I have got three business units in this room, you all do the same job, yet you all do it differently. You are all right in a way but why should the bank do it in three different ways? We want one way and we want you to decide what the one way is.' Now that is very time consuming and once you start working to budgets with people who simply haven't grasped the concept that they have to change the way they do their job; what we have said is 'right, we are not getting there, we'll cut corners, we'll tell you that we have synthesized the three views and this is one you can all work with'. Then it sounds as if we haven't listened and it is not real yet so the business don't believe it. (Simon, project director)

On time and budget versus functionality

That's the difference between delivering the project and delivering the benefit. The project to my mind bears none of the blame for that. The senior business people have given us the guidelines. We have a budget and we deliver the functionality we can to that budget. You distort that at junior level without understanding how the process works and that is exactly what you've got. You have got something that is done to time or budget but doesn't necessarily have all the functionalities they want. They – their business management – should decide how much money they want to spend, which functionalities they want delivered within that. The junior guys should be trusted more by the senior guys in there to define the functionalities in more detail, something they ought to put a lot more time into. Second, they should then be able to go back and say 'if we get that it is going to cost more, please up our budget'. It shouldn't be up to the project to do that. So the observation is correct. The understanding of why we are in that position is one we would widely differ on. (Steve, senior business analyst)

On relations between project team and business areas

I am conscious that there are times that the business gets very annoyed with the project. There is a goodwill that has been lost in that people think that the project is very demanding. Partly it is due to a different way of working; they work in a much less disciplined manner; not because they are personally less disciplined, but it is a different way of working. Very quickly we came to an antagonistic position with the business. Partly because we had different understandings of what we were trying to achieve, partly because the business did not quite believe in Spectrum ... . (Christine, business analyst)

CBG, the biggest group, have an innate caution. I don't think they have a climate that helps. We spend a lot of time in one-to-one discussions, saying 'what seems to be the problem here, knock that one off', what they call their 'barriers to progress'. CCG which has some wholesale changes going on tends to adopt a much more Stalinist approach. They just say 'we are doing this on Monday, and they do it. They ride over people, and there is some pain on the way, but they get there. They have to convince some people to get that far. In CBG the system covers a broad area of their business and therefore is seen as more critical to them, so you try to respond to their preconditions, etc. We can usually agree to disagree on the basis that I say 'philosophically, if I were in your shoes I would move to the next phase today'... I got a good quote in our last meeting, something along the lines of 'I think we are probably in sight of thinking about setting a date ...' Right! You've got to have a sense of humour about these things. (Simon, project director)

All the tribulations around project Spectrum had created a deadlock situation. Trust between the project team and a crucial user group had all but broken down. Feelings of frustration and rejection were abundant in all areas, including the project team. It was not at all certain whether the project would be implemented despite some operational successes and a serious amount of sunk cost.

Questions for discussion

1 Were there any inherent weaknesses in the project set-up itself which may have contributed to the current state of affairs (e.g. relations between key players, involvement of top management)?
2 Try to expose the logic of 'what is going on' in this case.
3 Assess the impact of 'culture' and 'politics' on the implementation of Project Spectrum.
4 Can a communal view on these issues be found, or at least are there possible actions which might lead people to move into the direction of getting a communal view?

Appendix I The business areas – background information

The three departments featuring in the case constituted effectively the non-high-street banking arm of a major UK financial institution (excluding merchant/investment banking). All were located in the City of London. Their customers were large corporate organizations (e.g. Procter and Gamble UK), and financial institutions (banks, building societies, insurance companies). Business areas had been encouraged to be autonomous, with their own leadership and culture, which was good from the business point of view, but it proved to be a stumbling block when trying to bring in a centralized IT function across all the groups.

Corporate Banking Group (CBG) dealt with the large corporate organizations and had traditionally been a powerful player within the bank. Their main product consisted of a loan portfolio. In recent years they had lost a big part of their business to other parts of the organization as customers demanded more and more sophisticated financial products which CBG could not or would not offer. Numbers had declined sharply and at the time of the implementation of Spectrum about eighty people worked in CBG. The head of CBG – a stubborn man – was known to be highly sceptical of Spectrum.

Financial Institutions Group (FIG) dealt with banks, financial institutions, and insurance companies. Their operating environment was more stable than CBG's. Approximately 200 people worked in FIG at the time of the Spectrum implementation. The head of FIG was known to have made some 'silly remarks' about Spectrum to score points with his people. Both FIG and CBG were users of the GCIS system which Spectrum was eventually to replace. It took years to get it operating at a satisfactory level but people were now well accustomed to the system.

City Corporate Group's (CCG) customers were mainly located in and around the City of London. They held 'big accounts' and to a certain extent their business overlapped with CBG's. Traditionally they had been a rather small unit but were fast growing. Seventy people worked in CCG at the time of the Spectrum implementation. The head of CCG was known to have a no-nonsense approach to business and appeared to be supportive of Spectrum in public. CCG had no IT system in place prior to Spectrum.

The typical structure of the business areas was as follows:

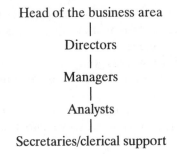

Head of the business area

|

Directors

|

Managers

|

Analysts

|

Secretaries/clerical support

Appendix II The project team: background information

The number of people on the project team varied over time (never more than sixty). In the summer of 1995 the team counted about fifty members (business analysts, programmers, system analysts, system developers, testers, managers). The project director had worked in one of the business areas a few years prior to the implementation of Spectrum. There was a strong feeling among members of the project team that their work rate was a lot higher than that of the business areas (especially FIG and CBG). They felt they worked within a 'meritocracy' while, especially in FIG and CBG, the 'old boys network' was still very much in operation.

> *Overall, the quality of personnel we are working with in the business is lower than the quality of personnel on the project. By and large we are a very hard working, integrated group of people. If we have a deadline, we'll achieve it. People will work long hours; if they have to, they will get answers very quickly. People are very flexible and will manoeuvre to get things done. It is very frustrating for us to bump up against 'oh well, I can't discuss that because I can't stay past 5 o'clock' or 'we can't run that application because we are all very busy right now'. It is quite peculiar how people who run 'the business' look down on other people for being 'techies'.* (Sarah, business analyst)

Appendix III maps the structure and reporting relations of Spectrum. The structure was perceived as awkward and not working particularly well by most key players.

> *The whole structure of the project is very awkward. We have got a steering committee at the top – the project director reports to it – with very senior people and heads of the business areas. In the project review group (PRG) sit directors or assistant directors. Then you have the business reps. We as the project prepare a lot of reports for the steering committee and are aware that a lot of our approvals come through the committee; the*

way in which we spend the money and how much we are allowed to spend all comes from the steering committee which represents business ... People in the steering committee are not feeding messages (e.g. we had given the project only to December to complete this much work and this is what the project agreed to do) to the PRG or the business reps. (Duncan, senior development manager, head of development team)

Appendix III Reporting lines and information flows

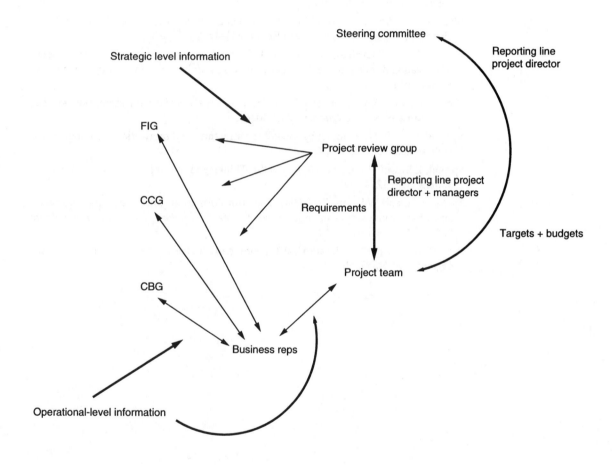

Further Reading

Barley, S.R. (1986) 'Technology as an occasion for structuring: evidence from observations of CT scanners and the social order of radiology', *Administrative Science Quarterly* 31: 78–108.

Hammer, M. and Champy, J. (1993) *Re-engineering the Corporation: A Manifesto for Business Revolution*, London: Nicholas Brealy.

Huff, A. S. (1988) 'Politics and argument as a means of coping with ambiguity and change', in L.R. Pondy, R.J. Boland and H. Thomas (eds) *Managing Ambiguity and Change*, Chichester: John Wiley, pp. 79–90.

Myerson, D. and Martin, J. (1987) 'Cultural change: an integration of three different views', *Journal of Management Studies* 24: 623–47.

Noble, F., and Newman, M. (1993) 'Integrated system, autonomous departments: organizational invalidity and system change in a university', *Journal of Management Studies* 30: 195–219.

Sackmann, S. (1992) 'Cultures and subcultures: an analysis of organizational knowledge', *Administrative Science Quarterly* 37: 140–61.

Schneider, S. (1993) 'Conflicting ideologies: structural and motivational consequences', *Human Relations* 46: 45–64.

Sproull, L.S. and Hofmeister, K.R. (1986) 'Thinking about implementation', *Journal of Management* 12: 43–60.

Taylor, J. A. and Williams, H. (1994) 'The "transformation game": information systems and process innovation in organizations', *New Technology, Work, and Employment* 9: 54–65.

Westenholz, A. (1993) 'Paradoxical thinking and change in the frames of reference', *Organization Studies* 14: 37–58.

Part four

Government service organizations

Case 4.1

Satisfying the customer/satisfying the staff at City Museum

The City Museum is a small, local-authority-financed museum. In the face of budgetary cuts imposed as a result of central government policies, the museum is struggling to maintain its position in the local council's priorities. In competition with hard-pressed services such as education, the museum's service is vulnerable to financial cut-backs and even closure.

The City Museum has for a long time offered an 'on demand' enquiry service to members of the public. This service requires the museum's professional staff to be available to deal with face-to-face enquiries about objects possessed by the public and the museum's displays during opening hours. Recently the volume of enquiries has increased markedly. The professional staff feel that they are subject to excessive demands as a result of the current organization of the enquiry service and wish to see its availability reduced. The museum director, however, believes that it is important to maintain the service in its current form.

The case describes the divergent views of the problem as seen by the director and the professional staff. Readers are asked to consider ways of reducing the discontent which is being experienced by the professional staff. The case raises issues of conflict, divergent organizational perspectives, leadership, professional orientations, organizational goals and priorities, environmental change and the role of stakeholders.

Case 4.2

Change in the police: a case of arrested development?

The East Wessex Constabulary is one of the numerous police forces to be found in England and Wales. Recently, the organization of policing has been subject to substantial attention by central government in the form of the Home Office and the Home Secretary. Radical 'reforms' have been advocated in an attempt to improve the economy, efficiency, and effectiveness of the police service. In keeping with the Government's overall philosophy, private sector management practices and attitudes have increasingly been held up as models which public sector organizations should follow.

Superintendent Cowan is reviewing the changes which have been proposed and those which are being implemented in the East Wessex Constabulary. He identifies a number of problems associated with performance management, workloads and management competence as well as a series of strategic issues. He is, at best, unsettled by his observations.

The case invites readers to consider such matters as: the pressures both promoting and inhibiting organizational change; the management of the change process; and the appropriateness of applying private sector practices to 'not-for-profit' organizations such as the police force.

Case 4.3

'We've got no time for that: we've got people dying' – introducing IT to a social services department

This case looks at the ways in which social care is provided and financed in the UK, and is set in the context of recent changes initiated by central government, whereby responsibility for many services has been devolved to a local level. The case focuses on the social services department of one city council and the introduction of an IT system (the Social Services Information System – SSIS) intended to help the department deal with the care of the elderly.

The case describes the development of the SSIS by a project team and its efforts to plan and implement the new information system. The responses of managers and social-work professionals to the project are described.

Readers are asked to consider the appropriateness of the strategy adopted for the introduction of the new system, the sources of conflict surrounding its adoption, and the problems of managing the project team's work. The case raises issues on the management of change, managing professionals, the introduction of new technology, conflict and the design and implementation of management information systems.

Case 4.4

Performance, Pay and Privatization in the Civil Service

During the 1980s and early 1990s central government in the UK has sought to reduce the scale of the activities of the traditional Civil Service and to introduce to it new structures and management processes derived from private sector practice. A number of Civil Service functions have been transferred to novel, quasi-autonomous bodies. The Investigation Service Agency is one such devolved body.

The Agency is governed by a supervisory body, the Investigation Service Authority. At the instigation of its chief executive, who has a record of successful management in industry, a series of changes are proposed in the way the Agency is managed. The case focuses in particular on the introduction of a performance-related-pay (PRP) system and its attendant appraisal scheme. The structure of the system and the problems associated with its workings are explored. The reactions to the system on the part of the Agency's staff are described in their own words.

Readers are asked to consider the continuing viability of the PRP system, the problems inherent in such systems, and the relationship between the Agency's culture and the response to the system. Issues raised by the case include the appropriateness of private sector management practices in government administration, the management of professionals, leadership, conflict, organizational culture, career management, and the design of reward systems.

Case 4.1

Satisfying the customer/satisfying the staff at City Museum

ALAN B. THOMAS

Following the 1852 Libraries Act, many local authorities in Britain established libraries for the benefit of the local community. In time these libraries became repositories not only for books but also for archives and artefacts donated by Victorian philanthropists and travellers. In this way, by the end of the nineteenth century many local councils had established museums as a separate service. Unlike the great national museums, such as the British Museum, the Victoria & Albert Museum and the Natural History Museum, all located in London, these local institutions were relatively small and primarily provided displays on the natural and local history of their area. In some cases they also assembled collections of more exotic objects from ancient civilizations and foreign countries. This was all an expression of the Victorian love of collecting and the dissemination of information before the days of film and television. For working people this provided their only opportunity to experience aspects of their past and foreign cultures.

In those days a curator and assistant curator, who had charge of the collections, were expected to be experts in the full range of fields represented in their museum. Growing specialization and the expansion of knowledge and research in the twentieth century made this increasingly unrealistic. Thus the era of the generalist museum professional gave way to the curator dedicated to a particular subject.

Most local authority museums today employ professional staff who are predominantly graduates in an appropriate field and who cover the major collections. Their task is to care for those collections and ensure their preservation, to present them to the public in displays, and to carry out research upon them and make them available to scholars. However, for the public, museums remain important sources of information, education and leisure. The growth of interest in antiques and the natural environment has meant that the public frequently wants to learn more about any items they possess or about what they have seen in their excursions into the countryside.

Local authorities have traditionally seen their museums, like their libraries, as an important part of the cultural resources they provide for the populace. However, as their budgets have come under ever-increasing strain as a result of central government policies, many museums have had to fight to maintain their position in local authorities' financial priorities. This battle against philistinism has not always been successful. Some museums have been closed as a result of these pressures and many more feel that their future is in doubt.

The City Museum

The City Museum was opened in the heyday of Victorian England. It is now housed in one part of a large complex, built in the 1930s, which also includes offices for other local services such as police and various local government departments.

The museum is open to the public five days a week, including Saturday (closed Wednesday and Sunday), and displays collections of two main kinds: natural history (rocks, animals, insects, birds, etc.) and human history (archaeological objects from Britain, South America and Egypt as well as coins and medals, industrial artefacts, and so on). An art gallery, which is organizationally part of the museum, is located in areas of the building adjacent to the display areas for the museum collections.

The museum is headed by a director who has been in post for some twenty years. As a graduate in one of the natural sciences, he previously worked in the natural history department at another museum where he carried out various research projects derived from his doctoral studies. Although the City Museum is somewhat smaller than the one he had previously worked in, he had felt pleased to have 'made it' to the position of museum director.

The museum has twenty-three staff members including the director as shown in Figure 1. With the exception of the clerical staff (one secretary and one inventory clerk) and the security staff (two security officers and five attendants) each member is attached to one of the museum's departments (including the art gallery).

At one time the security staff were twelve in number. They patrolled the galleries providing members of the public with the opportunity to approach them and ask them questions. Latterly, following cut-backs, the number of security staff has been reduced to seven. This means that CCTV cameras are now watched in a security office, located at the entrance to the display areas, and

	Natural history	Human history	Art gallery
Professional	3	3	2
Technical	3	1	1
Clerical		2	
Director		1	
Security		2	
Attendants		5	

Figure 1 Staff distribution at the City Museum

security staff are less in evidence in the galleries. In consequence, many general enquiries that previously would have been dealt with by the security staff, such as opening times, where to find particular exhibits, and general questions about the collections, are now finding their way to the professionals.

The enquiry service

For many years the City Museum has offered an enquiry service to the public. This service was intended to enable local people to bring in objects for identification and to receive information about the objects in the displays. Since the bulk of the museum's collections (around 70 per cent – the total collections are valued at around £15 million) are held in store, due to restricted display space, enquiries about these are also often handled by the service. The service receives enquiries both by mail, telephone and personal application.

The enquiry service operates on all of the days on which the museum is open. On Saturdays only one member of the professional staff is present. This means that while he or she can receive enquiries, most of these cannot be dealt with on the spot. Instead they are recorded and passed to the appropriate staff member for attention the following week. In addition, if that staff member has a problem in relation to an enquiry – some members of the public can be 'difficult' and potentially violent – they have to cope with this on their own. However, a 'panic button' can be used to alert the security staff if an enquirer 'turns nasty'.

Until a few years ago, dealing with face-to-face enquiries took up only a small proportion of the time of the professional staff. Only the professional staff have an obligation and the requisite knowledge and expertise to handle enquiries. However, they have received no formal training in dealing with the public and rely on their experience and sense of professionalism to manage these encounters. On the whole this task was regarded by them as a peripheral element of their job, whilst they saw their main duties as cataloguing (identification, description, measurement, etc. of the items in the museum's collections), display, research and acquisition. The museum has a backlog of uncatalogued items amounting to approximately one million objects accumulated over a period of a hundred years, so this presents the professionals with an ongoing task that they regard as both important and daunting. Cataloguing is important in terms of the museum's ability to respond to enquiries from scholars both in Britain and abroad, and for purposes of security, insurance and stock control.

Even so, they have always recognized the importance of publicizing the museum and its collections through direct contact with the public. Most staff devote evenings and even weekends to giving talks and conducting guided tours for the benefit of local societies and organizations, including schools. This work is unpaid and there are no provisions for overtime, so this aspect of the museum's operations relies heavily on the professional commitment of its staff. They also realize that the enquiry service is part of this important process of maintaining contact with the public, whose support is crucial to maintaining the viability of the museum.

Current developments

Recently the number of outside enquiries received by the museum has been rising. This is believed to be due to such factors as higher levels of unemployment, which tends to increase the use of the museum's facilities, growing public awareness of and interest in archaeology and natural history, due to increased media attention (popular television series such as The Antiques Roadshow, The Living World and Timewatch), and reduced competition from other leisure services, since the museum remains free whereas these services have often introduced admission charges. In particular the number of face-to-face enquiries from visitors has increased markedly.

The professional staff in the natural history and human history departments are located in an office space at the rear of the museum's main display area. The director and the two clerical staff have offices in another part of the building. Two of the technicians in the natural history department work in the basement two floors below and the third in the building next door. The security staff are based in an office near the entrance to the display areas. The entry to the natural and human history departments' offices is in the main display area, and the door is flanked by a bell-push and a large notice reading 'Enquiries. Please Ring'.

At present this bell rings about thirty-three times a day on average. No formal analysis of the pattern of demand, in terms of type, day or time of day, is available but they are generally experienced as random events. Responses to the bell are handled as follows. An informal arrangement, agreed in the absence of any formal policy, operates whereby a natural history professional answers the bell in the morning and a human history professional in the afternoon. The person answering the bell receives the enquiry, identifies the relevant member of staff who can deal with it, locates them, and hands over the enquiry to that person. The art gallery and its offices are located some distance away from the enquiry point. Therefore any enquiries for the art gallery, of which there are many, must be notified by telephone to the gallery staff who must then leave the gallery and make their way to the enquiry point.

Because professional staff members are not necessarily always to be found in their offices – they may be out on site investigations, attending meetings, working at off-site museum stores (there are three of these), or visiting enquirers in their own homes – locating them is often a time-consuming and fruitless process. If the appropriate staff member is not available, the person dealing with the enquiry has to complete a record detailing its nature and pass this to the office of the relevant professional. Occasionally the public are disappointed to discover that the person they need to speak to is not available. Some enquirers will happily leave their objects to be studied and reported on, but others insist that they want to be seen personally and therefore make an appointment.

The growing number of these enquiries has been associated with rising discontent on the part of the professional staff. In particular, although they believe that the total amount of time spent by any one member of staff on enquiries is relatively small, their dispersed pattern tends to prevent concentrated attention on other work. The staff feel that their work, which they already find taxing, is constantly being interrupted by the demands of the enquiry service. As one of them put it, 'That bell is ringing every five minutes!'

Furthermore, not all enquiries are seen by the staff to be legitimate. They see them as falling into four categories:

- *Legitimate* – e.g. an object is brought in for identification (as a matter of policy, no valuations are given).
- *Trivial* – e.g. a school student, having been set a homework assignment on 'Roman history', asks for 'Roman history please'!
- *Misdirected* – e.g. a number of enquiries are believed to be best handled by library staff (the City Library is housed in the same building). Museum staff believe that library staff frequently direct enquiries to the museum which should be handled by the library. This is a source of considerable concern.
- *Social work/'loony'* – a certain proportion of enquiries are believed to be made by lonely or 'disturbed' people who are seeking attention or who are so eccentric as to be considered as being of unsound mind. For example, one enquirer asked (five minutes before closing time) 'Is it true that all primitive men were women?' These enquiries are recorded unofficially and confidentially in a special 'loon book'. No one is too sure why this is done; in part it is a matter of security, for these enquirers are regarded as potentially dangerous people. One enquirer, who had been sentenced to a term of imprisonment for inflicting grievous bodily harm, continues to appear regularly at the enquiry point.

Addressing the issue

Some members of the professional staff have communicated their dissatisfaction to the director about the growing amount of time they spend dealing with enquiries. A senior staff meeting is held once a month for two hours and the matter has been raised there. The staff's view is that the public enquiry service could be operated on only certain specified days of the week rather than at all times. This would leave more time for uninterrupted work on the major tasks of cataloguing, display and research.

The director's view, however, is that it is important to the museum's reputation in the city that it maintains its 'open' enquiry service. He is acutely aware of the museum's vulnerable financial position in the context of continuing pressures on local authority budgets. He has said that he regards the problem as 'complex, with no easy solution' and he sees no way of solving it. In effect he has indicated that the staff will just have to put up with the situation as it is. The staff continue to regard the matter as an important issue and are far from satisfied by his response to their concerns.

To make matters worse, because of recent cuts in public expenditure staff numbers at the museum have been reduced. No money is available to allow, for example, for the employment of a receptionist to filter and direct enquiries. There is a feeling among the professional staff of stalemate and a continuing worry that, if the number of enquiries continues to increase, their central tasks will be increasingly compromised. While recognizing the fragile position of the museum, they feel that something must be done about the enquiry service.

Questions for discussion

1 How can the discontent engendered by the existing organization of the enquiries service be reduced? Identify as many solutions to this problem as you can and assess their advantages and disadvantages.
2 What should the priorities of the City Museum be? Should the museum be concerned chiefly with conservation, scholarship and display, or dealing with public enquiries?
3 If you were the director of the City Museum, how would you deal with the dissatisfactions expressed by your staff?
4 If you were one of the professional staff, what further steps would you consider to resolve the problem?

Further reading

de Varine Bohan, H. (1976) 'The modern museum, requirements and problems of a new approach', *Museum* 28(3): 131–43.

Hudson, K. (1978) *A Social History of Museums*, London: Macmillan.

Lewis, B.N. (1980) 'The museum as an educational facility', *Museums Journal* 80: 151–5.

Morris, B. (1984) 'A method of recording public inquiries in a museum', *Museum* 41: 30–2.

Will, L. (1994) 'Museums as information centres', *Museum International* 46(1): 20–5.

Williams, R. (1991) 'Museums: education or commerce?', *Museum* 43: 113–4.

Wittlin, A. (1970) *Museums: In Search of a Usable Future*, Cambridge, MA: MIT Press.

Yates, B. (1993) 'Coming to terms with change: the new curator', *Museum International* 45(4): 41–5.

Yorke, D. and Jones, P.R. (1987) 'Museums and marketing techniques', *Management Decision* 25(1): 25–32.

Case 4.2

Change in the police: a case of arrested development?

KEVIN C. GASTON

Superintendent Cowan sat in his office contemplating the task before him. He had recently moved on promotion to East Wessex Constabulary to fill the post as head of the management services department. The first assignment that he had been asked to undertake by the chief constable, Sir Frank Craft, was a review and appraisal of the restructuring which the force had recently undergone. He had collected a mountain of data including documentation concerning the restructuring of the force and had conducted many interviews with personnel across a broad spectrum of functions and levels within the organization. It was now a case of pulling the various threads together into a coherent report. But therein lay the problem – much of the information that he had collected was ambiguous and even contradictory.

The following pages outline the background to and nature of the changes, and the views of those interviewed concerning their effects.

Background

All police forces in England and Wales – and East Wessex Constabulary was no exception – had undergone significant changes in the last decade.

The old structure

East Wessex was a large force covering the geographical area of several counties and a number of cities. For policing purposes the area was divided into twelve territorial divisions. Each division was controlled by a divisional commander. Both uniformed and detective officers were assigned to a particular division. In addition some specialist operations were based at the force headquarters. These included the drugs squad, fraud squad, serious crime squad, and the specialist teams that used dogs and horses. Force headquarters was also the base for many of the centralized support functions. These were referred to as departments and included personnel, training, criminal records, press office and Superintendent Cowan's own management services branch. Headquarters was also the location of the chief constable's office and the offices of the assistant chief constables who had overall responsibility for operations, crime and administration. Figure 1 shows in diagrammatical form the organizational structure of the force prior to the changes which are described in later sections.

In organizational theory terms, the structure was a mixture of the 'machine bureaucracy' and 'professional bureaucracy' models advanced by some writers. There was a clear division of labour with specific spheres of activity; sets of rules

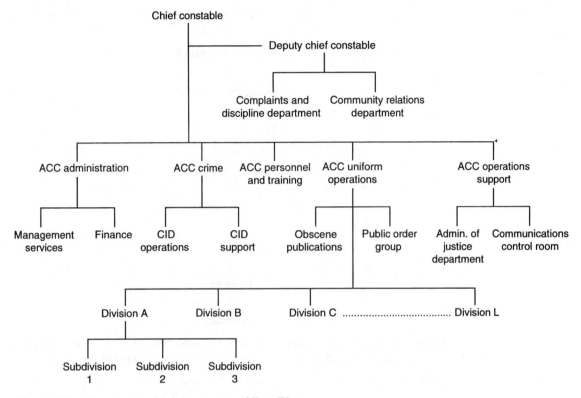

Figure 1 Pre-change organization structure of East Wessex

uniformly applied; a clear hierarchy; centralized control and decision-making, and promotion based on assessed competence. Individuals could be transferred readily from one job to another – a role-based system was very much the order of the day. This set-up was reinforced by the rank structure which was common to all forces. There were nine ranks in all (see Figure 2). Apart from overtime working, which was available to the lower ranks, increased earning power was linked to promotion. With promotion came increased power and status. The organization was very status conscious.

A 'dual' command structure was in operation. Functional resources based on divisions were under the control of local senior officers (divisional commanders) who had the power to allocate them according to local need. However there was a dotted line relationship with headquarters' commanders (assistant chief constables and their deputies, normally chief superintendents) who required to be 'consulted' about the deployment of resources together with issues concerning recruitment, training and transfer of personnel.

Headquarters generally, and the chief constable's office in particular, concerned itself with matters of policy rather than operational matters. However, it would be fair to say that the organization as a whole was very hierarchical. Real power definitely resided at the centre of the organization. Any initiatives or

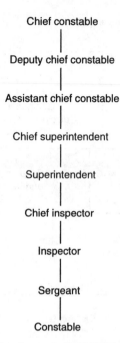

Chief constable

Deputy chief constable

Assistant chief constable

Chief superintendent

Superintendent

Chief inspector

Inspector

Sergeant

Constable

Figure 2 Rank structure of police forces (as at 1 June 1994; there has been a proposal to abolish the ranks of deputy chief constable and chief superintendent)

changes to existing patterns of operation had to be sanctioned from headquarters either by the appropriate assistant chief constable or by the chief constable himself.

Pressures for change

The old structure outlined above had served the organization well in the past when it faced a largely stable and predictable environment. However, stimuli for change had been increasing in the past decade and had come from a number of different sources. Perhaps the most significant impetus for change came from decisions and initiatives taken by central government and transmitted through the Home Office, Her Majesty's Inspectors of Constabulary (HMIC) and the Audit Commission.

The police service had not escaped Central government's preoccupation with getting 'value for money' from public sector organizations and the emphasis on market-based initiatives. Circulars from the Home Office to all police forces indicated that applications from chief constables for additional resources would be scrutinized very closely. A quotation from Circular No. 114/1983 illustrates the point:

> ... he [the Home Secretary] will not normally be prepared to authorise additional posts (i.e. the employment of more personnel) unless he is satisfied that the force's

existing resources are used to best advantage. He will look to HM Inspectors for their professional assessment of whether, for example, resources are directed in accordance with properly determined objectives and priorities. ... It will not be sufficient for applications to be cast in general terms: a specific case for additional posts will need to be made.

The circular went on to emphasize the three 'Es' of economy, efficiency and effectiveness. This search for improved performance gained momentum from other initiatives such as the government's Financial Management Initiative (FMI), the Citizen's Charter and the work of the Audit Commission which focused on getting value for money from public sector organizations.

The 1980s and 1990s also saw a rise in the reported crime rate, especially in relation to drugs, violence, public disorder and house burglaries. At the same time fear of crime rose sharply while respect for and confidence in the police declined markedly. Indeed, respect for many public institutions waned during this period.

At the same time the government set about privatizing a large number of organizations which had been in public ownership. The disciplines of and the competition in the private sector were regarded as more effective than the ways of working to be found in the public sector. Organizations which found themselves still in the public sector were exhorted to adopt private sector management practices. This led to the rise of what some observers dubbed 'the new managerialism'. Mission statements, strategic plans, goals, action plans, performance indicators and performance-related pay (PRP) were some of the terms which typified this approach.

Not all of the triggers for change were external. Some chief constables had themselves initiated changes within their forces. Some were at the forefront of adopting the latest IT to aid strategic planning and resource allocation. Some had employed more civilians to carry out a wide range of support tasks thereby freeing police officers for operational duties. A few had even restructured their force, devolving power and responsibility for all operational matters to territorial divisional commanders.

Wider changes were also happening which affected the police service. Changes to the criminal justice administration system had an impact. The founding of the Crown Prosecution Service (CPS) had removed from the police the decision to prosecute in criminal cases. There were inquiries into police responsibilities and rewards (the Sheehy Report) and a government white paper on police reform which, amongst other issues, emphasized quality of service initiatives. It indicated that the current number of forty-three forces may be reduced by amalgamation and the redrawing of force boundaries.

Understanding the changes in East Wessex

Superintendent Cowan was well aware of the countrywide change initiatives which had been affecting police forces generally. His first step had been to try to understand the nature of the response which his new force had adopted. He approached the task by reading all the relevant internal documents and then by interviewing a number of people who had either been involved in the changes or had been affected by them. The following sections are transcripts and notes of those data-gathering activities.

Looking through the relevant documents it was clear that the plan adopted was in fact a modified version of a much bolder set of suggestions for change.

The rejected plan

The more adventurous proposals entailed the reduction of the twelve territorial divisions to just three. These would be known as the Basic Command Units (BCUs). These would be the primary tier of organization which would provide locally agreed standards of policing in line with the suggestions laid out in the Citizen's Charter. Each of the three units would have a headquarters from which all operational and most strategic decisions would be made. Force headquarters would be much reduced in size. It would focus on strategic issues which affected the whole force and act as a resource and support centre for the BCUs. The changes were justified by the argument that they would encourage a proactive rather than the traditional reactive stance towards policing activities. It was suggested that the bureaucratic model would be replaced by a management arrangement in which the force headquarters would support rather than control activities (see Figure 3). All this was in line with the current Home Office, HMIC and Audit Commission philosophies. Key to the new arrangements would be the building of strong BCU management teams.

Superintendent Cowan was curious as to why this plan had not been adopted. There was no documentary evidence to indicate why this plan had been passed over in favour of the less radical course of action outlined below. It was not until the later interviews with personnel closely connected with the changes that reasons for not proceeding with this plan came to light.

The accepted plan

The plan that was eventually adopted required that the number of divisions or BCUs would be reduced only to six (see Figure 4). Much of the reasoning advanced in the more radical proposals was used to justify these more limited changes. For this plan, too, the justification centred around the need to devolve day-to-day or operational responsibility away from the centre of the organization and closer to the point of service delivery. Functional resources were to be based on the territorial BCUs under the control of BCU commanders. It was for these commanders to exercise their judgement over their deployment in the light of local policing needs. The 'dotted line' relationship with headquarters senior officers was retained. Even the same phrase – '... who should be consulted about their [i.e. the resources'] use along with recruitment, transfers and training' – was used. Some specialist functions remained located at headquarters. It was

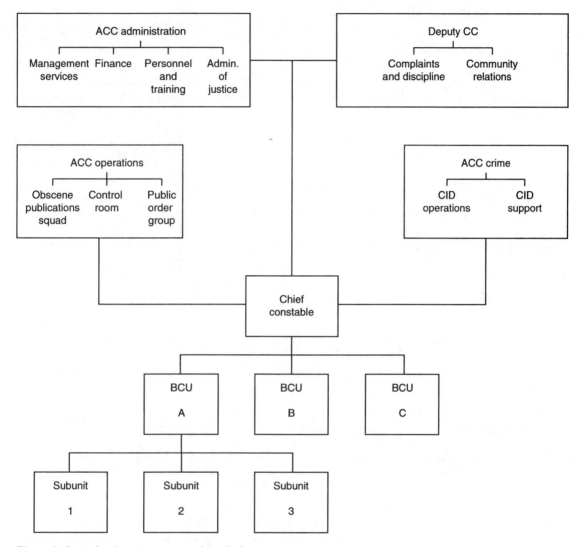

Figure 3 Organization structure – rejected plan

the intention that both the specialist functions and headquarters staff were there to support territorial activities. It was clear from the documents that the change was an exercise in the decentralization of power.

The plan went on to outline how the changes were to be brought about. The use of internal change agents was the preferred method. A small group of senior officers was briefed on the aims of the reorganization plan. They were then asked to develop small teams which would spread the word throughout the force. A series of seminars was held to inform the lower echelons of the force and to engender understanding of and commitment to the new arrangements. The implicit model was one of 'cascading' the information downwards. It was also

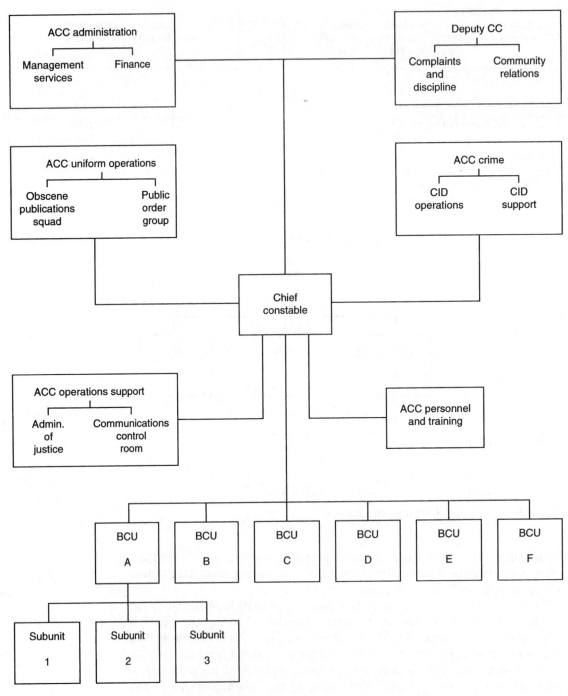

Figure 4 Organization structure – accepted plan

anticipated that useful feedback would be gained from the lower ranks on how the detail of the changes could be operationalized. A form of feedback loop or two-way vertical communications channels would develop. The document contained numerous references to 'paradigm changes', of a move away from 'public sector models of administration' to the more popular rational management or new public management approach favoured by central government. There was much play made of the need for the centre to 'let go' with the top management team spending more time on developing the vision for the force and concentrating on broad strategic issues. There were references made to the changes made and methods used by private sector organizations. In particular an example was made of the approach taken by Tom Farmer, chief executive of ATS (Associated Tyre Services – the vehicle tyre and exhaust replacement company). In this case the imagery of turning the hierarchical organization pyramid on its side had been used. The base of the old triangle or pyramid was turned into the vertical plane and was depicted as being the boundary of the organization which interacted with the external customers. It was this point of contact between the service providers and service users which was depicted as the most important part of the organization. In the jargon, it was seen to represent the organization/environment interface. The middle and upper parts of the old pyramid, when rotated through 90 degrees, then assumed a position behind the front-line officers. Symbolically they are seen to be supporting the customer interface activities (see Figure 5).

Internal documents showed that over a six-month period prior to the formal start of the new structure a large number of briefing meetings with middle-ranking and junior managers and supervisors had taken place. However there did not appear to be any minutes of these meetings nor any details of feedback or suggestions coming back up this communication conduit. This lack of evidence of the views of those personnel who were to be directly affected by the changes troubled Cowan somewhat. It occurred to him that in order to make his report and assessment as complete and balanced as possible it would be necessary to interview a representative cross-section of the force staff. By doing this he could

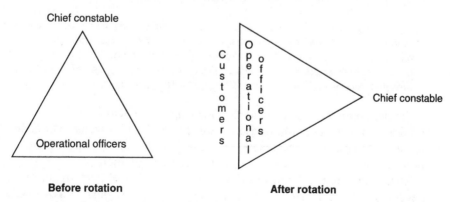

Figure 5 Rotation of the organizational pyramid

build up a picture of their initial response to the changes and, since the new format had been running for just over a year, their subsequent and more up-to-date views. The interview transcripts together with the background documentation led Cowan to discern a number of interrelated issues. The themes fell into two broad categories. The first category could be termed more immediate or operational issues. The second took a broader perspective and could be regarded as touching upon strategic matters.

Operational issues

As part of Superintendent Cowan's investigations he set about trying to measure the impact on performance that the restructuring had had. This proved somewhat problematic because there had not been any attempt to construct a detailed pre- and post-change study. Data on crime rates, clear-up rates and the number of complaints could be compared, but these indicators are, by common consent, held not to be very accurate indicators of performance and at best only give a partial picture.

On operational performance

As part of the decentralization of power and responsibility to BCUs there came an accompanying increased emphasis on performance and performance monitoring of these units and of the sub-units (based on smaller geographical areas and associated with individual police stations). It was too early to come to any definitive conclusions but some emergent issues had become apparent.

Although formal performance targets had not been issued by the centre, all BCU commanders knew that the performance of their area and the sub-units within it were informally monitored. This had led to a degree of resentment because the demographic and other factors varied both between and within BCUs. Arrest rates were particularly prone to distortion. For example, in urban areas arrests were disproportionately high compared with rural areas especially for minor public order offences (e.g. drunk and disorderly, and using insulting language or behaviour). As one long serving officer pointed out:

> *It's easy to get arrests for rowdiness if you've got a couple of nightclubs and lots of pubs in a big town. In rural areas like ours you don't get the same concentration of youths and therefore you get less trouble. Unfortunately this tranquillity, this absence of arrests, is not as easily measured or interpreted. When the figures are aggregated it just looks as though we are being less productive.* (Sergeant – 18 years service)

Similar points were being made by the management team of a BCU which was predominantly rural in comparison to some other BCUs which consisted in part of large towns. The increasing emphasis on the monitoring of individual performance was also the subject of differences of opinion.

There appeared to be mixed views about the merit of performance targets. Several of the constables who had completed a few years service broadly welcomed the targets. One commented that:

It's much better these days. You know what you are being measured on and therefore you can concentrate your time on those activities. There is a problem, however, that occasionally you are called away to deal with other incidents which don't count for much when it comes to meeting targets. For example, being whisked away from your normal area to spend a day escorting a public march demonstrating about the building of a bypass through some ancient woodland area stops you building up your number of process reports for traffic offences and reduces the chances of getting crime arrests for things like shoplifting and other theft. (Constable – 3 years service)

Another observed that:

Overall it's quite good. It shows more clearly what we all suspected – some people put themselves about, keep active and turn in a lot of work. The only ones who have anything to fear are the shirkers and uniform carriers. In the old days they could 'hide' by using various ruses and thereby avoid doing their fair share. Now it's easier to square them up – to show that they are underperforming. (Sergeant – 5 years service)

However the sentiments expressed by some officers with a significant number of years service seemed to run counter to those expressed above:

Concentrating on a few measurable activities at best misses the point and at worst is downright counterproductive. A lot of what we should be doing, and indeed what members of the public contact us about like asking for advice and help, isn't capable of simple measurement. Yet doing this informal stuff is vital in developing and maintaining the goodwill and cooperation of the local community. Occasionally some of my younger and more enthusiastic colleagues jump feet first into a situation and make an arrest which only makes matters worse. This is particularly so with crowds coming out onto the street at night when the pubs and clubs close. A softly softly approach in which restraint rather than a high profile is shown is often more effective in defusing situations. However it means the arrest rate – a performance indicator – remains rather low. (Sergeant – 22 years service)

On workloads

Part of the rationale for forming BCUs was that by placing power and responsibility lower down the hierarchy increased responsiveness to the customer would be achieved. This in turn would ensure that the deployment of personnel would change in order to meet the more accurately perceived demands of the public. Fewer officers would be assigned to clerical and desk jobs and fewer would work normal office hours. More officers would be available at times of peak workloads. In this way increased efficiency would be the result. In other words more output could be obtained from the same number of police personnel. As with almost all the other aspects of Cowan's investigations there were conflicting data on this facet of the organization's activities.

Almost everyone agreed that workloads had increased in the recent past. There was disagreement as to the causes. Some were of the view that the force reorganization had not helped as there was an increased demand from headquarters for a wide range of information to help their (i.e. headquarters') 'monitoring and collating responsibilities'. Others pointed to the recent changes in legislation including the setting up of the CPS. The aim of this was in part to remove from the police the decision as to whether to prosecute in criminal cases. The CPS now decide the issue; the police merely investigate alleged offences and collect the evidence. In reality this had created more paperwork for the police. The standard of the paperwork required by the CPS was high. On occasions, either because of lack of experience or competing demands on the time of the officers involved in a case, the paperwork was either incomplete, substandard or submitted too late. This led to prosecutions not being brought or being discontinued. Inevitably this tended to have a deleterious effect on morale and a souring of relations between the police and the CPS. The compilation of files also resulted in officers spending more time in the station than out on patrol. This ran counter to the intention of the new BCU set-up which had envisaged an increasing number of officers being released for patrolling duties and for increasing the amount of time when individual officers would be 'on the beat'.

This increased workload had other knock-on effects. Recent recruits who joined their first station were not receiving adequate on-the-job training because experienced officers were too busy to devote time to guide the new arrivals. This in turn led to the new recruits not performing to the required standard. When they made arrests or investigated offences standard procedures were not always followed. This caused extra workloads later on to put things right.

Even more worrying was the report from some quarters that some officers were using the demands of paperwork as an excuse to minimize the time they spent outside on patrol. As physical risks such as assaults had increased in recent years there was an understandable reluctance to get involved in potentially violent incidents. The real concern was that the old unwritten rule that an officer would go immediately to the aid of another officer who was in need of urgent assistance was gradually being broken. The very heart of operational police culture, namely the spirit of camaraderie and cooperation among officers engaged on operational duties, was falling apart. Cowan had noted elsewhere that cooperation between BCUs was under strain. This strain was now also apparent within individual BCUs and sub-units.

On management competence

Part of the new force strategy accompanying the structural changes was the formation of committed and competent BCU management teams. Most of the team members were drawn from the management ranks of the old structure, although in a few instances officers had been appointed from other forces. After interviewing a number of members of these teams Cowan was a little less than reassured. He had found a marked variation in both ability and enthusiasm. In one instance a BCU commander had had the foresight and determination to put in place a hand-picked management team. He had got less committed or less competent officers transferred out and more able officers transferred in. In this BCU the morale seemed very high although the workloads were high. Delegation of responsibility and freedom of action were the hallmarks. The management style was one of support and enabling. In contrast, in another BCU the commander was the same person who had been in charge of an old divisional area which the BCU had incorporated. He was known as having a somewhat authoritarian and autocratic style. His immediate subordinates also varied in their apparent ability and willingness to make the new system work. In off-the-record conversations Cowan was told by several officers that the morale of street officers in this BCU was extremely low and that work standards were slipping.

What was clear from all BCU management teams was that they felt very stretched. The delayering of intermediate ranks had led to increased reporting ratios. It was no longer possible to get to know one's staff well. Additionally, the increased involvement with other public sector organizations such as the courts, the probation service, social services and local government departments – known as the inter-agency approach to community problems – had placed further demands on management time. Officers further down the police hierarchy had observed that contacts with their managers were less frequent and more fleeting in nature.

The views of officers at the bottom of the organization on the competence of middle and senior management were largely not very complimentary. They pointed to the increased usage by management of what was termed 'corporate speak'. This was the use of words and phrases more commonly found in private sector businesses. One officer remarked:

> We are supposed to prioritize, be proactive, give quality of service and be responsive to community needs. In reality we just rush from one job to another doing a sticking plaster job. My strategic plan is just to get through the shift unscathed and not too exhausted.

Strategic issues

Looking through the notes it was clear that some longer-term issues were beginning to emerge. It was too soon to discern definite trends connected to the reorganization but Cowan considered it important to flag up some broad headings which would need further monitoring as they went to the heart of the issues of organizational leadership and effectiveness.

Integrating the BCUs

Instances had come to light which suggested that cooperation between BCUs was not always as good as it could be. Criminal enquiries which offered high chances of success in terms of numbers of arrests and recovery of property were being investigated by detectives from one BCU when for geographical reasons the enquiry should have been undertaken by another BCU. Intelligence about criminals and their activities was not always being shared between BCUs. The following quote illustrates this point:

> We received information that a drugs processing operation was being conducted centred on a house in another BCU area. Most of the villains involved lived in that area too. Luckily, one of those involved lived on our patch. So we set up a covert observation on the drugs house without informing the other BCU management. We justified this by saying that utmost secrecy was paramount as any leaks would jeopardize the whole

operation. Once we had got enough evidence we raided the drugs house, nicking the four main gang members. Simultaneously we arrested the villain who lived on our patch while he was still at home. We used this arrest to justify bringing all the prisoners and the recovered drugs and cash to a station on our patch. That way we could count the arrests, charges and associated property all as activities attributable to our BCU. After all, it all helps to improve the performance indicators. In the old days we would have either passed the whole thing over to the other BCU or division as it used to be, or at least we would have taken the prisoners and property there. We would still have got the glory but the other division would have counted the arrests as theirs for statistical purposes. (Detective sergeant – 15 years service)

This lack of inter-unit cooperation was not confined to criminal matters. It had also occurred across a number of other policing activities such as major searches for missing children. There were also examples reported where cooperation between BCUs had worked well and relations were good. This came about in large part because of the good working relationships developed by the individual BCU commanders concerned.

Relations between BCUs and headquarters

This was a very touchy subject. Comments from BCU managers highlighted the tensions between the centre and the operating units which came to the surface from time to time. The issue was clear in principle. Headquarters was to concentrate on broad strategic issues leaving the BCUs free to concentrate on operational matters. Additionally, headquarters was to be the place where specialist resources would be based which could be called upon by the BCUs when needed. In practice the distinction was blurred. It was not at all clear where strategic matters finished and operational matters began.

There were many occasions when policy guidelines developed at headquarters and disseminated to BCU management were so tightly drawn that there was little scope for operational discretion. Financial budgets were also a bone of contention. Sanction limits were imposed whereby approval for expenditure above a relatively modest limit had to be referred to headquarters for authorization. In the matter of personnel transfers either within or between BCUs, headquarters required that they be 'kept informed and advised'.

When requests were made from BCUs for services from the specialist resources and squads based at headquarters the issue of prioritization arose frequently. The centre saw it as its job to decide between competing claims from BCUs for such services.

Some BCU managers offered the view that it was not particularly difficult to manage relations with headquarters. One stated that 'you could get what you want from headquarters as long as you knew your way around the politics and were prepared to fight'. However one example had been cited which suggested that the influence of headquarters' departments was re-emerging, especially in relation to specialist groups such as the criminal investigation department (CID) and traffic officers who were based within BCUs. One BCU commander had three major criminal investigations occurring simultaneously which was stretching the CID staff resources. As there were no major traffic management difficulties she decided to redeploy temporarily some traffic officers to CID duties to take over the more routine investigations. Shortly afterwards at a meeting of BCU commanders at headquarters, the assistant chief constable in charge of traffic matters countermanded her decision in front of the other commanders. He was heard to remark subsequently that he had humiliated her publicly as an example to the other commanders not to exceed their authority. It seemed to some that the informal dotted-line relationship between specialist officers (e.g. detectives and traffic officers) based on territorial BCUs and the reciprocal headquarters departments was as strong as it always had been prior to the structural reorganization. At the general level it raised the issue of whether there was any serious intention of decentralizing power to the operating core or whether the strategic elite based at headquarters intended to retain in large measure their power and influence.

This observation led on to Cowan considering the role and motivation of the force top management team and of the chief constable, Sir Frank Craft, himself.

The leadership of the force

Recent press and media coverage had portrayed the chief constable in a very favourable light. In the local newspaper there had been a long article reporting the new working arrangements between the force and the local government authority via the police committee. The piece highlighted the increased emphasis and resources being placed on the inter-agency approach to community problems. The chief was reported as saying that the new structural arrangements in the force meant that more power was being given to the operational units so that 'we can be nearer the customer and thereby be in touch with local needs'.

The force had attracted national coverage too. In a recent article in one of the broadsheet newspapers the chief had been pictured with the junior Home Office minister with responsibility for police matters. The latter was lauding the strategic plan developed by East Wessex and the swift way in which it had been implemented. The minister remarked that 'It [the strategic plan] is a model of forward thinking; it shows the way ahead for the police. Other forces would do well to follow this innovative and sophisticated approach'.

Internally Cowan found a much more unclear and less positive picture. He had noted that the force *Statement of Purpose and Values* (see Appendix 1) had been displayed prominently in all stations. However these exhortations had not always been well received. In periods when workloads were very high, when it was a case of 'fire-fighting' – dashing from one incident to another – constables would use black humour to draw attention to the gross disparity between the lofty ideals of the mission statement and the reality of police work as they experienced it.

Perhaps the most worrying observations came from Cowan's immediate predecessor in management services. She was a superintendent who attracted much respect for her perceptive observations and reflective and analytical approach to policing activities. She observed that the department rarely carried out any research or development in the sense of thinking proactively about ways of doing things better and more effectively. Most of the time was spent handling an avalanche of requests from the most senior ranks at headquarters for information and for guidance in the development of force policy in response to initiatives and changes announced summarily by the Home Office.

We spent all of our time dealing with 'crises' identified by ACPO* ranks. We were asked to develop guidelines on a whole range of activities such as performance-related pay, performance indicators, inter-agency cooperation, relations with the private sector, and so on. The environment is changing faster than headquarters can keep up with especially in relation to changes in legislation and government policy. We were little more than a management services department. In fact I managed to get the name of the department changed to just that. R&D was a misnomer as we did not do any real research or development. (Superintendent Rachel Cohen)

She was also able to shed some light on why the more radical reorganization plan, which she had played a leading role in developing, had not been adopted. Her view was that having only three BCUs would have made them too autonomous and too powerful in relation to headquarters. Decentralization may well have become a reality. By adopting the plan which created six smaller BCUs, headquarters could pursue an informal policy of 'divide and rule'. Inter-BCU rivalry and increased competition for scarce resources held at headquarters would tip the balance of power back to the centre. Additionally, by having six rather than three commander's posts and an increased number of subordinate managerial positions within each BCU meant that the opportunities for promotion were greater. And, of course, it is in the gift of the chief constable to allocate these posts. Power to reward is a great lever with which to control subordinates' behaviour.

Some final observations

Rereading his notes Superintendent Cowan was overcome by feelings of tiredness and unease. Was this just because he had worked extremely hard on this appraisal of the force changes and yet had not found clear evidence of marked organizational improvement? Or was it because he was becoming infected with the cynicism and anxiety that he had detected in others? Certainly the potential benefits which had been held out in the force reorganization plan and much spoken about by the chief constable were to be observed only patchily. The delegation of power to the BCUs had occurred to some degree but the reassertion of traditional dominance by the chief officers at headquarters was also in evidence.

His final task was to review the traditional morale indicators to try to discern any trends. A quick flick through the computer printouts seemed to indicate that

---

*ACPO = Association of Chief Police Officers. The membership is made up of chief, deputy chief and assistant chief constables of police forces in England and Wales.

sickness and absentee rates were indeed rising as were the number of early retirements and retirements on ill-health grounds. The ill-health retirements seemed to show a move away from the usual causes of physical disability and an increase in stress-related factors. The increase in retirement of officers in their thirties was also disconcerting especially when unemployment levels nationwide were high and showing no signs of significant decrease. Cowan made a note in the margin of his draft report to investigate whether these surrogate morale figures varied between BCUs or whether they were uniform across the force. An inter-force comparison would also be revealing.

And what was he to make of the latest piece of unofficial intelligence? A contact in the Home Office had intimated (off the record) that the chief constable was at the head of a very small shortlist for promotion to become one of Her Majesty's Inspectors of Constabulary. Apparently the appointments committee were very impressed with the organizational and strategic changes which he had masterminded in the East Wessex constabulary.

Questions for discussion

1 What were the main factors in the case which were driving the changes? And what were the main restraining influences?
2 How was the main change process managed? Can you suggest any ways in which it could have been handled better?
3 To what extent do you think it is appropriate to organize and manage public sector service organizations along the lines found in private sector profit-orientated companies?

Appendix I Statement of common purpose and values

1 Uphold the law firmly and fairly.
2 Prevent crime.
3 Pursue and bring to justice those who break the law.
4 Keep the Queen's Peace.
5 Protect, help and reassure the community.
6 Reduce the fears of the public.
7 Reflect public priorities in actions taken.
8 Respond to well-founded criticism with a willingness to change.

Further reading

Anthony, P.D. (1994) *Managing Culture*, Buckingham: Open University Press.

Bate, P. (1994) *Strategies for Cultural Change,* London: Butterworth-Heinemann.

Buchanan, D. and Boddy, D. (1992) *The Expertise of the Change Agent*, London: Prentice-Hall.

Ezzamel, M., Lilley, S. and Willmott, H. (1994) 'The "new organization" and the "new managerial work" ', *European Management Journal* 12: 454–61.

Flynn, N. (1993) *Public Sector Management*, Hemel Hempstead: Harvester Wheatsheaf.

Halford, A. (1993) *No Way Up the Greasy Pole*, London: Constable.

Home Office (1993) *Police Reform: A Police Service for the Twenty-First Century*, London: Cmnd. 2281, HMSO.

Johnson, L. (1988) 'Controlling police work: problems of organizational reform in large public bureaucracies', *Work, Employment and Society* 2: 51–70.

Mintzberg, H (1983) *Structure in Fives: Designing Effective Organizations*, London: Prentice-Hall.

Morgan, G. (1986) *Images of Organization*, Beverly Hills: CA, Sage.

Ott, J.S. (1989) *The Organizational Culture Perspective*, Pacific Grove, CA: Brooks/Cole.

Pettigrew, A., Ferlie, E. and McKee, L. (1992) *Shaping Strategic Change*, London: Sage.

Sheehy, P. (1993) *Inquiry into Police Responsibilities and Rewards* (Volumes I and II), London: Cmnd. 2280, HMSO.

Stewart, J. and Walsh, K. (1992) 'Change in the management of public services', *Public Administration* 70: 499–518.

Thompson, G., Frances, J., Levacic, R. and Mitchell, J. (eds) (1991) *Markets, Hierarchies and Networks: The Coordination of Social Life*, London: Sage.

Case 4.3

'We've got no time for that: we've got people dying' – introducing IT to a social services department

HEATHER SALT

Introduction

Since April 1993, there have been important changes in the way in which social care is financed and provided in Britain. Before then the Department of Social Security (the central government department responsible for making public provision for the economic welfare of the elderly, unemployed and people with disabilities through pensions and other monetary assistance) paid for care in residential homes for people who could not afford it. This money has now been transferred to local government social services departments, who are now responsible for organizing all care. These departments will provide some services themselves and buy-in care from a variety of private and voluntary providers.

One of the major aims of the changes is to make sure that help goes to those people who most need it. In order to do this social services will have to find out a lot about the people who ask for help. Community care services are provided to anyone who needs help with day-to-day living and to those who look after them. This could include elderly people; people who require rehabilitation services because of alcohol/drug misuse or whilst recovering from a major illness or injury; the chronically sick, disabled or mentally ill; and carers of people in the above circumstances. A detailed assessment will then be made so that a care plan can be devised.

In order to help with the new assessment procedures, the social services department in the city of Sewingbury had been given funding for the procurement of an IT system which would assist in gathering data for community care monitoring and planning purposes. The project was originally called the Information Needs Project, but later became known as the Social Services Information System (SSIS). The concept of SSIS as a one-stop computer-based information system which included an office automation package (word processing, e-mail, diaries, spreadsheets) was procured at a time of uncertainty in local government. Changes included reorganizations in roles and responsibilities, new legislation, and movement towards the enhancement of quality within public service sector organizations generally.

The social services department

The social services department provides services to the central district of Sewingbury. The administrative functions – central and operational services,

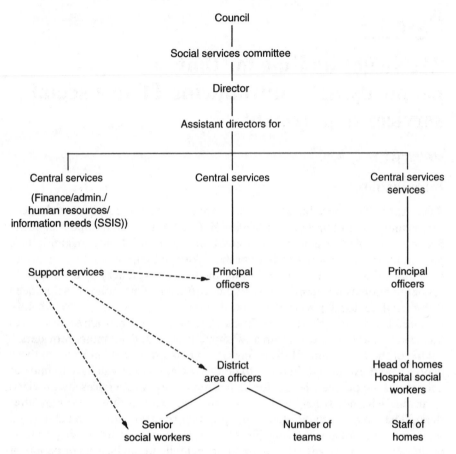

Figure 1 Functional structure

finance section, personnel section, registration and inspectors unit, external services unit and SSIS – are located within the Town Hall, the City Council headquarters. The services provided to 'users' operate from six district offices within the city (see Figure 1).

Social services are welfare activities organized by the state and carried out by trained personnel, notably social workers, and over the last few years have undergone major revision. The biggest changes in social care for 40 years came into effect on 1 April 1993, when the new community care proposals became law. The main principle behind the law is that people will receive support and care in their own homes. Community care arrived when reductions in local authority budgets were cutting deeply, and only heightened the challenge for City Council, health authorities and the voluntary sector to work together to use available resources more effectively. For social services to plan various services and examine how effective social services are in meeting peoples' needs, personnel need to be able to extract accurate information. In the past, information strategies to assess whether the various services are meeting peoples' needs have had a low priority, and the strategic vision behind SSIS is that, whilst it follows politically imposed legislation, it will be practitioner led and lead to more efficient use of information and standardization across the district sites.

Planning information – SSIS

The *Community Care Plan* states that the major financial and organizational change to be implemented following the Community Care Act is to transfer funds, which were previously distributed through the Department of Social Security for private residential and nursing home care for the elderly, to the social services department. This means that people who have their own financial means can still apply directly to a private home and request a place, but those who need financial help to pay for residential care must apply to the social services department and be assessed. This requires a lot of extra work carrying out assessments which is a process dependent on coherent information.

In order to help develop the ethos of more effective and efficient information usage, the social services department appropriated funding for the procurement of an IT system which would assist in gathering data for monitoring and planning purposes. The new information system (SSIS) would record and maintain a centralized index of all information relating to clients known to the social services department. It would also provides a centralized register of available resources which could be used to provide for the needs of those clients. The IT director asserted that:

> *The information should be recorded as part of the process which generates it for accuracy and completeness. SSIS, coupled with management procedures, can guarantee the quality of input.*

Project organization

A dedicated development/implementation project team was established (see Figure 2). Originally it consisted of only three people, who had social services managerial backgrounds and who had developed an interest in computers over time. However, the team was awaiting the arrival of eight additional members who would bring with them a diverse mix of computing and inter-personal skills. The team stressed it was impossible to continue with only three people. The rigorous recruitment strategy, which conforms to local government equal opportunity policy, had meant a six-month delay in the recruitment of this new team which hindered the implementation of SSIS. Eventually, the new team members were recruited in January 1994. However, problems arose when trying to integrate the new members into the existing team unit.

A paradox emerged because the original team had continually complained that lack of human resources was having drastic consequences, but when the resources arrived the original team members were reluctant to delegate.

> *When there was the three of us we had a colluding agreement that we just exploited each other ... and if you had to work till 9.00 at night you would ... .* (Project manager, May 1994)

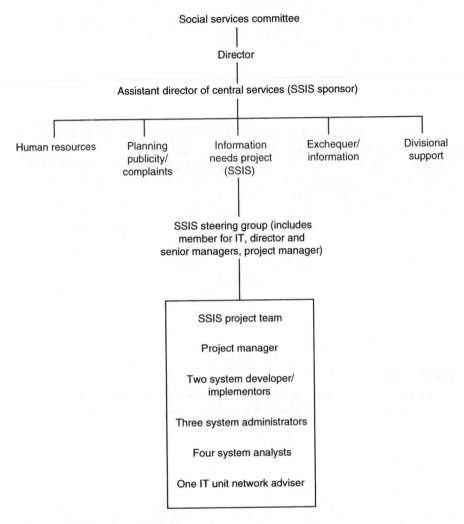

Figure 2 SSIS project structure

The original SSIS project manager remained, and after he discerned the problem he was able to move to a healthier approach. He was establishing a 'task-based' project management method and was beginning to trust and delegate some of the operational work to the team so that he could focus on strategic issues.

> *Nobody wanted more than us to shift things on to other people because we were getting worn out, but we had ownership of the project and determination to make it carry. There is a conflict between continually achieving the goals and letting them slip and allowing time to hand over.* (Project manager, May 1994)

The structure of the project team is shown in Figure 2. The project manager reported to the assistant director of central and operational services who was also the project sponsor, although he did not use the title officially:

> *I've basically inherited a role that wasn't there. Basically it's self-interest that got me involved. I didn't feel the project would work unless it got support from the senior management team and that wasn't apparent at the time.* (Assistant director, central services, May 1993)

The project team had identified the needs of the department and the benefits a new information system could give, but top management did not appear to be actively supporting and communicating the concept and vision behind SSIS. However, it was difficult to communicate SSIS which was still an imaginary concept in that the team had a theoretical understanding of the system but had not seen it as a fully working system. The vision started to drift. A steering group was thus established and the sponsor, whose main role in the department was finance, helped the project become concrete by helping to dismantle blocks on the way so that City Council members would acknowledge the seriousness of the venture and commit monetary and human resources to it. Social services had traditionally been pushed back as far as IT was concerned and implementation was new to the culture so this support was deemed crucial.

However, whilst recognition had been given for the need of top management to visibly support the system, it was the project team who actively had to try and sell the concept to others as well as develop the system itself. It became apparent that there were some serious blockages around issues of control, resistance to change or general indifference and scepticism which meant the implementation of SSIS was going to prove far more complex than initially envisaged. However, the needs of the department and the information it required in order to plan services with the introduction of the community care assessments and packages meant that the current, traditional manual systems were no longer a real option. Hence a persuasive communications exercise would be needed for SSIS to be effectively utilized as an operational rather than merely an administrative tool.

> *Community care is about utilizing information to the best. We can't answer the basic questions in life that an organization like social services should, so then, we in a way capitalized on that in generating fear. But here in Sewingbury the culture's been that social services has been pushed back as far as IT development [is concerned].* (Project sponsor, May 1993)

To clarify the above quote, the project sponsor may mean that whilst many social workers enter this realm for ideological reasons, in the hope that they will help empower those less fortunate members of society, they can actually end up as agents of control because of their concealment or lack of efficient information and service, which then encourages client dependency.

> *If the information we put on is correct and we utilize the systems fully we should be able to plan services a bit better. For example, we seem to collect manual statistics for the hell of it, not for a particular reason and it seems to be ... 'Well we've collected it for years so why don't we carry on?'... and we churn out all this information and yet I'm not sure that we do anything with it.* (Administration team leader, May 1993)

Implementation strategy

The new system was to be part of a new IT strategy and it was the first time that IT had been centrally coordinated. However, as one administration team leader stressed, the system would only be as good as the information put on it.

> *I know with any system you are bound to get a few mistakes, but really I think you need to start off with each individual record as accurate as possible.* (Administration team leader, May 1993)

Hence, the system would be dependent on the emergence of a new culture based on a task-centred approach, tied into departmental service plans so that the service plans became more definable, measurable and deliverable and therefore capable of being monitored. The project manager and project sponsor stressed that whilst it was government legislation that was forcing this change in public services management, the system they had picked to help the change was one that followed operational management processes as opposed to imposing things on practitioners:

> *It will impose strict ways of actually doing it which is no bad thing. But it follows the thinking of an operational manager and a process assessing someone's needs and converting that into resources and so on. Its logic is based within the work of Social Services.* (Project sponsor, May 1993)

Operational managers had to encourage staff to adapt to a change in role and functions. The project sponsor commented:

> *... their thinking needs to change to 'I'm not just a social worker any more, I'm actually a manager of resources'.* (May 1993)

The project sponsor and manager conceded that there had been resistance, not just to the IT changes but to changing roles.

> *There is resistance. Whereas social workers were multi-purpose if you like – they identified a person, their need and gave it them – we are no longer operating in this way because of the purchaser/provider split.* (Project sponsor, May 1993)

Social workers and managers needed to be convinced of the benefits of moving in that direction. For example if they could be encouraged to view the system as a tool to enable them to access information they hitherto did not have which would ultimately help the end user, the client, this might detract from the notion that IT was just another form of electronic surveillance.

> *Social workers like to see it as 'well how is it going to benefit me?'. And to be fair to them, actually going out visiting, doing the casework, sorting out emergencies, they are under a lot of pressure. They are understaffed, but I think if you can sell it to social workers as less of a piece of paper or a form to fill in, and there is an absolute mound of forms at present, I think even though they might be very apprehensive about operating it, I think it will sell itself once these benefits are seen.* (Administration manager, May 1993)

However, there were also genuine fears about technology, especially from some older members of the department. Many social workers and managers had very little, if any previous experience of computers due to indifference and/or lack of access to computer terminals at the district sites. IT development had been pushed into the background in social services, and staff generally saw themselves as providers of care. Statements such as: 'we deal with people, not computers ...' continued to be prevalent. Yet support and commitment from social workers and operational managers is fundamental if procedures are to be standardized. Practitioners have to share their knowledge and expertise with the implementation team:

> *We need them because they've got to talk us through the process. And then there are decisions to be made – you know, if Site X are doing it one way and Site Y another, which way is going to become standard because the system will only do it one way. So we'd need fairly senior people who could argue the case at senior management meetings. But all the way with this computer system it's: 'we've got no time for that: we've got people dying ... '.* (Project manager, December 1993)

The impetus would need to come from operational managers after demonstrations and discussions of what SSIS was capable of when working at full speed. The project manager clearly understood why there was ambivalence.

> *It is understandable when someone can't afford a new carpet for a day nursery and they see someone who wanders in with a £2,000 laser printer even though the money is from a different budget and cannot be transferred.* (Project manager, December 1993)

The moaning from the, in the words of the project manager, 'more radical' of the social worker professions filters down, with expressions such as:

> *What are they wasting all that bloody money on this lot for when they haven't money to provide basic services?* (Project manager, December 1993)

It was therefore seen to be crucial to communicate the system as something that the department had invested in, something that would improve the service rather than hinder it. For example, a practitioner would be able to say: 'I'm assessing you as a client. Right, I can give you a search now, its ordered – you'll get your home help next week', which cuts down on the telephoning backwards and forwards and searching for information on the old system which is not there. A clear example of this was provided:

> *The other day a lady who was mentally ill was demonstrating some quite bizarre behaviour and she was not very well. An information advice worker spent an hour-and-a-half with her, only to find at the end of it that this client was an open case to a social worker on a team and it hadn't been updated on the computer.* (Office manager, December 1993)

The implementation process begins

Office Power was a word-processing and business communications package which formed a part of the SSIS project and was intended to replace the word processor, Wordplex. The expectation initially held by the project team was that Office Power would develop only as and when SSIS demanded that function to be there. However, because of external constraints, notably budgetary constraints, Office Power was rolled out before schedule.

Basically, before the end of last financial year, the politicians were looking for expenditure cuts. My boss said: 'Can we, insofar as Office Power will replace Wordplex, can it happen now! Can we avoid a year's maintenance costs on this other system?' And I stupidly said: 'Yes'. I should have said: 'no'. And what it meant was we went out there to six main offices with a system that hadn't been tested properly and we regretted that. (Assistant director of operations, June 1994)

Whilst Office Power had the added benefits of spreadsheets, email, and a diary which the team hoped operations managers and social workers would be motivated to use for personal purposes, heavy-duty word-processing operators initially found it a disappointment. They compared it with the previous system and found response times very slow. The technical problems were eventually resolved. The underlying problem appeared to be that the new computers had been installed without any consultation.

We were told originally that we would be left with some of the Wordplex until we had sufficient training on Office Power. What actually happened was the IT team had been given instructions that all Wordplex had to be out because it had been given up as savings ... ours were all taken out one day and all these Office Powers put in the next. (Management team assistant, June 1994)

So we were left with great anxieties, the actual response on the screens was very, very slow ... that wasn't just happening here, it was happening all over. (Team leader, June 1994)

The management team assistants (MTAs) felt that they had been dumped with the system and really needed some more 'handholding'. In consequence some MTAs reverted to old typewriters to get the work out. Word-processing operators did not have sight of the long-term vision; their only vision was one of wanting to be able to do their daily tasks. Project IT developers, on the other hand, saw the delays as teething problems. However, the team conceded that they had not adequately tested the system before the launch because of constraints from top management who needed to save on their budget.

Moving everyone over to a new package meant, however, that they had to persevere with the new systems; in effect there was no turning back. Further, the department had an opportunity to standardize word-processing across the whole department and could create a new, valuable resource – an office systems manager who would take on a strategic role developing corporate standards in documentation and continuing training programmes in office skills.

The second part of SSIS to be implemented was the financial assessments module. Again mistakes were made by implementing a particular module early. Within SSIS, to be financially assessed for a service you had to exist as a client, the social worker had to exist and the resource to which the person was being admitted, for example a residential nursing home, had to exist. Staff in the financial assessment section would not normally input any of this information themselves, but at this stage client demographic data had not been entered into the system elsewhere. Hence the financial assessment team had to be trained to do the audit and inputting. It proved a lot of extra work for what should have been a basic financial calculation. The resultant frustration and lack of tangible benefits demotivated this section to continue with SSIS. However, a positive outcome was that they became more interested in examining other financial information solutions than in wanting to revert to old manual systems, and this was a major attitudinal shift. Again the team admitted that they had made a mistake:

> *With hindsight, we picked the wrong part of the system to start off with but we thought it was going to be the biggest pay-back. However, there were no clients on the system. They had to do the reassessments manually and then put the information on afterwards. We are not saying it hasn't been a success because that part of the system needs to be built, but we need something a bit more tangible, so people can grasp benefits. I think the referrals part of it will be a greater success, because we've got the client index and can download it. We want a kickstart.* (Director, central operational services, June 1994)

The project manager now decided to reschedule plans in order to have all the clients on the system by the end of 1994, utilizing extra staff from the resources available for SSIS and focusing priority on the strategic role. The project manager realized he had become too involved in the day-to-day hands-on work: fire-fighting, fixing machines, ordering equipment, answering all queries on computers and consoling users.

> *What is happening to us is that because we are in existence, we are suddenly like a magnet – we attract other things. There has never been any IT coordination, so as soon as the centre starts to coordinate – who is the IT coordinator for the department? Me!! Because we are the bulk buyers the systems are now built round us, so we now waste time ordering crummy bits of software for stray outposts of the department.* (Project manager, June 1994)

Although in one way, this corporate role was seen as a good thing, enabling IT to be controlled and integrated with present systems, it could also distract attention from the IT strategy.

> *The difficulty is actually controlling it and stopping the operational side from skewing the project priorities.* (Project manager, June 1994)

Relaunching SSIS, or the launch – take two

Communication

The project team had decided that by July 1994 they would finish work on Office Power, even though it had still not been implemented at every site in the district, and concentrate purely on SSIS. As a team they were going to establish headline tasks and form a detailed project plan. They had started a process of demonstrations of the system to managers across the department, from the team manager upwards, which provided an overview of what SSIS might do. So SSIS, whilst initially driven by central services, had reached departmental level and operations managers were becoming more involved.

> *... to start with, it's going to be crude, although in their operational divisions they should come up with some overall priorities of areas of work for us for the next year. Because the one thing I'm adamant about is that this team will not decide social services' priorities. We will respond to what they want.* (Project manager, June 1994)

It appears that whilst management staff/directorate were attending presentations and were forming strategies and policies about care management plans, these were often devised in isolation and were not aligned to the information systems.

Management staff need to firm up procedural guidelines aligning business requirements with the system and identify roles/responsibilities for maintaining data. (Systems analyst, June 1994)

The team agreed on the importance of communicating with remote sites so as to move away from the notion that SSIS was something isolated, only taking part at the 'centre'.

We've got to rely on people to change that and now we've got the team who are going out talking to people, working with them, helping them to get what they want by better communication, by being able to put their needs forward; and the system then giving them this in order of priority, they should then see some pay-back relevant to their job, and how that information will ultimately help the end user. (Assistant director, central services, June 1994)

The fact-finding and interviews would be carried out by the new team members:

The people who will be doing the exercise don't have the baggage of ten years in the department. If I, for instance went out, my previous social services managerial role would hinder communication and they'd tell me what they thought I wanted to hear. (Project manager, June 1994)

Communications between team and operational managers had been difficult initially:

Some of the new team were a bit frustrated with operations managers where different mind-sets clearly emerge. Getting operations managers to think in the same way as systems analysts is very difficult but they are working very closely now with different groups and different parts of the system so relationships are being built. (Project manager, June 1994)

A team leader explained that whilst referrals would be used for administrative purposes, for example to hold up-to-date demographic details, it would be social workers who would key-in and use the information directly. As soon as a referral goes in, an assessment is needed and so the information must be entered in a standardized way, hence the importance of communicating with users.

The social services department had used some other formal methods of communication, such as questionnaires asking about training needs and levels of computer skill, and the use of a quarterly bulletin, *ISIT*. However, these were often ignored, sometimes deliberately:

People receive so much paper – and when you are dealing with a crisis of a situation and are having to go out and take an elderly person into a home or do a compulsory admission on someone who is mentally ill, the last thing you are needing is bits of paper. (Administration team leader, May 1993)

Communication between districts and head office was felt to be poor and the usual way of gaining information was more likely to be informal channels:

When our present director came, I recall in a meeting him making a remark that the informal networks were the way in which people found out what was happening in this department and that the informal communication networks were far superior to any formal channel of communication, and I don't think anything's changed from that observation. There is very little of a participative nature in our present culture. (District manager, May 1993)

I think a lot of people in the hierarchy know what's going on but to everybody sort of down below it just appears ... they say 'right we want you to do this now'. We are district based. I think a lot of people in the Town Hall will know what's going on, but when you are out in the district, you only get the odd letter here and there or a phone call. (Administration team leader, May 1993)

Training

The project team leader, supported by the project sponsor, stipulated that everyone must be trained before going onto SSIS, and he set up a new, centralized training suite in the Town Hall:

Some people at present don't go near computers, partly because of previous lack of terminals but also because they just don't want to use them. Others have a personal interest in computers and are familiar, but really it doesn't matter how computer literate you are, you've got to be trained how to use SSIS. (Sponsor, May 1993)

Some staff were looking forward to training but others who had previously witnessed poor training programmes were more sceptical.
Training for Office Power hadn't been entirely successful for all districts.

All the MTAs who were currently using Wordplex went off for two days training at the Town Hall and three did advanced training. But because our site was the last to come on line with Office Power some of the people who were trained in March couldn't put this into practice until May, which left them feeling very disappointed and inadequate. (Team manager, June 1994)

This was supplemented with an hour's on-the-job training by the head of the typing pool who had previously trained others on Wordplex.

The comment I've had back from the staff was that they learnt more in that hour than they did in the two days because this trainer had a social services background ...

Our plan was to train the people so they could train others – we think it's better for people to have the same background than be trained by an outsider, but because the Office Power facilities were rolled out quicker than we had anticipated, we hadn't a training package ready. We are now devising our own training modules and manuals, but again it's the wrong way round. We should have had a training manual up front, but to save some money on the budget we had to roll out! (Project sponsor, June 1994)

The sponsor stressed that as long as you realized why these things had happened you could still control what was going on.

And we are learning from the mistakes all the time. What emerged is the need for someone to overview the whole of Office Power, so we've got a new post of 'Office Power manager' who will oversee developments and establish standard formats for documentation. So the mistake actually generated that resource. (Project sponsor, June 1994)

The training plans for the rest of the system were being developed in parallel with the information collecting exercise on work procedures and processes. It becomes clear that the project team and managers wanted to implement training that was accessible and relevant to people's actual jobs.

The centralized nature of the training suite had two purposes. One was symbolic: it showed that the department was investing in its people by enabling them to train away from their workstations uninterrupted. Second, it could be hired out to other departments. However, not everyone appreciated a centralized strategy:

> *My point about a centrally-based training approach, I fear, is I have doubts about its absolute effectiveness because the best training after some very basics is practice. When you drive a car you learn how to drive and use road networks by practising, not by an assimilated environment, and it's very much the same with computers because you learn by making a mistake!* (District manager, May 1993)

Again, the district offices felt isolated from corporate plans, something which seemed to have its roots in a culture whereby implementation policy was completely separate from execution:

> *I think if it's going to be successful a lot of effort and a lot of training has to be devoted out in the operational offices where the work is done ... where the actual systems will have a bearing and not in a centralized office in the Town Hall.* (District manager, May 1993)

Expectations

With the raising of the profile of SSIS, more people became aware of the vision of an improved service and need for efficient information. At the same time their expectations had risen and this had been noticed by the project manager:

> *Managing the expectation levels is actually quite difficult, to try and get them to understand what it might do, when they have no understanding of the labour and skill level needed to produce what they come up with ..., but I think that will change over the years when they get a better grasp and we ourselves get a better grasp of it.* (Project manager, June 1994)

The current situation

Whilst the department had to overcome software functionality and corporate networking difficulties, the major problems appeared to be associated with the management of change. Staff were often operating in crisis situations and had to contend with large budget cuts to services which resulted in some tragic cases highlighted in the media. These professionals were largely uninterested in IT, seeing it as something abstract and irrelevant to them.

The SSIS director became more aware of the seriousness of SSIS as the process of implementation continued. He brought managers together and stressed that the 'absolute priority of the department is the information systems'.

However, another manager later said that in social services 'everything is an absolute priority because of the very nature of the work'. The project manager became increasingly aware of the need for a communications/information strategy which would be supported by top management.

It became clear that the unintended consequences of certain actions meant that strategy was more likely to emerge as the implementation process continued. A good example of this was the launch of Office Power before plans for training modules and consultation with users had been enacted. Whilst this action caused some problems in the short term, it also generated the need for an extra, valuable resource of an Office Power manager. This position was created to overview Office Power and develop a long-term corporate strategy for all documentation. Furthermore, management control issues, the need for communication and information to be documented to help further projects, came to the forefront. Previous reorganizations and restructuring of the whole department meant various roles had changed; some managers had been given roles that were unclear to them, valuable information on computer needs had been lost as people left or changed position; roles and responsibilities with the vendor were also ambiguous.

The implementation deadlines started to slip at least eight months behind, and major technical problems and relationships with suppliers were blamed. Some disillusionment had set in because the project team were trying hard to align organizational issues with technical implementation, but when installation commenced, the management of change issues became increasingly abandoned or 'put on hold' because of the flaws in software and hardware. However, the team continued to be optimistic and the successful side of the launch was still being portrayed. For example, the project manager had been asked to give advice to City Council members and senior managers because from their perspective SSIS was seen as a great success even though it had not been fully implemented. What the IT group saw was that after a few months slippage of the initial dates, social services had at least 130 people using the new system, Office Power and e-mail. The project manager commented:

> The city has whole project teams sitting doing nothing and systems sitting there that are now five years old and still haven't got a PC on the desk, so when they see one where part of what we bought is working, fine ... 'they must be good, let's bring them in to advise!'.

Both the project sponsor and manager believed that the first year after the procurement had been a familiarization exercise. They perceived that they had been building the foundations of the system launch. The implementation of a corporate system had been new to the culture of the department, who had over the years been without effective information technology, and they had clearly underestimated the complexity of the process. However, as the implementation process commenced they had started to appreciate the need for an information strategy and the importance of investing in equipment and training time. But it seems that budgetary savings continued to be the top priority of local government, and investment in people, the most important resource of any organization, again took a back seat.

Slippages in the original timetable meant that bidding for further revenue had to be postponed as the team could not ask for ongoing revenue until they showed that they had a working system. Hence, it proved difficult to comply with a strategic plan when resources were allocated on the basis of past results and were stopped and started. Furthermore, the operational side of the project became the priority in order to get the promised system tool onto desks and any technical faults cleared; hence, wider changes in organizational processes, culture and training had to be delayed.

> *It has been an eye-opener on this project – the emotional highs and lows are so notable, things just stand still or move ahead so quickly you can't stop to reflect, and these emotional swings seemed almost to be contagious. Having said that, there is always work going on, things like devising training manuals, flowcharts of the care management process which will be helpful for later implementation.* (Project manager, November 1994)

At this stage, the project manager and project sponsor both felt that they had paid a price for wanting a one-stop information data-store, and that with hindsight they might have opted for a less complex product as a solution.

Interestingly, the project team are now 'selling' the benefits of the other new systems (financial information management system and the human resources information management system) within the city, and are examining where these may be used instead of SSIS. If this were taken on board, it would allow the team to concentrate on unique areas for development in SSIS rather then duplicate what is already available.

The project manager concedes, however, that he was at fault in not buying-in some project management from the suppliers. At the time he felt that a contracts manager who could manage some of the day-to-day problem-solving would be sufficient, but it emerged that this resource did not have a high enough profile in the company. The other major difficulty is portrayed as communication. The project manager stressed that there is a difficulty in communicating delays to users without using complex terminology and imparting a negative picture. He also found IT people are reluctant to document changes and give exact dates of when things will be solved, which further hinders the communication process.

Questions for discussion

1 Would project implementation have been improved if senior management had developed a management of information systems strategy at the beginning rather than taking the more flexible approach to strategy – following a broad vision, managing change as it evolves?
2 Why do problems arise when trying to integrate new members into an existing, well-established team unit? What help can be given to overcome this?
3 Why did the views of social-work managers, practitioners and IT specialists differ over the benefits of SSIS?
4 How could communication be more effective between IT developers, professionals and suppliers?

Further reading

Handy, C. (1994) *The Age of Paradox*, Boston, MA: Harvard Business School Press.

Hirschheim, R. (1985) *Office Automation: A Social and Organizational Perspective*, New York: John Wiley.

Knights, D. and Morgan, G. (1991) 'Corporate strategy, organizations and subjectivity: a critique', *Organization Studies* 12: 251–73.

Lucas, H.C. (1986) 'Utilising information technology: guidelines for managers, *Sloan Management Review* 28: 39–47.

Markus, M.L. and Pfeffer, J. (1983) 'Power and the design and implementation of accounting and control systems', *Accounting, Organizations and Society* 8: 205–18.

Mintzberg, H. (1973) *The Nature of Managerial Work*, New York: Harper and Row.

Mintzberg, H. and Waters, J.A. (1985) 'Of strategies, deliberate and emergent', *Strategic Management Journal* 6: 257–72.

Mumford, E. (1983) *Designing Human Systems*, Manchester: Manchester Business School.

Mumford, E. and Pettigrew, A. (1975) *Implementing Strategic Decisions*, London: Longman.

Pettigrew, A. (1972) 'Information control as a power resource', *Sociology* 6: 187–204.

Pettigrew, A. (1987) *The Management of Strategic Change*, Oxford: Blackwell.

Thompson, L. (1985) *New Office Technology – People, Work Structure and the Process of Change*, Work Research Unit, Occasional Paper.

Walsham, G. (1993) *Interpreting Information Systems in Organizations*, New York: John Wiley.

Case 4.4

Performance, pay and privatization in the Civil Service

IAN TANNER

A view of the problem

Interviewer: *You're in favour of individual payment for performance?*

Interviewee: *I don't think I really do like it, not as a bonus. I think though, to be honest, that part of that is being in the Civil Service a long time. We're not used to it; it's a strange idea. Extra payment is a bit suspicious, particularly when it's all secret.*

We have had a tradition in the Civil Service that the rewards for good work were promotion – and people had a successful career and they ended up at the top and it's a very long-term thing. Some were always much more ambitious than others.

It should be team based, if you have to have this type of bonus. The team gets so intermingled that you can't really separate us. Individual bonus introduces competition. We work together; we have got to work together otherwise you have a collection of individuals who are working for their own good and to hell with the others, basically, which is a problem. You've got to pull together. What are we supposed to be doing?

The thing that worried me and I think a lot of others was job security which had gone because in the Civil Service you were safe for life – short of some hideous crime. That worried everybody and I think it has got worse since. I have no real conviction that there is a long-term future – so vulnerable to politics. For many people in the Civil Service the job security was an important factor and that's gone; bound to feel it perhaps a bit more than other people.

Background

During the period of the Conservative Government in the UK in the 1980s and 1990s there was a continuing policy of reduction in the number and scale of functions carried out by the Civil Service. Quite typically this reduction was brought about by the creation of a more or less autonomous entity which took over the functions of what was formerly a Civil Service department. These newly formed bodies employed the existing staff, each person being given the choice of transferring to the new body on new terms of service or remaining with the Civil Service to be assigned to some other department. The proportion choosing to transfer was generally very high as a result of favourable financial inducements and the uncertainty of reassignment within the Civil Service. The emergent organization could subsequently be requested to compete for the work, which it formerly undertook as of right, against firms from the private sector. In this way the apparent scale of central government bureaucracy was decreased and the door opened to the private sector to demonstrate greater efficiency in the provision of the services hitherto provided exclusively by Civil Servants.

In many instances this process led to the creation of completely new entities with the task of developing and managing the offshoots. In this way the administrative control to which they had been subject within the Civil Service was replaced by a more overt managerial structure. These bodies were variously titled directorate, authority, office or agency. The people brought in to staff these supervisory elements within the new structures were characteristically not Civil Servants but men and women with proven experience in private industry and commerce. They were intended to provide the leadership and know-how to bring about a fundamental change within the operations of the newly devolved bodies to enable them to compete successfully with their private sector competitors. This reflected the contemporary Government ideology in which it was held to be self-evident that public (i.e. Civil Service) management was less efficient than that in private firms.

The Investigation Service Agency

The Investigation Service Agency (ISA) was one such spin-off from the British Civil Service. It was responsible for a number of functions at local community level which it had been carrying out for over a century. At the time of the devolution there were some 2,000 people employed in these tasks, of whom 1,500 or so were professionals. As a result of the local focus of the work, these people were located at regional centres throughout the UK. Each such centre had relative autonomy under the control of the regional director to continue to fulfil the functions of the former Civil Service department in competition with the private sector within the region.

The Investigation Service Authority

In the ISA, devolution had led to the creation of a supervisory authority to control the regions and to provide general management functions formerly provided from within the Civil Service. The ISA was supervised by a board comprised of non-executive ministerial appointees with two or three executive directors drawn from the newly created head office. This head office employed about thirty people – half of these were professionals, some of whom were seconded from the regions for set time periods. The chief executive was recruited from private industry. He had no specific professional qualification relevant to the work of the authority but he had a very successful record of management in a variety of different industries.

The Authority was thus totally new, most of its staff were new to the organization and it had no history of past practice to constrain the way in which it operated. The chief executive soon established a very open style of management; individuals were recruited for their proven expertise and were very much left to get on with their jobs without interference from above. The offices were bright, modern and well-equipped with computer systems for data analysis and report production – which were the major components of the Authority's output. The Authority developed a new strategy and policies for the Agency regional organization, and was engaged in pioneering new developments in the professional methodologies which could be taken up by the regional units in their everyday work. Visitors were struck by the ambience of hard-working informality which pervaded this office – people were busy, involved and very productive.

In common with many managers of his generation, the chief executive had become an enthusiastic disciple of the McKinsey company's ideas about excellence in managerial practice which had received wide circulation following the publication of Peters and Waterman's *In Search of Excellence*. He was determined to bring the principles embodied in this thinking into the newly formed Authority and into the working practices of the former Civil Servants in the regions. Within a very short period of time he had good reason to feel that excellence was being demonstrated in the everyday activities of the Authority's head office. His own presence in these offices had much to do with this – he was outgoing, very capable and an able communicator – he enthused people.

The regions

In contrast, regional directors were generally a rather staid and aloof set of men. The average length of service for regional directors was in excess of 30 years and even the youngest, whose progress through the old Civil Service promotion ladder had been regarded as exceptionally rapid, had been working his way up for over 25 years. They regarded a certain social distance between themselves and the junior staff as both proper and necessary for the maintenance of discipline and control. This distancing was reinforced by the frequent relocations required of all members of the professional staff. Promotion invariably meant a move to a different region and as a result the regional director was always an outsider in the sense that he had not recently worked in the region he now directed. These frequent changes in personnel were quite typical in British Civil Service life.

Curiously, in the light of this bureaucratic structure, the work of a regional office was frequently described by the incumbents in terms of teamwork, albeit a team with clear hierarchical separation of responsibilities and involvement. The work of the professionals involved investigation and preparation of technical reports which eventually were published and delivered to relevant parties. In the course of preparation a report would be drafted by the junior staff, passed up through supervisors and seniors to the regional director himself, each person checking and amending the report as they thought necessary. After the director had seen and commented upon the document it would be passed back to the original writer for redrafting. This process was repeated until a draft met with complete approval and was considered fit for distribution. Teamwork was a matter of joint responsibility for the product rather than joint action in its production.

The Agency's task was of a complex technical nature. A report might represent two- or three-months' work, or occasionally longer, for one or two of the juniors, with the appropriate supervisory input from the rest of the team. Some of this required the juniors to be out of the office, but when at the regional office they generally worked in open offices in which the supervisor could literally oversee their work. In at least one office this was further aided by placing the supervisor's desk on a dais in the corner of the room: no one could escape his gaze!

These regional offices were facing a period of major organizational change and adjustment. The change in formal status from Civil Service department to semi-autonomous organization was accompanied by a requirement to extend and modify the nature of the work undertaken. There was also a question of trust and confidence in the new structural arrangements which threatened to stand in the way of radical change.

The great majority of those who worked in the regions were very positive about the fact that they belonged to the Agency regional organization rather than to the Authority. The Agency was an entity which commanded their loyalty and respect. This entailed a set of attitudes to the role of the Agency, the professionalism of its officers and the independence of its judgements. This appeared to be as true of new entrants as it was of the longer serving survivors of the former Civil Service department.

This sense of belonging to the Agency also implied a degree of antipathy to the Authority. This appeared to have several sources. The Authority was a politically conceived instrument, seen to be born of a lack of faith in the old department. Its very existence was seen as a challenge to some of the old values of the service. The Authority was required to monitor the work of the regional organization and was empowered to redistribute that work to private competitors. In this sense it represented the threat of reduced workload and thus job insecurity. In addition, the lack of clarity in some areas of policy *vis-á-vis* the development of the Agency led some people to suspect that there may be longer-term plans to reduce the role of the regional organization. Where the Authority acted in ways which altered the day-to-day priorities in the conduct of the work, some people resented the incursion into their professional independence. These things affected different people to different degrees but the overall effect was a fairly widespread lack of trust and confidence in the Authority and a reinforcement of the traditions and values of the Civil Service.

The agenda for change

The views of the chief executive about the need for excellence in all aspects of the organization's work were well known. He had taken the time, soon after his appointment, to visit all of the regions and to spend time talking to all levels of staff about his vision of the possibilities for the future. He even joined groups of the younger professionals for a drink at the local pub after work in a very informal exchange of ideas, the first social contact any of them would have had with senior staff. The chief executive's views included a dislike of 'bureaucracy', a belief that organizational excellence would result from individual competition, and, furthermore, that this should be encouraged through performance-related pay (PRP). In his previous jobs in manufacturing he had been responsible for the introduction of several PRP schemes and believed that they had induced necessary changes in the attitudes and behaviour of those involved.

Before the separation from the Civil Service, pay was strictly related to grade according to scales established for the Civil Service as a whole. There were no bonuses or personal elements in the salary although, under general British Civil

Service rules, extra payments were made for subsistence and travel when the staff had to work away from their base office.

The new chief executive announced his intention to introduce a PRP scheme soon after taking up his post. It was part of a package of measures designed, as he put it, 'to bring the Agency into the twentieth century.' The package also included the introduction of promotion on merit without regard to seniority or length of service and, more radically, external recruitment of professionals directly to senior posts. Both of these innovations were totally alien to the former Civil Servants of the Agency.

The PRP scheme

PRP was introduced after a few months rapid preparation by the personnel specialists. The intention was to encourage a change in attitudes and behaviour within the regions in which excellence of personal performance would become a goal for all members of the organization.

Performance marking was to be made by the individual's superior against a four-point scale. The points were labelled: 'excellent', 'superior', 'normal' and 'inferior'. The 'inferior' grading was to be taken as a clear indication of a need for improvement – disciplinary procedures were to be instituted for continued performance at this level. The gradings were linked to one-off payments for the year under consideration, paid as a lump sum a month or so after the grading had been confirmed.

The reviewer, or reporting officer in Civil Service terminology, was required to make a judgement as to which marking each of his or her immediate subordinates merited. The scheme incorporated, as part of the review process, a form which had to be completed and signed as agreed by the reviewee. Part of this form was devoted to a set of key tasks for the coming year to be recorded as a basis for future evaluation.

The scheme was intended to proceed in the following way: for every grade key tasks were to be established within the job descriptions of the staff at the beginning of the year. Objective descriptions of expected performance had to be stated for each level. These key tasks were to be agreed between managers and their staff. Feedback on performance against these measures was intended to be provided at quarterly intervals by the appraiser, which was an opportunity for praise and encouragement, where appropriate, or for discussion of the reasons for any shortcomings. This discussion would emphasize the actions that might be taken by the appraisee or his manager to improve performance in the future. At the end of the year new targets would be set and agreed for the following year. At the end of the annual appraisal there should also have been a discussion of training requirements in the light of performance and career development needs.

The operation of the PRP scheme

For many people the actual experience of the scheme differed substantially in one way or another from the description above. Because of the speed of introduction of the scheme as a whole, the reviewers had been given only minimal guidance and no training in the conduct of the review meetings which formed the basis for the whole process.

The existing promotion and review procedure required an assessment of the character and capabilities of the reviewee but had no assessment of the performance of current tasks. The judgements demanded in the Civil Service process were concerned with suitability for higher-level posts – performance in the current post, while relevant, was not regarded as central to this judgement. The PRP reviewers thus had to come to this as a quite new area of judgement and there was substantial diversity of interpretation of the scheme in practice.

There were those who ruled out any consideration of effort (i.e. the attempt to improve or achieve something) because they believed that the scheme should be measuring performance (i.e. what was actually achieved). There were others who placed the emphasis on the effort which individuals expended and attempted to reward people for 'having a go'. An internal attitude study revealed that half of the respondents reported effort to be of some importance in determining the assessment while the other half reported that it was not.

In addition to these differences in the basis for measurement there were differences in the processes which reviewers adopted in the monitoring of performance. The better reviewers did this through frequent contact with the reviewees during which the quality of the work was reviewed and assessments communicated to the subordinate. There were some people who took the time to do this as part of what they regarded as their normal management duties. Their reviewees were not surprised at the end of the year by the assessments they received.

There were others who, for whatever reason, did not devote time to the processes of review and feedback during the year. Their reviewees remained uncertain about what to expect at the year end, and had grave doubts about the basis for the judgements which were made. In the worst of cases, experience of this process confirmed the reviewees' fears that these subjective judgements could be ill-informed, partial, prejudiced and unfair. In one instance the reviewer admitted to the reviewee that he had not even looked at the major report which she had spent six months preparing!

The new scheme required the reporting officer to establish key tasks with the reviewee annually and to use these as the basis for an objective review of performance. The form of management by objectives implied by the key tasks was quite new to the staff of the regions and they experienced some difficulty in formulating appropriate objectives. This difficulty stemmed in part from the absence of any really measurable elements of the work. Certainly it was possible to set time deadlines and assess some financial outcomes of the work of the Agency but these did not directly reflect what the professionals believed was important about their work. As a result the objectives, if they were written down at all, tended to be rather general and vague.

Many of the reporting officers regarded key tasks as an inappropriate way of judging the performance of a subordinate and did not use them at all. Others ignored the appraisal form completely for purpose of assessment but filled it in 'for the records'. One reviewer admitted that he marked his reviewees on two or three attributes which he felt relevant and then 'scattered the rest around the middle' to complete the marking. One group within a region had interpreted the key tasks as a measure of personal improvement in which the tasks were specific aspects of the individual's behaviour judged to be in need of improvement by the reviewer.

In the absence of concrete, measurable outcomes from the work, some reviewers resorted to a generalized subjective assessment of the overall contribution of the reviewee. Different reviewers emphasized different things and as a result the basis for comparison across the organization was undermined.

The problem of the grades

The scale labels themselves were intended to guide reviewers, although, because of the aspirations of the new chief executive, 'normal' was to be considered as 'slightly better than' general Civil Service performance for the grade! This tended to confuse the issue for many reviewers. This probably contributed to the expressed criticism of PRP that everybody was more or less around the boundary between 'normal' and 'superior' and that the dividing line was purely arbitrary. Certainly, a large proportion of reviewees fell into the central categories.

A number of people expressed concern about the effects that their rating behaviour had on other's opinion of them personally. Most frequently they did not wish to be seen to be too generous, which they felt would indicate weakness on their part and somehow count against them. It was this which led people to let it be known that they were tough markers – as a reflection of their high personal standards. These defensive responses were clearly encouraged by the uncertainties of the measurement on which the assessment had to be based.

The validity and therefore the equity of such judgements became a matter for growing dissension among reviewees. This was exacerbated by the stark difference that this individual, public, subjective judgement represented when seen against the pre-existing formalized systems of the British Civil Service in which fairness and impartiality were highly valued features. Reviewees' suspicions that this process was arbitrary and open to bias and personal distortion were fuelled by what they saw as 'obvious anomalies' in the results as they became known.

Equity between regions

The delay in payment of the performance bonus following the review was necessitated by the perceived requirement to coordinate the gradings between the different regions. From the outset, in order to increase the motivational aspect of the scheme, it was intended to publish the results so that each region's overall performance could be compared with the others. But because of the mistrust of the actual grading measurements, regional directors thought that they should informally review the results before they were finalized in order to 'consider how to resolve any anomalies'. A further consideration was the degree to which the distribution of gradings in each region corresponded with the profile which had been used as a basis for projecting the likely costs of the scheme (W per cent excellent, X per cent superior, Y per cent normal, Z per cent inferior).

At the inter-regional level the directors compared the regional results and treated as anomalies any deviation from the projected 'ideal' profile. The errant region then had either to justify the deviation or to amend the results. In some instances, individuals had their gradings amended in order to 'normalize' the results. Within the regions practice differed; in some, reviewers independently marked their reviewees and were unaware of any pressures to find consistency within the region. In others, reviewers worked within a framework of comparison across the region which provided them with 'guidance' as to the level of marking to be applied. As the scheme developed, many reviewers adopted the practice of telling reviewees that they were borderline between two grades until the distribution became known – only then was the grade confirmed or amended to maintain the conformity of the distribution.

It was hardly surprising that there was a widespread belief that the PRP ratings for each grade in the job hierarchy should exhibit a distribution including a proportion of the incumbents in each rating category. This belief was given credence in places by the fact that some reviewers had used it as an argument for the award of particular ratings to individuals – 'someone has to be "inferior" and this year it is you!' Consequently staff found it difficult to understand how it was possible for all of the regional directors to be "superior" (see Appendix I) or to believe that the staff of north-west region (whose appraisal ratings were clearly better than those of other regions) were really so much better than the rest. On a more personal level they expressed disbelief about the gradings of others whom they 'knew' to be worse, the same as, or better than themselves. Many of these 'anomalies' may, in fact, have been entirely justifiable differences between groupings and individuals, but that was not the perception. The majority of the participants did not think that this was likely and this reaction was an expression of their lack of faith in the system.

The effects

The majority of the staff felt that PRP had only served to worsen relationships between colleagues. There were also a significant number of people who held that PRP had increased stress, decreased job satisfaction, reduced job security, and adversely affected the professional judgement of colleagues. Indeed some individuals were almost reduced to tears when explaining the vicissitudes of the appraisal process to the independent expert who was assessing the impact of the scheme. Relatively few believed that PRP had led to increased effort, increased work output, and increased quality. There were very few people who would say that PRP motivated them to alter their behaviour in any way. Many volunteered their view that PRP had no motivational impact at all. Most made the point that the money itself was comparatively insignificant but that it was not a question of money. It was quite simply that as professional people they always tried to give their best contribution and that the offer of a financial carrot was not only unnecessary but also slightly insulting.

The appraisal form also included a section in which the reviewer was required to mark the reviewee against a set of traits such as 'gets along well with colleagues' and 'writes clear reports'. These were included because the merit review interview was also to be used as an occasion to assess the individual's suitability for promotion and to develop a plan for the training which might consequently be required. The traits reviews were part of this promotion review and had been retained from the existing Civil Service procedures. Unsurprisingly, the desired separation in principle of performance review from promotion assessment became very obscured by this pragmatic amalgamation of the processes, with important consequences.

Promotion in the past had followed a clear Civil Service pattern. Interested candidates would go before a promotions panel which would assess their general 'fitness for promotion'. If successful the candidate's record was marked 'fit for promotion' to the next grade and then he or she could apply for posts at that level if they became vacant. This would then be on a competitive basis against other applicants who had expressed an interest.

Promotion was not rapid and for many of the middle-level officers there had been periods of ten or more years without any promotion at all. There was a prospect of some early promotions as a number of regional directors were due to retire within five years, but after that it was difficult to see much scope for movement. This had prompted the new chief executive to propose the idea that some people could be promoted within their current posts. This was not taken seriously by staff with experience of the Civil Service. They could not envisage how this could be possible since the job descriptions of the different grades were quite specific, and in any case this might mean that a supervisor and his subordinate were both on the same grade which would clearly raise all sorts of problems of authority and responsibility.

In this context, the fact that the promotion prospects for individuals had come to be associated with the PRP rating was highly significant. It was widely believed that you had no chance of being 'fitted for promotion' if you had not been marked 'superior'. Because of this, the PRP rating had a very great impact on the interests of some staff. The differentials between the grades were substantial, there was keen competition to get promoted, and it was therefore perceived to be crucial that the judgements made about you were equitable. If they were not, one of your peers might be promoted on the basis of lenient markings while you languished in the lower grade. To have had a reviewer in those circumstances tell you that he was a 'tough marker', which was not uncommon, was a matter of more than passing interest.

This uncertainty and perceived unfairness struck at the core of the policy of recruitment and promotion of capable young people which was part of the new strategy of the Authority. After two 'normal' markings, an ambitious junior would begin to look for opportunities elsewhere. This was especially unfortunate if these ratings appeared to be arbitrary and inequitable. A system in which promotion prospects were felt to rest on the results of a lottery, as some referred to PRP, was not likely to retain the most talented of its recruits.

Speaking for themselves

On the meaning of grading labels

Interview 1

Interviewee: *The emphasis has moved from characteristics to what they are actually doing. I could visualize how there would be differences in different places about how the scheme works. Most of us of the old school will have the weightings in our mind which we used to put on.*

Interviewer: *What is 'normal'?*

Interviewee: *I don't know what 'normal' is; it varies. I mean 'normal' in Yorkshire, for me, is quite different to 'normal' in Shropshire and Cheshire even. If you keep your head above water in Yorkshire then you're doing well – you're certainly 'superior' – if you don't actually sink in Yorkshire you're probably 'superior'.*

Interviewer: *Has anybody provided a coherent view of 'normal' or 'superior'?*

Interviewee: *It has tended to be related to what we were already using as Civil Service benchmarks, and it was put over as being something like half-a-mark above what one would have thought was a standard for good average performance in the Civil Service. If you took a good acceptable standard on the Civil Service benchmarks and moved it half a notch higher that was deemed to be what was expected from 'normal' performance; I think. That's what I've tended to think of it as.*

Interviewer: *Where does the notion of 'normal' come from for you?*

Interviewee: *That's the crunch question isn't it. That's the real difficulty; what is 'normal'?*

Interviewer: *No one has given you a guiding note?*

Interviewee: *Not really; left to work it out for yourself. Whatever touchstones you can use at the end of the day. I am pretty sure that what I see as 'normal' is different to what other reporting officers see as 'normal'.*

Interviewer: *How do you reach your conclusions about 'normal'?*

Interviewee: *Mmm ...well ... subjective judgement.*

Interviewer: *Is there an absolute standard applied to all or are you doing this comparatively?*

Interviewee: *Well its got to be a mixture of both, then it becomes very difficult. If you've got two people the same grade under you that's something; you can at least compare them, but then you've got to try and think about what other junior staff are doing. You have no idea what their performance is like. You have to take into account that your views and attitudes have changed or what you thought was good about them may not be what they are doing now and obviously relate it back to when you were a junior with all the prejudices and colouring that that brings to bear. An amalgam of the lot and then you make the dreaded judgement. It is done in the dark: it's done with a lack of knowledge of what is expected or what the standard really is – you just do the best you can in isolation.*

When it comes down to it, it's a subjective judgement by individual reporting officers and any semblance of standards or uniformity between regions and sections is almost impossible to achieve and the results seem to bear that out.

Interview 2

Interviewer: *What is 'normal'?*

Interviewee: *That is where the Authority has failed and we are not good as an organization. There is no common standard. The Authority should have specified a standard for each grade – they could have given some indication of what they would expect a 'normal' postholder for each grade to produce. A definition of 'normal' was put about as the average performance for the grade. Now, you as a reviewer never know what the average performance for the grade is and so you can never measure against that. So the goalposts are always moving or perceived to be moving.*

In the November before the scheme started we had a trial assessment run and in fact at that run I was marked ('normal') – that was 'normal' in brackets because immediately after that they brought out a new set of standards and I was reassessed. What happened was that there was a hardening of the Authority's attitude towards the performance standards generally. That was announced in a memo just after the trial assessment and we all had a reappraisal in the light of the new attitude very early the next year. I had my formal appraisal and it was explained to me that, although I was marked 'normal' in November, because of the new attitude to performance unfortunately now I was considered to be 'inferior' for my previous year's work. It was a two-month gap then I was dropped – the explanation was that I was just inside the 'normal' marking in November, but because of the new attitude to standards I now fell just below that mark.

On the perceived anomalies in grading

Interview 1

Interviewee: *Equality of standards throughout the country must be a superhuman task given the different personalities. It does seem to me that you get bunchings in certain regions, in certain markings, you suddenly get a whole batch in one region who are 'superior', in the next region you got most on 'normal'. Well, postings (appointments to jobs) being what they are, it makes me a little bit suspicious of the sort of levels in some regions. If I was judging it as an impersonal thing I wouldn't be happy with that set of results without further investigation of standards.*

And the other thing is that if you look at some of the markings that were given to grades I think that all but one of the regional directors received 'superior'; now, how all but one of them can be above average for the grade defies logic for me, so the definitions that are used by people are not common. When you look at the balance of gradings, the senior grades get a greater share of the higher markings. It may be quite difficult to say to somebody as powerful and with as much authority as a regional director, 'I think you are only "normal" or even "inferior"', whereas it's nice and easy to say to six or seven juniors down there, 'you're not as good as the rest so you only get "normal".'

Interview 2

Interviewee: *The major issue is it appears that directing staff are getting a higher share of the bonuses than the junior staff. Creates a degree of tension.*

Interviewer: *Why?*

Interviewee: *People who make it and are successful are the ones who get promoted and the ones who are performing better. I know this is intended and a senior gets judged against a senior and not a junior, but this is where we go back to what I said; whether you should assess on a team basis.*

Interview 3

Interviewer: *How can all the regional directors be 'superior'?*

Interviewee: *If you look at regional directors, yes there has been an inequity in the marking. You could have a 'normal' regional director. A regional director would be very reluctant to mark down his deputies because it would be a reflection on him if his deputies aren't performing the way he expects them to perform. If they aren't he should be kicking them to kingdom come throughout the year to make sure they do perform. Regional directors and their deputies should not be in the system at all – the scheme should stop at middle management level.*

Interview 4

Interviewee: *Strangely enough I was thinking about this the other day. In any system you have got to have some sort of structure so the Authority must have a few people 'inferior', they must have about 60 per cent 'normal' to fit in with known groupings of people and performance factors. Possibly, given any situation, you're going to get these strata. So I say to myself, 'I've been picked on as one who's got to be in that position [inferior] for a while and then someone else will come along and they will probably slot them in there to keep the balance right'.*

On the process of appraisal

Interview 1

Interviewer: *What is the process of assessment?*

Regional director: *When you get to the position of regional director ... I don't really think the regional directors expected the full panoply, every letter, of the system would be applied to them. Certainly it hasn't applied to the regional directors; it tends to be informal – there isn't formal counselling – you don't spend half a day agonizing. It isn't a question of agonizing at that stage. In my case it was made very clear that the region as a whole had been looked at as well as the individual in charge; which I, for my part, found acceptable. I thought that was right. There was a measure of informality – a matter of minutes rather than hours. No more or less than the regional directors expected would happen.*

Interview 2

Interviewee: *What we've got is a hybrid of the old Civil Service annual report and the so-called objectivity – the key activities and the measurement of them. They're a nonsense because the nature of our work is qualitative. That's not to say that there are not quantitative aspects, but the true assessment of what somebody means to you in the organization is what have they produced for you. Now, whether it's because of our inabilities with the system or whether it's because of our inabilities as managers to plan ahead, when we have to put in performance targets it's a chore at the end of the year: 'I've got to get this done, let's agree some targets that the reviewee will agree', and it's very much a generalized sort of thing. It's not a measure for what someone is intended to do and they are not a measure for what they have, or are likely to do, and although we review them – I mean I've tried this year to make this system work – when I come to do people's assessments at the end of the day it won't be an objective assessment against what I targeted them to do and what they failed on or achieved on those targets. We could probably put some numbers on our work but the better the numbers you get probably the further away from the judgement of the work you get. The major thing that is going to determine what they're worth to me is the quality of what they produce.*

Interview 3

Interviewee: *It is a conflict of running two systems. The old is giving way as judgements are coming along. Increasingly regional directors are having to respect [that] the judge-ments that are coming up the system are the results of this new system and can't be influenced directly. At the same time it does seem to me to be a bit dangerous to leave the thing to the end then come along and say that you've got one section which is completely out of line because somebody is over generous. Whereas if you can trap that – if you can have words of discussion – the difficulty is that the appraisal in the new system comes so early on, if the result of that appraisal is communicated to the reviewee on day three of the process, then it seems to me to be completely wrong to go back and tell the man that somebody has had second thoughts and that he isn't to be regarded as outstanding, he is to be regarded as standard; because that is counterproductive. It raises hopes and makes everybody apprehensive.*

The mechanics are that you get a spreadsheet and you set all the people down on the spreadsheet and before anything happens to the reportee himself you get the reviewer to say what they intend – what their snapshot is, based on counselling. Then we have a round-table discussion just to see that before the thing gets launched we are not going to be faced with something unacceptable at the end.

The match with existing values

Interview 1

Interviewer: *How well does PRP fit with the work here?*

Interviewee: *I don't think one can argue against the proposition that those who work very well for the firm or perform better than others should be paid more. I think that's right. What I have great difficulty in accepting, no not accepting ..., is putting it into practice in an organization such as ours. For example, we are going on a course on report writing, the tutor wants examples of our work and she accepts that it is unlikely that many of us will have written a whole document by ourselves. Normally most of what we do is a team effort which goes up and down a string – so almost nothing that she will get will be the work of one person – that's the point. ... We work in teams and in regions and anything that is published, which is the extreme end product if you like, will be a composite of the work of the most junior to the work of the most senior, including my threepence worth. So it is a team and one works in a small group and one relies upon a team working as a team ... It's been said you can have team bonuses and regional bonuses but that again creates this choice and to my mind if it is difficult to choose between people and that is said to cause problems ... certainly in my experience the most horrendous episode I have ever experienced was bringing this in for the first time. If you accept that we are a service and it's 'all pull together chaps'; it's the end product that matters and you have got to keep everybody's spirits up because you have only got to have one person out; you know we work in teams of five, six, seven and eight, we are very small teams and we work as a team and it's a team spirit; you have only got to have one person who can bugger up the team.*

Interview 2

Interviewee: *I am in favour as a general concept of pay for performance but I am not sure if it is relevant on a personal basis in our work. Generally we operate in a team environment. People are given individual jobs but the results are a team effort. I am not sure that rewarding each individual for his effort is a just and a fair method of assessment.*

Interview 3

Interviewee: *I am not so sure that I want to know that people in another region are better than me – publishing the results leads to questioning: why do certain grades get boosts at the top? There should be some sort of statistical distribution within each grade.*

The general feeling on this is that the chief executive is sold on PRP and we are stuck with it for better or for worse. All we can do with it is tinker with the edges and ... I am not sure that I am for the payment aspects – senior staff I don't think warrant it and I am not sure that for junior staff individual bonus is the right method.

Interviewer: *What about a team bonus?*

Interviewee: *I am not sure that it's a job which really on the whole is suited to a bonus type of system. The outcomes of the work depend on luck to some degree.*

On the effects of the scheme

Interview 1

Interviewer: *Does it motivate them?*

Interviewee: *No, I don't think so – they tell me it doesn't and I can believe that because it doesn't motivate me. They tell me it's not the money – I would hate to think it did because I am a professional man with professional integrity and I do the job because I have professional integrity.*

Interview 2

Interviewee: *PRP has a negative effect on relationships with colleagues. That's where it does have a detrimental effect. People see other people getting and not getting; the public sector is an area where everybody knows what everybody earns because they know the rate of pay, whatever. So there has never been ..., it's one attractive aspect in one respect, there is no suspicion, 'is so and so, at the same level, being paid more than me?'. You know Ian Rush might be getting more than Gary Lineker but that's private and between them; but the bonus scheme ..., since we've had open reporting, the markings that people get on report are never kept secret. You know people will talk openly, 'I got a 'normal', I got 'superior', so people know about their bonus and things like that. It's an extra divisive factor between people.*

Interview 3

Interviewee: *Quite honestly, the fact that I've been marked 'inferior' has had a bad effect on my performance. It makes me both anxious and depressed sometimes. So one tends to think 'I've got to put the main thrust into the job', and in doing that you're probably missing a lot of interesting side issues that if your mind was settled about your own situation you'd be more broadly interested in things, I think. That's as far I'm concerned really. Obviously I read everything that's circulated, I appreciate what the Authority is trying to do, obviously, but being so much out on a limb it takes a lot of one's mental energy. The other rather off-putting thing can be the continuous daily judgement of work that you're doing. If a small thing goes wrong you think, 'Oh my god! this is another black spot', whereas, if you've got a good 'normal' you can take a few mistakes. One gets the feeling that the slightest thing that goes wrong is almost confirming to them what they are thinking. I'm probably over-reacting – it has a very adverse effect all this sort of negative feedback that's coming over. We work in such a close proximity; he's there, I'm here day after day. We share a telephone, all the conversations are overheard so I have to think, 'what am I going to say if this happens', its very nerve-racking.*

Interview 4

Interviewee: *I don't go along with this fully open reporting (i.e. showing reviewees what is said about them). The parts of the report which try and pick out people's innate characteristics will become more and more valueless. People will not want to complete them; there are things about people which they can't change. It doesn't do them any good; it doesn't do the reporting officers any good. People will just steer down the middle to avoid problems.*

The grades were published by region and by grade – so individuals who were sole representatives of a grade in a region were publicly exposed.

Interview 5

Interviewee: *It was even suggested at one of my appraisals that I had been marked 'inferior' to make me push myself harder.*

Interviewer: *Do you think it has had that effect?*

Interviewee: *Not in a positive sense – I've tended to rationalize that; to take the whole thing and see how it fits into my situation, whether I needed to push myself in view of my age and family circumstances. I have tried.*

Interview 6

Interviewee: *In Civil Service days there was annual appraisal but very little apart from promotion depended on it. As long as you were doing a good job, a reasonable job, and you weren't in arrears with your work, you hadn't got this financial thing.*

It creates a lot of anxiety in me I can tell you. It's results – 'go out there and get it' – a change from the way it was and a lot of it is PRP orientated, I am sure. The fact that people up the line have to show results and the pressure goes down the line for results. It is a very stressful situation – obviously a person does not get considered for promotion until you're 'superior' so all the 'normal' people are trying to get 'superior'; so the more senior you are the more pressure there is for the people down below you to produce the results to go up through the system and one's own situation comes into this – there is me, 'inferior', producing what results I can, which are all going feeding up through the system, and you see the people above you benefiting and one is still struggling along on the bottom.

Interview 7

Interviewee: *I am not sure that the architects of the scheme thought that much about what they were doing other than they wanted to have PRP – because its a dynamic thing, a progressive thing to say that we've got. The problem is that you've got a dynamic idea in what is still a hierarchical Civil Service organization and the mechanism for doing it is still the old Civil Service mechanism with the extra bit [key tasks] grafted in. So it leads to it being suspected. There is this great sort of desire in the public service for fairness, and fairness is not overt with this system. In fact I don't think it even exists – regions are seen to be good regions to work in, maybe because they have a better balance of people but it may be just that their marking standards are different – and as long as you have that lack of feeling of fairness there's going to be suspicion about it. There is still a certain amount of feeling that the natural order of things must take its course ... there are people who look at age and seniority profiles and say, 'he'll slot in there – he'll slot in there'.*

Interview 8

Interviewee: *PRP tends to be a thing which is sworn at once a year – I think it is extremely divisive. I don't know whether you've seen the statistics for last year's PRP but they make interesting reading – percentage-wise it's amazing how the higher up you get the more 'superior'. This is something that shouldn't be in. It allows favouritism, it divides staff. You spend a hell of a lot of time arguing about it and getting nowhere.*

Interviewer: *Do people in the section talk about PRP?*

Interviewee: *Of course they talk about it! Never mind the section, it's what's happening in other regions ... I know exactly who got what where, the nearer you are to the central office the better. This is the thing; people do talk. If you look at this region, of 'normal' ratings, more than 75 per cent are located near this office which leaves only three people outside this office rated 'normal'; the rest are 'superior'.*

Questions for discussion

1 If you were the chief executive what would be your reaction to the facts presented in the case? Should the PRP scheme be abandoned? Should the Authority press ahead with its intention to radically alter the ISA using other methods?
2 In the light of the evidence presented, what would need to be done to improve the PRP scheme? Is the lack of meaningful objective measures an insuperable obstacle or is the subjectivity of judgements a factor which all assessment schemes have to recognize and incorporate?
3 At the time of this case report a management consultant related the problems of the payment scheme to the culture of the ISA. What credence should we give to his assertion that the culture could be a substantial obstacle to the operation of such a payment scheme? If he is right, what should be done to negotiate the obstacle?

Appendix I Performance assessments in the ISA (percentages)

Job grade	Assessment*				
	P	I	N	S	E
Directors, senior managers	—	—	—	100	—
Regional directors	—	—	—	95	5
Deputy regional directors	—	—	24	65	11
Senior professionals	—	—	42	50	8
Professionals	—	3	48	38	11
Junior professionals	—	6	52	40	2
Trainee professionals	38	2	60	—	—
Managers	—	—	50	38	12
Assistant managers	—	14	54	32	—
Clerical grade 1	6	—	51	43	—
Clerical grade 2	—	6	56	38	—
Clerical grade 3	—	4	70	26	—
Secretaries	25	—	46	29	—

*Key to assessment categories: P = probationary, I = inferior, N = normal, S = superior, E = excellent.

Further Reading

Brindle, D. (1987) 'Will performance pay work in Whitehall?', *Personnel Management,* August: 36–9.

Davies, A. (1991) 'Restructuring, pay and grading in a Civil Service agency', *Personnel Management,* October: 52–3.

Frost, P.J., Moore, L.F., Louis, M.R., Lundberg, C.C. and Martin, J. (1985) *Organizational Culture,* Beverly Hills: Sage.

Harrow, J. and Willcocks, L. (1990) 'Public services management: activities, initiatives and limits to learning', *Journal of Management Studies,* 27: 281–304.

Kilmann, R.H. (1989) *Beyond the Quick Fix,* San Francisco, CA: Jossey-Bass.

Marsden, D. and Richardson, R. (1994) 'Performing for pay: the effects of "merit pay" on motivation in a public service', *British Journal of Industrial Relations* 32: 243–62.

Perry, J.L. (1986) 'Merit pay in the public sector: the case for a failure of theory', *Review of Public Personnel Administration* 7: 57–69.

Pollitt, C. (1990) *Managerialism and the Public Service: The Anglo-American Experience,* Oxford: Blackwell.

Procter, S., McCardle, L., Hassard, J., and Rowlinson, M. (1993) 'Performance related pay in practice: a critical perspective', *British Journal of Management* 4: 153–60.

Schein, E.H. (1985) *Organizational Culture and Leadership: A Dynamic View,* San Francisco, CA: Jossey-Bass.

Part five

Spiritual service organizations

Case 5.1

The diocese of Carbridge: crisis and change

This case examines the problems faced by one diocese of the Church of England in the context of a major financial crisis in the Church as a whole. In concert with the economic recession of the late 1980s and early 1990s, the Church of England suffered a severe shortfall on its investment income. At the same time, changes in the pattern of recruitment to the clergy has placed increasing strain on the Church's pension funds. As a consequence a substantial gap has emerged between its income and expenditure.

This case describes the structure of governance and authority in the diocese, and outlines the alternatives it faces in managing its financial difficulties. The consequences of the adoption of new structural arrangements for diocesan management are illustrated by their impact on its services group.

Readers are invited to examine the effect of the original authority structure on the diocese's problems and the management of working relationships, the likely consequences of the new structural arrangements, and possible alternative structures. The case is also concerned with the process of managing change, and raises issues of leadership, management and motivation in 'not-for-profit' organizations, crisis management, power and authority.

Case 5.2

Piety, power and progress

A group of MBA students and their tutor are in a pub discussing the field project they are about to begin somewhere in rural Lancashire. Remarking on a nearby medieval hall, their conversation turns to medieval times, the role of the monasteries and their eventual suppression in Britain.

In the company of Simon, we visit a Benedictine abbey at a time near to the end of the fourteenth century. Simon is conducted around the abbey buildings by the cellarer, Bernard, the abbey's chief administrator. Bernard explains many features of monastic life and organization that Simon finds both baffling and fascinating. The monastic life was not at all what it had seemed from the outside: it was more worldly, more complicated and more contentious than he would ever have guessed, and very different from the life Simon knew as steward to his master, Guy of Langho. He is particularly intrigued by Bernard's account of the meeting of a special synod at which the issue of organizational renewal had been debated before Cardinal Henry of Norwich. The rest, so to speak, is history.

The discussion in the pub continues animatedly, and the example of the Cistercians is introduced. The talk centres on questions of organizational adaptation, growth, renewal and change, leadership, goals and objectives, reputation, innovation, success and glocalism. This case raises these and other issues – such as organizational culture, authority and power, regulation by rules, goal displacement, and performance evaluation – and invites the reader to compare and contrast the principles and practices of a medieval monastic organization with those of modern times.

Case 5.1

The diocese of Carbridge: crisis and change*

ANTHONY J. BERRY

In the Autumn of 1993 the diocese of Carbridge was facing some difficult decisions about its organization structure and patterns of work. While the diocese had been suffering a long and slow decline in its active membership, it had managed to maintain its patterns of work largely because it had been able to rely on the income from historic resources. However, an expectation that these historic resources were to 'run dry' had triggered a crisis. To adjust to the new financial resources would require changes in work and its organization.

The place of the Church in England

The diocese of Carbridge is one of the forty-four dioceses in the Church of England. For over five hundred years the Church of England has been the established church in England. Establishment carries considerable legal implications as the Church requires its internal arrangements to be approved by Parliament. For example the decision of the Church of England to allow women to be 'ordained' as priests could not be implemented until Parliament had approved the legislation and the Act of Parliament signed by the Queen.

Unusually for churches and religious organizations, the Church of England has as its head, the Queen of England. This curious arrangement was created by the action of King Henry VIII as he set in motion the separation of the Church in England from the jurisdiction of the Bishop of Rome, the Pope of the Roman Catholic Church. This movement, triggered by the problems that King Henry had in producing a male heir, was the product of half a century of debate within the European churches and was part of the movement known as the Reformation. The principal bishop in the Church in England, the Archbishop of Canterbury, Thomas Cranmer, was appointed by the King to be the spiritual head. Other bishops and priests who would not recognize the changes or recognize the King as head of the Church in England were executed.

These were troubled times of religious passions, passions that were underlined by the order of Henry's successor, Mary, that Thomas Cranmer be burned to death for not recanting his acceptance of the changes of King Henry. After Mary's death the Crown passed to Elizabeth, who restored the policy of Henry. In the following 500 years, apart from the time of the English revolution (1640–62), these arrangements have, with very few alterations, been maintained.

---

*This case study is designed for teaching purposes to demonstrate the problems within an organization. Any similarity to any person is accidental.

Over the last century there has been a decline in membership of churches in England. By 1945 this decline was marked and then accelerated until 1985 after which the rate of decline slowed. Even so the Church can claim approaching two million members. Furthermore, over half of the population regard themselves as in some way associated with the Church, having been baptised into membership as children, taken a further step of commitment as young people (known as confirmation) but no longer enrolled in or directly contributing to any particular church. In 1992 the figures were as follows:

Live births	650,000	
Baptisms of children	170,000	
of adults	46,000	
Confirmations	52,000	
Adult attendance	1,430,000	(Easter Day)

These figures show a continuing wish of many parents to have their children acknowledged by the Church of England as in some limited way members of the Church.

The Church of England is also part of the worldwide Anglican communion of churches (membership of about 100 million) and has good relationships with other Christian churches, though relations with the Roman Catholic Church are still cool. Such was the schism and such was the power of the State and the Church that 400 years were to pass before, in the mid-nineteenth century, Roman Catholic bishops were allowed in England.

The organization of the Church of England

The primary principle for organization in the Church is geography for the Church claims to be coterminous with the boundaries of the kingdom of England. Within England the Church has two provinces based upon the ancient centres of Canterbury and York, an arrangement which echoes the centres of civilian and military governance of the Roman occupation of Britain in the fourth century. While both provinces are headed by an archbishop, the Archbishop of Canterbury takes precedence. Indeed one sign of the establishment of the Church in the nation is that both archbishops are members of the House of Lords and that the Archbishop of Canterbury outranks everybody in the country except the Queen.

Within each province there are a number of geographically defined units called dioceses, each headed by a bishop. There have been bishops in the Christian Church for almost 2000 years and the bishops in the Church of England are proud of their standing in a continuous line of descent from St Peter, the first bishop. Only bishops can create other bishops. The diocesan bishop has the support of other assistant bishops, called suffragans.

The next level of organization is the parish, also geographically defined, headed by a priest. Each priest has to be ordained to the office of priest by a bishop. Within a typical diocese there are about 300 parishes, although the numbers range from 150 for a small diocese to nearly 600 for a large one. So within the forty-four dioceses there are over 12,000 parishes and serving them there are over 10,000 ordained priests, almost a thousand of whom are women. All of the priests are of graduate status, with first degrees in a wide variety of subjects. They also have up to nine years of theological and practical training before appointment to a parish.

Many people hold the view that the parish is the real centre of church life and work. A parish would have about 150 members on its roll about half of whom will attend regularly on Sunday. It is in the parishes that people become members of the Church, gather for worship and celebration of the Christian life and witness, are married, have their funeral services and are buried in the church-yard. The parish is the place where the members focus their commitment to their religion, work at pastoral and social concerns in their community, serve in local schools and community organizations, care for each other, raise monies for the Church, for charities, for missionary work in the parish and in the world, raise money to keep ancient buildings in repair and pay for some of the costs of the priests, the diocese and the wider national and international Church. In addition there are a large number of voluntary organizations connected to the Church including children and youth organizations such as scouts, special guilds of bellringers, men's groups and women's groups, missionary societies and para-church organizations to serve members with particular interests in aspects of Christian theology. There is something for everybody. Local loyalties are very strong and schemes to merge with other parishes are always resisted until inevitability takes over. Sometimes neighbouring parishes agree to create a ministry team for mutual support and development, to share resources and to undertake work over a wider area.

The parish is governed by an Act of Parliament which defines the powers of priest and members. The priest holds his or her office from the bishop as a shared 'curer of souls' but otherwise is given the freehold of the parish and hence can only be removed by resignation or by complex and expensive procedures in eccle-siastical courts. Within the parish there is an annual general meeting, a parochial church council and numerous other committees to which people are elected.

Each parish priest, with about fifteen other parish priests, forms a 'deanery chapter' which exists for mutual support and development of the priests. The deanery is headed by one of their number who after a full consultation is appoint-ed by the bishop as dean. This dean has influence but no executive authority.

Finance

The Church through the centuries has been the beneficiary of a large number of bequests of land, property and taxes levied upon the population, though in the nineteenth century the Church was prevented from collecting taxes and had to rely upon voluntary contributions. This meant that some dioceses were much richer than others. Following a series of reforms in the nineteenth and twentieth centuries, much of the inherited wealth of the dioceses was concentrated in the hands of a body called the Church Commissioners. This body, with about £2.5 billion of assets (1994) was responsible for providing money for stipends (that is the pay) for housing and pensions for all of the diocesan and parish clergy.

Stipends and pension arrangements for the 800 or so clergy engaged in chaplaincy (hospitals, armed services, prisons, industry, universities and colleges, schools) are met from a variety of sources as well as by the commissioners.

In the 'Great Depression' of 1989–92 the investment policy of the commissioners led to a book loss of £500 million with a consequent loss of dividend, interest and rental income. In parallel, clergy were living longer and retiring younger than they once did (now fixed at 67 years old). So three problems emerged: first, the demand on the commissioners' funds to pay pensions was increasing (note that there is no separate contributory pension fund); second, there had been changes in the pattern of entry to the ordained ministry for, by 1990, a large number of people were becoming priests in their mid-life rather than in their mid-twenties (this means fewer years of service per priest and a greater need for pensions); third, the members of the church had become accustomed to not paying for the full costs of having ordained clergy. Hence the annual 'giving', as it is called, of the parishioners is much less than needed, creating a financial shortfall in parishes and in dioceses.

The problem for parishes is seen starkly in the fact that an average parish needs some £35,000 to support itself. Parish income comes from voluntary contributions, 'giving' by the members, special fund-raising and fees for services such as marriage and burial. On average, parish incomes in 1994 were about 20 per cent less than the costs. The difference is currently paid through the commissioners. However by 1997/8 this source of money will have dried up.

The impact of the financial crisis

The diocese of Carbridge will have to either 'save' or find some £2.5 million of its approximately £14 million budget (see Table 1).

Table 1 Diocese of Carbridge income and expenditure

	1995	1998 projected (at 1995 prices)
Total income of parishes	£10,500,000	£10,700,000
Parish expenditure	7,100,000	7,200,000
Parishes to diocese	3,400,000	3,500,000
Diocesan funds	1,150,000	1,250,000
Church commissioners	2,950,000	
Diocese income	7,500,000	4,750,000
Diocese expenditure		
Salaries of clergy	5,200,000	5,400,000
Buildings	600,000	400,000
Other	300,000	200,000
Synod boards	900,000	600,000
Central Church	500,000	600,000
	7,500,000	7,200,000
Total income	£14,600,000	£11,975,000

Of the total parish income in 1995 some £3.4 million is to be paid to the diocese. Together with the money from the Church commissioners this provides the central diocese resources for paying the priests and the other staff. Almost 85 per cent of all diocesan costs are wages.

Of this £7.5 million budget about £500,000 is transferred out of the diocese to the central Church organizations, some £300,000 for training and £200,000 for central services. These central contributions can be compared with the cost of repairing and maintaining clergy housing which was £600,000 in 1994.

The 400 parishes in Carbridge have considerable historic assets in the form of buildings but they are prohibited by central Church legislation from selling these to raise money. If they wish to sell assets they have to go through a complex and lengthy legal procedure. A parish with an 800-year-old church building might have to generate over £650,000 for essential repairs. The parishes cannot afford the cost of insurance to replace the church buildings. However in Carbridge diocese there are some 400 clergy houses which are worth about £75 million, but they can only be sold to provide more housing.

It is ironic that the Church of England has 10,000 churches which are priceless, 10,000 houses which are worth £2 billion and the commissioners have £2.5 billion. But the system is asset rich, income poor, with future costs higher than apparent future income.

Each diocese, and Carbridge is no exception, has a central staff group who provide resources for parishes: clergy training; youth work; children's work; adult education; legal and other professional services; witness to the wider community in industry and commerce; research; financial advice; links to the worldwide church; mission; interchurch activities; publicity and communications; etc.

The governance of the diocese

The governance of the diocese has been developed over the last four centuries to reflect the interests of the twin leadership – the king/queen and the bishops. In a diocese this now means reflecting the historical succession and spiritual leadership of bishops but also the authority vested by the State in individual members of the Church and their rights and obligations of membership.

The diocese of Carbridge is typical of dioceses in the Church of England. It is has two main strands of authority, the episcopal and the synodical. The Church is often described as being episcopally led and synodically governed. However these two strands can have a very uneasy relationship to each other and are described below.

The episcopal system

The episcopal system of authority (Figure 1) shows that the diocesan bishop has three suffragans, which in this diocese work mainly in a specific part of the diocese, east, west and south (Figure 2); in addition there are three archdeacons who are specifically located in the three areas. These seven people comprise the

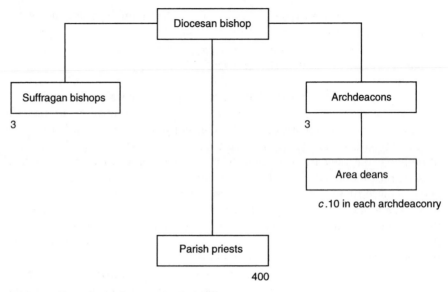

Figure 1 The episcopal system in Carbridge

senior staff and, whatever might be said and written in other places, they are the most powerful group. Their power does not so much come from the Charism of the Bishops but from the very traditional pattern of authority which they carry.

The senior staff decide who is allowed to officiate as a priest in the diocese; strongly influence the selection of persons to be trained as clergy; with some limitations from historical arrangements, they decide who can be offered which jobs, who can be promoted to more exacting jobs in parishes or in diocese roles; establish appraisal and development programmes, arrange for training to be available; manage the budgets; and exert influence over every aspect of church life. Their power is limited by a long string of Acts of Parliament which maintain the separation of powers of the clergy and the members. These Acts of Parliament clearly put the church members outside of their immediate control and indeed give the members considerable authority over money and forms of church activities and worship in the parish churches. However the ordained clergy take an oath of obedience to their bishop which gives the bishop considerable ability to influence clergy.

The synodical system

The synodical system of authority (Figure 3) is rather complex in this diocese. Starting at the bottom:

1 Each parish has an annual meeting of enrolled members which elects a church council and elects, based upon a weighting formula, representatives to the next level, the deanery synod.

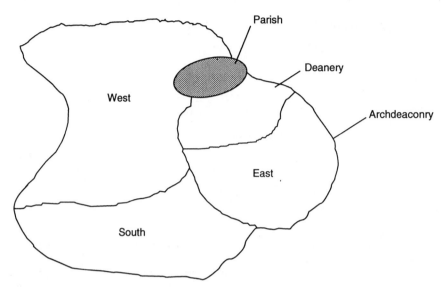

Figure 2 Map of diocese

2 The deanery is comprised of a number of parishes, depending upon geography, but usually between ten and twenty-five. The deanery synod has as members all of the parish clergy and the elected members, which means a body of between thirty and ninety members. Each deanery synod elects clergy and other members to be members of the diocesan synod.
3 The diocesan synod comprises three groups, the bishops and archdeacons, the elected clergy, and the elected members, and will have hundreds of members.

This diocesan synod has a number of standing committees (called boards). The most significant of these is the bishop's council which acts as an executive committee and prepares agendas and reports for the Synod itself.

4 There is a national body, the General Synod, which governs the whole Church of England, but this concerns itself with general policy and does not directly interfere in the affairs of a particular diocese. The General Synod is made up of the two archbishops, all of the diocesan bishops and elected members of the clergy and members of each diocese.

The boards of the diocesan synod

These boards act as standing committees for the diocesan synod taking their terms of reference from the synod and reporting to it on a regular basis both for ongoing work and for the special projects which are created. Membership of these boards is made up from elected members from the deanery synods and from the diocesan synod together with a small number of co-opted members (see Figure 4). Hence these boards have up to forty-five members. So they meet three

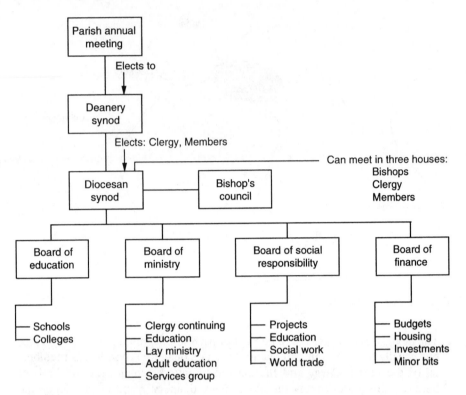

Figure 3 The synodical system

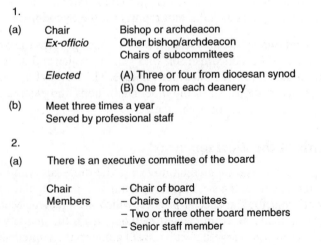

Figure 4 A typical board

times a year and delegate the day-to-day management of the work to an executive committee which will have about eight members. Each board has a group of permanent professional staff to undertake the specific work and to advise the board on policy matters. Normally a member of the senior staff will take the chair role of a board and will also chair the executive committee. In this way some internal coordination is maintained, a coordination which is enhanced by a parallel meeting of the senior members of the professional staff.

The bishop's council

The bishop's council is made up of the senior staff together with some twenty other elected members, who might be clergy or lay members. This council acts as the executive body for the diocesan synod, preparing its agenda. Only business approved by this council can be tabled at the diocesan synod meetings. However matters which are raised for debate are usually allocated time. The bishop's council must work together with the other rather independent boards.

The diocesan board of finance

The diocesan synod has the power to decide expenditure and budgets and to decide what level of financial contribution it will require from the deaneries and parishes. In practice this power is delegated to the board of finance and heavily influenced by the budget committee, which is the creation of the diocesan bishop as a means of exercising more control than the chairman of the board of finance. This contribution from the deaneries is then allocated *pro rata* to their qualifying income and the deaneries allocate to their parishes in the same manner (some of their income, like giving to overseas and UK charities is excluded from these calculations; some parishes give away as much as a third of all the money they raise).

These allocations of required money are called quota. Here there is representation and taxation. In the last ten years diocesan quota has been increased mostly as a result of inflation, an inflation which has hidden the slow-down in the growth of the real income of parishes. Many parish councils have been sending strong messages that they will not be willing to raise more money. Within the diocese there is cross-subsidization from the richer and larger parishes and deaneries to the less well-off and smaller parishes, although this is always a matter of debate.

Board of education

One of the boards of the diocesan synod has a statutory role (established by an Act of Parliament) as an education authority. This is because the diocese owns and manages over 100 schools, mostly primary (5–11 years of age) but with a largish number of secondary schools (11–18 years of age). The money flows of this board are protected and are very considerable; most of the money comes from the government via the Department for Education.

Board for training

This board through its twenty-two staff provides a wide range of training for both priests and members, in theology, in aspects of Christian life, in taking the Christian message to the world about them, in managing in church structures, in managing parishes, in working at specialist jobs within the church communities, and so on.

Board for social responsibility

The board for social responsibility involves itself with a wide range of concerns within the wider society, including issues of social deprivation and poverty, issues of drug abuse, conditions of employment and wage levels, race relations, and so on. It also offers a counselling service and an adoption agency supported by family social workers.

Diocesan pastoral committee

Technically this is not a board of the synod, but has representation upon it from diocesan and deanery synods. It exists to advise the bishop upon matters relating to the deployment of the ordained clergy across the diocese and has some influence upon the selection and training of clergy. It acts also as a kind of personnel body for the bishop. This committee (together with archdeaconry and deanery pastoral committees) also advises on changes in the boundaries of parishes, upon mergers of parishes and on the creation of groups of parishes (known as team ministries). Such changes must go through a lengthy process of proposal, consultation and higher level appraisal before they can be enacted.

The perceived effectiveness of the boards

The boards of the synod were both supported and heavily criticized by parish priests for doing things of little direct relevance to parish work, of creating highly paid diocesan jobs and broadly of spending scarce money on marginal activities. The boards were supported by their members, especially those elected from deaneries and the diocesan synod as they felt able to influence the work, to participate in policy formulation and to bring their gifts and experience into the work of the church. However the meetings of the boards were held in the daytime and each member had to travel over 50 kilometres to attend. Attendance was only ever about 50 per cent and most of those were retired people. Further the bulk of the 'real work' was done by the executive committees of each board and nearly all policy and work initiatives were created by the professional staff.

The crisis

The failure of the investment policy of the commissioners brought forward the gathering crisis of required or desired expenditure and actual income. In the diocese of Carbridge the expected shortfall of £2.5 million several years away induced, at first, a kind of inertia coupled with a sense of foreboding and worry. It was a problem that could be wished away by the difficult strategy of increasing giving or in the hope that the commissioners sums were wrong. In any event 1992 and 1993 passed without much debate in the diocesan synod or in the board of finance. This was compounded by the diocese practice of one year budgets and no formal or, it seems, informal programme of financial planning.

The response

In December 1993 to February 1994 the senior staff undertook the task of reorganizing the budgets, already agreed by the board of finance and the synod, with a view to cutting £500,000 of expenditure. These figures have been included in the budgets for 1995.

Choices

The financial choices facing the diocese of Carbridge are:

1 To begin the process of making priests redundant and amalgamating parishes.
2 To amalgamate parishes and staff them with non-stipendiary (i.e. unpaid) clergy who will have other sources of income either through their own work or through their spouses' work.
3 To reduce the costs of the central staff groups through a programme of redundancy as individual contracts (normally from 3 to 5 years) run out.

The strategy appeared to be as follows:

(a) To protect work with schools.
(b) To protect the parishes and maintain parish clergy.
(c) To stop unnecessary expenditure or discretionary expenditure.
(d) To reduce the level of diocesan central services.

This was to be followed by a second-wave strategy should the income not rise, which would involve both (2) and (3) above and then cut into the parish clergy.

During this period a scheduled meeting of the diocesan synod was cancelled due to lack of business. The whole exercise of internal consultation was handled by the diocesan bishop and the senior staff; the board of finance was not formally involved and the available opportunity to take the views of the diocesan synod was not taken. The chairs of the other boards of the synod were consulted on an individual basis.

In addition to these imperatives was the creation of a strategy for increasing income in the medium-term through a programme of fund-raising in the parishes. On average each parish was going to be asked to find another £10,000 a year (individual parishes' contribution ranged from –£3,000 to +£35,000) and send that to the diocese central funds. Reaction to this was muted and somewhat supportive. However some parishes were considering a policy of refusing to pay any more money, to take the responsibility of paying their own priests and acting themselves to provide financial support to poorer parishes. These suggestions, of parish independence, were a direct challenge to episcopal authority and to the diocesan work and its boards.

Structural arrangements

The organization structure of the diocese began to be the focus of attention for the senior staff. It was felt that the open, highly complex procedures were not helpful to effective or efficient management, leadership and control. It was felt that synodical governance was so much of a labyrinth that episcopal leadership was being made extremely difficult. Hence the following plan for reorganization was proposed.

1 Slim down, but keep the board of education (as required by statute).
2 Abolish all other boards of the synod, which would also save a mountain of paper, cut twelve meetings a year, cut travelling costs and save the time of the senior staff.
3 Give responsibility for all other work, finance, training, social responsibility, and, for the first time, the pastoral committee to the bishop's council.
4 Slim down membership of the bishop's council; it would comprise the senior staff, sixteen members elected from the diocesan synod and a few other officers.
5 Create work groups for each main area of work; each group to be chaired by a member of the senior staff except for finance which was to be chaired by a retired accountant.
6 Put the management of diocesan central staff into the hands of the senior administrator who through a liaison group would control the work and its coordination.
7 When priests left parishes to retire or to move to other jobs ensure that their successors were not appointed to the freehold but only as priests-in-charge for a contract of five years.

The advantages of this reorganization were that it took the democratic labyrinth by 'the scruff of the neck', cut it up and centralized power and control into the hands of the senior staff, albeit with the balance of influence in the hands of the elected members of the bishop's council. The proposals on staffing increased the flexibility for the bishops to adjust staffing to financial resources.

These proposals were formalized as follows. A diocesan review group had been set up by the bishop's council to consider the implications of the coming crisis. Its terms of reference were changed to address organizational issues. The group was chaired by a suffragan bishop and led by the senior administrator. The above ideas were fleshed out and presented as a paper to the diocesan synod, the members of which had six days in which to prepare. In the debate over the proposals the argument was substantially against the proposals on the grounds that centralization was not appropriate for a turbulent world and that the changes weakened the synodical source of authority and strengthened the episcopal source of authority; the proposals also removed most of the democratically elected members of boards and replaced them with appointees; those being asked to support the proposals had no moral right to disenfranchise their fellow members. However one of the suffragan bishops made a powerful closing plea for the clergy to be supportive of their bishops and the proposals were carried by 60 per cent to 40 per cent; about 80 per cent of the clergy voted for and 60 per cent of the lay members voted against.

An example of the consequences: the services group

Under the board of ministry of the synod was the services group, which was charged with the task of working to support Christian development in each of the three areas, west, east and south (see Figure 2), to support education and training of clergy and members of all ages. Further there had been developed some area initiatives which had staff attached to them. This group, with a full-time director, was now the largest staff group in the diocese.

In the process of consultation the director was invited to advise on how three, four or five jobs could be lost. The director's advice was taken and the bishop decided to cut five posts, including all the work in the three areas. Like all others, this process of consultation was conducted in absolute secrecy with the group director sworn to secrecy until the process was finished and announcements would be made. In addition, as part of the reorganization a member of the senior staff was given oversight of this work, one piece of work was transferred to a competing group and two pieces of work were added to this group.

When this news was broken to the staff of this group there was a sense of devastation, of loss, of guilt at survival. There was anger at the bishops for bypassing the synod and its boards, at the group director for colluding with the decisions, even though she had offered her resignation, frustration at not being able to influence the decisions, sadness and sorrow at the work that would have to be cut out. It was as though a bomb had exploded, shattering not only the work group but the basis of trust and the relationship among the staff. This sense of devastation was to continue to haunt the group as they prepared for some to leave and some to work at the task of planning the new order.

Questions for discussion

1 Was the dual system of authority the cause of the perceived structural problems?
2 How did this 'voluntary body' manage the relationships between the bishops and senior staff, the professional staff of the diocese and the members?
3 Were the new structural arrangements likely to add efficiency in the short term and what would be the possible consequences?
4 What was the process of managing change? What might be the consequences of the methods in use?
5 What would be an appropriate structure for the diocese? What steps would you take to develop a new or alternative structure and how would you seek a process of managing change?

Further reading

Batsleer, J., Cornforth, C. and Paton, R. (1992) *Issues in Voluntary and Non-Profit Management*, New York: Addison-Wesley.

Evers, S. (1992) *Managing a Voluntary Organization*, Corby: BIM.

Hull, B.B. and Bold, B. (1989) 'Towards and economic theory of the Church', *International Journal of Social Economics* 16: 5–15.

Laughlin, R.C. (1980) 'External financial control systems: theory and applications', *Managerial Finance* 6: 32–51.

Pearce, J.L. (1993) *Volunteers: The Organizational Behaviour of Unpaid Workers*, London: Routledge.

Reed, B. (1978) *The Dynamics of Religion*, London: Darton, Longman and Todd.

Stewart, T.A. (1989) 'Turning around the Lord's business', *Fortune* 25 September: 78–84.

Case 5.2

Piety, power and progress

GRAHAM BARLOW

Members of the MBA field project group from Manchester Business School had been checking the location of Ridgefields, the large factory where shortly they would be working together on their first field project. Now, they were relaxing with their tutor. At first their conversation had been occupied with impressions of their study to come. Then the topic swung to a discussion of the surrounding countryside. This had been rural and unexpectedly beguiling in the afternoon spring sunshine.

'Do you know anything about that large black and white house we passed?' one young man asked the tutor.

'The one close to the road on the left? That would be Samlesbury Hall. It's a fine house, though no longer what it was. It used to be pretty important once, but it suffered after the Reformation.'

'The Reformation?'

'Yes, the Protestant Reformation. A religious confrontation in the sixteenth century. Actually, it was as much about power and politics as religion. It was when the monasteries were suppressed.'

'Ah yes. In Yorkshire are found monasteries. I have seen one, an abbey at Rievaulx. It was a ruin.'

'Most of them are, now. Though you don't have to go as far as Yorkshire. There's an abbey – a former monastery – just round the corner.'

'That place with the big gatehouse and stone walls? I wondered what that was.'

'And it is a ruin also?'

'Yes, though the house which was built there is intact. It's used as a Church of England conference centre.'

'The Protestants ruined it and the Protestants have it now for their conferences?'

'Well, no, it wasn't like that, exactly. In some ways, the Church – the Catholic Church – was rather like a multi-national organization; monastic orders would be among its constituent companies. In England, they effectively became corporations owning between a quarter and a third of the country's surface. Their interests didn't coincide with those of the King and, on top of that, some monasteries were rich. So, the King plundered them for their assets, gave or sold off some of their estates to his chums, ruined the buildings and made the monks redundant so that they couldn't again be an alternative source of power and influence. Not unlike privatization.'

'And these troubles were because the monasteries by then had grown so rich?'

'Partly. Fundamentally, the confrontation was about authority, power and control. And some monasteries had been rich long before the sixteenth century. At times, they'd been pretty controversial, too. Really, it's quite an interesting story ... .'

Simon had been fortunate in meeting Bernard on the first occasion that he had
visited the abbey. After he had explained, twice, to the gatehouse porter that he
was not asking to be **given** ale but wished to buy some for his master, eventually
he had been led through the gate. As he was taken forward, he looked about
him with a mixture of curiosity and excitement. He had heard tales of the abbey
and its fine buildings and now, for the first time, he was walking within its
walls.

Outside, there had been little to see beyond the gatehouse and the high stone
walls. Now inside these, he initially felt overwhelmed by the scale of the abbey's
buildings. All were of stone and, just ahead of him, a new one was being built.
All were dominated by the great church to his right. Simon was led along a path,
into a large building and down a corridor. The servant in front of him paused at
a door, knocked and then motioned Simon to enter. He did so. A large man,
dressed in the habit of a monk, was sitting at a table, writing. The afternoon
sunshine streamed through a high window behind him. He looked up when
Simon entered. It was Bernard, who eyed the younger man inquiringly.

Simon introduced himself: he was steward to Guy of Langho. Though Guy
had ale enough, he considered it sorry stuff compared with the fine ale served
at the abbot's lodging. Moreover, he understood that some such ale perhaps
might be bought. Guy would esteem it if this could be arranged. 'Well, now,
we might be able to arrange something,' replied Bernard. 'A step outside for a
moment wouldn't come amiss: it's a fine day. Let us look into it.' Simon fell into
step beside Bernard and looked about him as he walked. Though no sound
came from the great church, there was plenty of other activity. Simon knew
a little of the abbey's reputation not only as a religious house but in particular
for its brew houses, guest house, and kitchens – better than Guy's, he suspected.
Now perhaps he might glimpse them himself. It was a prospect that excited
him.

Simon's interest was not lost on Bernard. He led the steward across a yard,
along a passage into a stone-flagged still room lined with casks, and sat him at
a table. After conferring briefly with a tall man, Aeldred, whom he later
explained was the head brewer, Aeldred drew two measures of ale, setting one
before Simon and the other, a smaller measure, before Bernard. Regarding
Simon quizzically, Bernard asked if the ale would be to Guy's liking. Simon said
that it would, and agreed to the consideration Bernard suggested. As he did so,
Simon again looked about him; at the still room, and at Bernard.

The room was large, airy, clean and, he noted, appeared to be provided with
a conduit for running water **and** a drain (water was carried in buckets at Langho
and thrown out after use). As to Bernard, he was less austere than Simon had
expected. He came across as a kindly man, capable of genuine warmth to those
about him and 'some of the unfortunates beyond our gates', a phrase he used
from time to time: Simon hadn't been sure whether that category included
himself. Certainly, there were times when he felt particularly unfortunate, chiefly
when Guy, his master, was in a fury (as he often was) over the shortcomings of
a capricious day or failure in the hunting field. He said so to Bernard, who
listened thoughtfully. 'Yours sounds like a power culture,' Bernard mused. 'Here

it's more of a role culture; or perhaps I should say a **rule** culture', he added with a smile. Observing the blank expression on Simon's face he added reproachfully, 'that was a joke'. 'Ha, Ha', Simon replied, seriously.

Bernard went on to explain that the abbey was governed by a monastic 'rule' or, more accurately, a set of rules which ordered every aspect of the abbey's life. 'For instance,' he said, 'you mentioned hunting. Our rule forbids the religious to hunt. Though it's not unknown for an abbot to keep a pack of greyhounds', he added, dryly. Simon was unsure how to take this last remark, but Bernard continued, 'the church and its services really are at the heart of things, with offices throughout the day: they begin in the small hours. But after prime, the first daylight office, there is breakfast; after high mass, dinner; then work until vespers, at the end of the afternoon. After that, supper and the last service of the day, compline; then bed'.

Simon was taken aback. It seemed very thoroughgoing, and to leave little time for anything else. 'And it's like that every day?' he asked. 'More or less,' Bernard replied, 'except on Sundays, saints' days, feast days, and so on'. 'What happens then?' 'Well, apart from offices, we usually eat and drink rather well. But at least the offices are manageable here. Some of the Cluniacs once used a continuous process system, the *laus perennis*. Their offices ran continuously, night and day, and they had to operate on three shifts.' Bernard smiled wryly. 'It's quite easy to become so busy being busy that you lose sight of your real purpose. And to become so involved with rituals that you forget what they represent.' He rose. 'Would you like to see the kitchens before you go?'. Simon assented readily.

As they walked together, he persisted. 'You have very full days. How do you manage to get everything done?'. Then, thinking of Guy, he added, 'and what happens if you don't?'.

'Invariably, we don't. We strive to live the perfect religious life and our horarium – the timetable which orders every day throughout the year – is part of the prescription for doing so. But as there's no limit to perfection, invariably we don't succeed fully, despite our vows of humility and obedience. The main thing is to keep trying: there's nothing like a performance-related evaluation system for inducing guilt and keeping people at it. However, we have our coping mechanisms.' Coping mechanisms? Simon certainly could do with some of those.

By now, they had reached the kitchens. Again, Simon was impressed – by their scale, their orderliness, the quality of the mutton and pig meat which he saw there, and their equipment which, he noted, again included running water and drains. He said as much to Bernard. 'Yes, the kitchens are kept busy,' Bernard replied, 'there are many mouths to feed. But we have up-to-date equipment: after all, it is nearly the fifteenth century. Would you like to see the services for tomorrow?' So saying, Bernard showed him some bills of fare. Simon took them diffidently and studied them with difficulty. He could read a little (which was more than Guy could), sufficiently to make out eggs, whiting, mutton, chicken and pork.

Simon's interest and laborious application were not lost on Bernard; nor was his apparent fascination with drains. Gathering up the bills he commented cryptically, 'We've come some way from our two cooked dishes and pint of ale.

But perhaps we can talk about that another time, for now I'm afraid I must leave you'. Indicating one of the monks present, he continued, 'Brother Martin will see you to the gatehouse. But if water supplies are of interest to you, if you come again I could show you a plan of them. Possibly we might be able to look at other things, too.'

Simon had accepted Bernard's offer with alacrity and, in the course of the year that had followed, he had learned a great deal. Thanks to Bernard, his reading also had improved considerably. Bernard had arranged for him to be kept supplied with small quantities of a premium ale which had found particular favour with Guy and gained Simon licence to make visits to the abbey to secure continuing supplies. But in the course of his visits, Simon had become increasingly aware of some puzzling contradictions. Indeed, Bernard himself had seemed something of a contradiction. While able instantly to produce scriptural quotation, he combined this with a worldly matter-of-factness and an ability to engage Simon on practical matters in ways which he understood readily. Simon was left in no doubt that Bernard possessed expert knowledge, not only of brewing but also of victualling, markets and supplies.

But how was Bernard able to reconcile such intimate knowledge of worldly affairs with the spiritual life of a monk? How did he attend all those church services? (especially the ones during the night: Simon had given much thought to those since his earlier visit). And then there were Bernard's vows of humility and obedience. In the company of the still room, Bernard had been very much an authority. Though courteous always, he left one with little doubt that he didn't care to be contradicted. Afterwards, Simon had raised these questions, tentatively. Bernard eyed him appraisingly for what seemed a long minute. Then, beaming suddenly, he stood up: 'Come! I think it's time that we looked into the drains', he said. From that point onwards, Simon began to have much to think about.

Bernard began by showing Simon the plans of the monastery's buildings. The abbey's drainage system was shown clearly; so were its water supplies. Each monastery was required to contain water, mills, granaries, brew houses, kitchens, and the crafts necessary to sustain it. It was to be set out in accordance with a standard plan with the abbey church, cared for by a sacristan, at its heart. It was to include an infirmary for the sick, in the charge of an infirmator: the building currently going on was for a new infirmary. The monastery also required an almonary to deal with the poor, supervised by an almoner; a guest house for visitors and better-off travellers, overseen by the hospitaller; dormitories and refectories, in the charge of a refectorater. Holders of these offices (otherwise known as obedientiaries) were subordinate to the cellarer, Bernard, who was the abbey's chief administrator (and who was assisted by a kitchener: Martin). While the drawings before them laid out the plan of this particular abbey, they corresponded with specified overall design requirements which were common to every monastery throughout the order.

Bernard explained that the rule prescribed not only the organization of divine offices in the church, but every aspect of the monastery's life. It prescribed not only monks' attitude, motivation and demeanour, but also the qualities required of the abbot, who was to be elected by his brother monks to work for the glory of God and the benefit of the community, not himself. (Simon found this a stark contrast to Guy.) The rule also prescribed obedientiaries' duties. It laid down the characteristics required to the monk chosen to hold the office of cellarer; also that the cellarer and other obedientiaries (who included the prior and sub-prior, the abbot's assistants) should together make up the abbey's chapter, or convent. Effectively, this was a combined advisory and executive committee, concerned with organizing the monastery's work. And work, Bernard had explained, was central to the rule's spiritual design: assiduous work cured most evils, whether of body or soul; idleness, on the other hand, tended to generate them. He quoted St Benedict: ' "Work! Work hard! Beware of wasting time! Idleness is an enemy to the soul!" '. Simon couldn't help contrasting this emerging picture of a hard-working, stable, well-ordered organization with Guy's erratic personal rule. Self-important and self-indulgent, Guy's narrow knowledge and overbearing ways often inflicted considerable damage upon his own interests.

Bernard's predecessors had found it impossible to meet all the rule's manifold exactions, the perfect religious life, 'especially if a community numbered only twelve'. Observing that Simon hadn't grasped his point he added, 'twelve apostles, you see'. Of necessity, monastic communities expanded. Monks brought to their work not only commitment but also education and other qualities of the upper classes of society, from which most of them came. They combined these abilities with the behaviours demanded by their rule: obedience, regularity, skill development, scholarship. Few others in any society shared such combinations of discipline, education, access to recorded knowledge and the prescriptions of what amounted to a comprehensive blueprint for designing and operating a self-sustaining organization, which existed within a network of similar organizations throughout the order.

Moreover, monks were required to consecrate not only their lives but also the monastery's property to the glory of God. They were enjoined to avoid negligence in its management and to regard the care and efficient ordering of monastic affairs as a holy duty. Monks' skills, of literacy and organizing, were scarce. Menial skills of husbandry and labouring were not. Accordingly, the rule permitted artificers to be engaged to take part in monasteries' work; it also allowed the goods which artificers produced to be sold. In doing so, it enjoined that care was exercised to ensure that the monastery was not defrauded; but at the same time, with regard to the prices of such things 'let them always be sold a little cheaper than by men in the world, that God may be glorified in all things'.

In the months which had followed, Simon had come to be aware of much that was new to him. For example, that the casks in which Guy's ale was supplied were made by the abbey's own coopers; carts on which it was transported could have been made by the abbey's wheelwrights. Goods produced from the abbey's resources generally had a reputation for quality and keen pricing, though this by no means always found favour with merchants, who did not welcome the competition the abbey could introduce into local markets. The abbey had its own vegetable gardens and fishponds, fowl, goose and pig keepers. It possessed cows and sheep, pastured on its own lands, some adjacent, some distant. The abbey's servants included not only lay brothers and artificers who worked within its walls, but also others far beyond. Simon had come to appreciate that it was lay brothers and servants who did most of the abbey's manual work. Cloister monks undertook services in the church and the holy reading that their rule required, though much of the labour of their hands tended to be undertaken in the library; some of the illustration and painting which was produced was exquisite. Simon discovered that Bernard, in common with other obedientiaries, took relatively little part in the life of the cloister: often, he was away from the abbey. He travelled widely, to the coast, to estates and woodlands which the abbey owned (and which often were managed by others, for the abbey had extensive contractual and commercial relationships which generated substantial income).

Simon subsequently discussed some of these matters with Bernard. He had begun by asking innocently, 'Doesn't the rule forbade you to eat meat?'. In response, Bernard pointed out that rules existed not only to be obeyed, but also to be interpreted; and that rules might be interpreted differently. 'For example, what do you mean by 'meat'? Should that include fish? Eggs? Certainly, it hasn't done; nor has it included stews: these have been quite acceptable where meat is only one of the ingredients. Offal isn't regarded as meat at all nor, according to some, is chicken: differentiation between two legs and four, you see. And rules not only require interpretation, they also can be extended – sometimes into grey areas. For the guest house, the abbot's lodging, there always has been a special kitchen. Visitors and paying guests can have a cut off of the joint there, and obedientiaries can dine with the abbot. They also can dine in the misericord: that's a room by the refectory where the rule is relaxed. And those eating in the refectory usually dine well on saints' days – which can be arranged to occur frequently, should need arise. You see, interpretations are often driven by questions of pressing necessity. If you rear sheep for wool, you're likely to find yourself with mutton, too. What do you do with it all? What do you do with the abbey's other beasts in winter, when grazing can be difficult? Meat is perishable and won't keep indefinitely. If we sell too much, it upsets local trade; if we give much away, we are held to encourage idleness in the naked poor – as we were considered to promote drunkenness when we gave them ale. So now, for the most part, we simply give them bread and other alms.'

Bernard's explanations had given Simon further food for thought. Initially, he had been attracted by tales of the abbey's operating systems and equipment and the lure of what he might learn from them. And he had learned a great deal. Moreover, through Bernard, he also had felt a seductive pull of scholarship. Over-responding, he had sought to visualize the cloister as a life apart, of austerity, reading and prayer, of disregard for worldly affairs in preparation for higher things in the life to come. Subsequently, he had realized that this view was inaccurate, romantic, oversimple. While, if anything, Simon had grown even more impressed with Bernard as he came to know him, he had also realized that Bernard was not a simple, humble, holy man as initially he had chosen to believe; on the contrary, Bernard was well born and well educated. Indeed, when discreetly probing prospects of entry to the cloister on his own account, Simon had discovered that virtually all the monks were of gentle birth and good education, and that only the most able and educated (and, often, noble) of them were chosen to become abbots. But Bernard had been kind and had suggested that a route to lay brother might be opened for him.

But it was with the span of obedientiaries' responsibilities (and particularly Bernard's) that Simon had greatest difficulty in coming to terms. He believed Bernard to be entirely truthful when he had said that, away from the abbey, he still considered himself to be under obedience; that he took account of the hours and offices of the day when on his travels; and that the paperwork which necessitated obedientiaries' dispensations from services in the abbey church was by no means always a preferable duty. Nevertheless, Simon had come to recognize that, far from Bernard's being a life of withdrawal from the world, he was very much of the world; indeed, he knew more of it and its commercial systems than anybody Simon had ever met. Gradually, it had dawned on Simon that, while the abbey's life ostensibly was one of contemplation and prayer, in fact it was part of an influential organizational network, rich in complexity, subtlety and material wealth. It enjoyed noble patrons. Its activities even extended to banking, fuelled by its reputation for probity, stability, and wealth.

Simon was not versed in casuistry, and found it increasingly difficult to reconcile these apparent contradictions. He also was aware that if they had occurred to him, they were likely to have occurred to others. What had happened then? One spring afternoon, Simon put this question to Bernard, who listened thoughtfully. 'It's called displacement of goals, I believe,' he replied, 'and you're by no means the first to point it out. There were great debates on just those points about 300 years ago. In fact, a monk who took part in one of them, Brother Geoffrey, came from these parts. He was a Yorkshireman.'

'What happened?' asked Simon, interested. Bernard looked about him; the sunshine which streamed through the high window was beguiling. Then he settled back into his chair. 'Well,' he said, 'if you've a little time, I'll tell you the story... .'

Bernard explained that the world had seen changes since St Benedict set down his holy rule in the sixth century. While the goal – to live a perfect religious life – remained unchanged, some had become rather flexible in interpreting it. Money certainly had become increasingly important. Not only cities and merchants had become rich; some monasteries had, too. Large monasteries employed retinues of servants, owned huge estates, and conducted their affairs with great style and splendour. They also had become politically powerful and important. But there was opposition from monks on the ascetic wing of the order, who believed that Benedictine practice had strayed too far from the founder's intentions. 'John Gualbert, Peter Damian, Stephen Harding, from Sherborne in Dorset, and later my own namesake, Bernard, from Clairvaux, all were monks who felt that there should be changes. There were hard debates about organizational renewal, and Stephen won a great success: he had support from the new Pope, you see. But his reforming ideas alarmed others, and afterwards a special synod was summoned to examine them.'

'What is a synod?' asked Simon.

'Well, in this instance, you might describe it as a committee of enquiry: Geoffrey was summoned to put Stephen's case before a cardinal, Henry of Norwich, and two assessors who were to consider its merits.'

'What was Stephen's case?'

'Fundamentally, that some monasteries were too worldly and rich, and that riches ran counter to monks' profession of asceticism, poverty and hard work. You see, in some quarters there already had been concern at the threat to established order posed by cults of hard work, poverty and simple living if they caught on. So some of those who hoped to counter the spread of Stephen's ideas insisted that Brother Johan should be one of the assessors.'

'Brother Johan?'

'Yes; a German monk reputedly of strong views and considerable experience in dealing with heresy.'

'Just what **is** heresy?' Simon asked.

'A good question, with long and sagacious answers', Bernard replied. 'But a short answer is anything which representatives of the Holy Father find doctrinally unacceptable. And one man's organizational renewal can be another's heresy. However, by acceding to Stephen the Church had shown that it was prepared to take renewal seriously. Hence, it was important that the synod's affairs shouldn't get out of hand; so an advanced thinker, Brother Peter of Warwick, was appointed to be the other assessor.

'Johan wasn't altogether pleased to find Peter one of his fellow assessors: in Johan's view, Peter talked too much and lacked proper experience. Johan believed that talk amounted to little more than waste of time; it was hot pincers and terror that brought results. And Peter was another Englishman. The English were nothing but trouble in Europe.

Henry, opening the synod, invited Geoffrey to make a statement. Geoffrey's case was simple. Worldly venalities were corrupting. The path to redemption lay before them clearly. Prayer, poverty and labour were essential steps upon it; but some within the Church appeared not to be following that path.

Geoffrey's last point was enough for Johan: "I beg you to notice the heresy of these troublesome people, who have set themselves against the Church and the authoritative statements of our faith; and I beg you to destroy them!".

Peter stepped in hastily. "Let's not jump to conclusions. Brother Geoffrey has just set out a very interesting agenda touching on two highly important core products – prayer and redemption."

"Products!" exclaimed Geoffrey, indignantly. "Redemption isn't a product! Redemption isn't something to be sold, with payment for prayers masquerading as gifts!"

Henry raised his hand soothingly. "Brother Geoffrey, the world is a vast and treacherous ocean. No one can avoid shipwreck and reach the shelter of the harbour unless he gives generously of his substance to those who are labouring in Christ's vineyard. And while we offer prayers for the good estate of the living, they yield best returns when seeking redemption of the dead."

"Very well. But generous giving can buy generous results. It can cancel outstanding penances!"

"We should all remember that the pecuniary penance is a great laxative for constipated purses", Henry murmured.

"Does that include buying redemption in advance by selling indulgences?" Geoffrey demanded.

Peter again intervened quickly. "Selling indulgences has been very localized, restricted to parts of France and Spain. As a fully-fledged voucher system, it scarcely got off the ground. But then, I think we must look at the real world and recognize that the Church is nothing if not a service provider. Futures markets offer great opportunities. There's a real demand out there for these products."

"Markets! Products!" Geoffrey expostulated. "Markets and avarice! Products and venality! They go hand in hand with the corrupting life of the cities! God would be served better by a life of silence and solitude!"

"Perhaps Brother Geoffrey's true vocation is to become an Anchorite," Johan interposed silkily. With narrowed eyes, he added, "I can arrange that immediately."

"Please, please, Brother Jon," Henry remonstrated, "there are other ways of dealing with these matters."

But Johan insisted. "If you don't deal with them firmly at the outset, you'll encourage further trouble. Shortly, you'll have Humiliati, Waldensians, no end of them. Mark my words, you'll end up by having to establish the Holy Inquisition on a permanent basis. Don't forget the trouble we had with the Evangelicals."

"What was wrong with the Evangelicals?" Geoffrey rejoined hotly. "They abstained from sex, earned their food by their labour and showed nothing but kindness to people. What was wrong with that?"

Henry stepped in smoothly. "Alas, they also preached the gospels in public and, most serious of all, they denied the authority of the Church. They had to be corrected."

"Corrected?"

"Their souls were freed from the corruptions which had infected their minds: they were released," Henry replied soothingly.

"How?"

"We burned them," Johan growled. "We had no more trouble after that."

"I do not deny the ultimate authority of the Church," Geoffrey declared, "nor do I deny the possibility that a rich man might enter the kingdom of Heaven ..."

"Good, good. A positive and practical approach", Henry interposed, smiling.

"Exactly so," Peter added. "The Church certainly shouldn't oppose the possession of riches, especially if a substantial proportion of them are devoted to the Church's purposes. In fact, it's important that people **should be** rich under such circumstances; the essential thing is to **legitimate** it with the right message. Something catchy, crisp and clean. How about 'piety to prosperity?' "

"**My** essential point", Geoffrey replied severely, "is that **we** should not possess riches on earth, but should seek higher ideals through discipline, labour and prayer. And the gap between the culture you describe, between what you and I consider essential, is too great to be bridged."

"That needn't be a problem," Peter assured him earnestly. "I can run you through the *Kilmann–Saxton Culture Gap Survey.*"

Johan sat up with sudden interest. "Kill who?" he asked.

"It's a survey tool. Part of a completely integrated programme for creating and maintaining organizational success", Peter explained enthusiastically.

Johan muttered something and turned away gloomily.

Geoffrey returned to his theme with quiet determination. "I'm sorry, but the gap **is** too great to be bridged: we need radical changes; a uniform policy; an integrative structure; standardized accounting practices. In the past, too many of our communities have developed their own forms of creative accounting. And far from denying the authority of the Church, we support it with vigour. But we believe we can serve the Church best by our example: an example of rigorous discipline; of hard labour of the hands, which is purifying; of eschewing riches and loving poverty; of relinquishing the follies of the world and seeking salvation by embracing hardship and building communities in lonely, deserted places, far away."

"Greenfielding, eh?" mused Peter, "that's good thinking. Site values could be for nothing in the right sort of area".

"You wish to go **far** away, to lonely, deserted places?" Henry enquired, cautiously. "**All** of you? **How** far?"

"The further the better!" Geoffrey exclaimed.

Henry smiled beatifically. "Dear Brother Geoffrey! I think we are agreed that you should proceed with your noble endeavour. We wish you all God's speed in your journey to **very** distant places." And with that, Henry declared the synod closed.

Those assembled rose and left the room in slow procession: Henry, Peter, Geoffrey. Johan, shaking his head, followed behind. As they passed through the doorway, Henry fell into step beside Peter and said quietly, "that message of yours really was most impressive". He repeated it softly, "piety to prosperity". Yes, impressive. Crisp and clean. And not too revealing. Henry paused as a sudden thought struck him. "It wasn't you who coined 'ethnic cleansing', was it?"

Simon gave a start. The afternoon sun had moved round in the sky and now it was playing onto his face. He rubbed his eyes; then sat up in astonishment. Bernard had vanished. In his place, his tutor was setting down a pint glass of beer. 'Rejoined us, have you?' he enquired. 'I thought that might wake you up. Actually, **you** were supposed to be getting the last round. I take it you were overcome at the prospect.' Disorientated, Simon didn't reply. Instead, he glanced hurriedly about him; then he recognized the oak-panelled interior and bar of the pub that they had entered earlier that afternoon. His colleagues were engaged in animated discussion.

'I was looking at it from an interpretative action perspective. Lip-service is paid to the intentions of the founder – especially in attempting to **legitimate** a course of action far removed from the original intentions. But successor-dominant coalitions impose their own situational definitions upon the others, who feel obliged to accept them, albeit with varying degrees of reluctance. It's phenomenological. You'll find it in Silverman.'

'I'm sorry, Peter; I have not read it.'

'Neither has he, Jon. He got that from my copy of Allaire and Firsirotu.'

'But you are talking about **adaptation**. About cultures running down, about trouble. I am talking about **renewal**. To regain the proper perspective strong change is needed. Leave the old places, close them down. Begin again, in different places with new people. There must be clear objectives, and plans to achieve them.'

'You missed out strong leadership, Jon.'

'OK, strong leadership, too. If they had done those things, they would have succeeded.'

'Succeeded in what?' the tutor interposed.

'In attaining their goals. The perfect religious life, hard work, loneliness, whatever it was they were wanting.'

'Actually,' the tutor replied, 'that is precisely what the Cistercians did. They split from the Benedictines and formed a new order, around the beginning of the twelfth century. They did impose rigorous discipline and hard work, and they set up communities in some pretty wild and remote places such as Skelldale, where Fountains Abbey was established. Fountains was a Cistercian house; so was Rievaulx, the abbey Jon visited.'

'And they achieved their objectives?'

'Probably, for some; at least, in the beginning.'

'What happened after that?'

'They got rich even more quickly than the Benedictines. You see, the Cistercians began with the reputation of being the new soldiers of Christ, dedicated to the disciplines of the religious life and noted for their piety and austerity. Their reputation brought them considerable goodwill. In the north of England, it also brought gifts of land from benefactors: Robert de Mowbray was particularly generous. Actually, several of the great northern aristocratic families vied to outdo one another's generosity.

But the Cistercians themselves brought crucially important attributes with them: thoroughness, dedication to work, and systems of uniform accounting and consolidated estate management which were radical and among the most efficient in Europe. They also had created a constitution and operational framework which balanced central authority with local autonomy in a new and highly effective form of glocalism. Hence, if land was poor, they developed other activities. For example, Robert gave the monks of Fountains the Forest of Nidderdale, including its mineral rights. The Cistercians had their own metallurgical specialists who examined ore veins, advised on their potential for exploitation, and trained lay brothers and other workers in extraction and smelting. At Fountains, they mined and smelted lead and iron. Furness, another Cistercian monastery just north of here, at Barrow, not only became the greatest producer of iron ore in northern England but also the richest and most powerful Cistercian abbey in the kingdom, after Fountains. Its hospitality was famous; it built ships in its own dockyards, capitalized on iron founding and was the economic powerhouse of the heavy industry which grew up in the vicinity. The abbey even raised an army in 1513 to fight the Scots at Flodden. The Cistercians were successful merchants, too. They dealt extensively; for example, in wool, which was another of their major products. They spent part of their income on extending and consolidating their estates, and on building: Furness came to own vast lands in Lancashire, Yorkshire, Ireland and the Isle of Man, while at Fountains the later buildings were lavish. Even ruined, they're still quite outstanding.'

'I've heard of Fountains,' Simon said, 'but what about this abbey here?'

'Whalley Abbey? That was a Cistercian house, too, though all its buildings weren't fully completed until the fifteenth century. But it certainly was successful, according to some criteria. Its abbots were noted for their prodigal hospitality, it employed many servants and its monks came to live pretty high. Indeed, in 1520, not long before the monasteries were suppressed, the monks at Whalley spent about two-thirds of their annual budget on food and drink, including sweet-meats, figs, dates and other exotic delicacies. They also spent substantial sums on minstrels, bear-baiting and other entertainments. By 1535, they'd reined back considerably, and gave nearly a quarter of their income to the poor; but time was running out. Two years later, the abbey was dissolved and its twenty-five monks were turned out. But at least most of them weren't executed, though their abbot was. So was the abbot of Fountains.'

'I should like to visit this Fountains Abbey. It sounds very great.'

'I recommend it, Jon; Fountains has been designated a World Heritage Site, and it's not as far as Rievaulx. And, if any of you do visit Fountains, be sure to look out for the message painted on the wall. I think you might find it familiar: **"Piety to Prosperity"** '.

Glossary of terms and supplementary notes

The Reformation (p. 197). Instituted by Henry VIII in 1537, when he set up a national church (the Church of England) with himself at its head. Earlier, successive English monarchs had imposed heavy levies or taxes on the monasteries. Now, Henry went a stage further: he suppressed them. In essence, this meant that the Crown (Henry) seized all their assets. Buildings usually were slighted (ruined); some land was passed to Henry's supporters but the greater part was added to the Crown estates. Crown ownership was short-lived, however, for most of the lands had to be sold off in the 1540s and early 1550s to pay for wars against the Scots and France. Within 20 years, little was left. The great plunder had become a redistribution.

The suppression (p. 197) eliminated a range of monastic functions, from provision of welfare and poor relief to record keeping. (The monasteries had relatively elaborate and sophisticated record-keeping practices, which the suppression eliminated at a stroke. The extensive monastic records which existed at the time of the suppression were dispersed and many were destroyed.)

Daily offices (p. 199)

Timetables: A principal point is that abbeys operated with timetables ('horaria') which **regulated** and **ordered** the activities of their days. While the sequence of daily offices was set out by St Benedict, attempting a contemporary translation of these into a timetable and set of activities would be influenced by several factors. **Measuring** the passage of time could be less problematic (monasteries developed clocks, including alarm clocks, for this purpose) than variations introduced by **concepts** of time.

The **structure** of the monastic day was divided into twelve equal parts (termed 'hours'). In the absence of modern artificial lighting, daylight was particularly important; hence, partly depending on where a monastery was located, summer 'hours' each could be perhaps some thirty minutes longer than winter 'hours', and could vary from abbey to abbey. Summer horaria thus were different from winter horaria, the latter operating from Holy Cross Day (14 September) until Easter Day, the placing of which in the calendar each year could vary by up to a month.

Beside the influence of the seasons, the **content** of the monastic day could be shaped by differences between the practices of orders, which resulted in more time being devoted to some activities than others. Also, with the passage of time, the tenor of monastic activities could change. For example, in Britain by the fifteenth and sixteenth centuries many abbeys had tended to move away from rigorous asceticism, to settle instead into more gentlemanly patterns of existence.

Water conduits and drains (p. 199). Monastic life-support systems were appreciably more sophisticated in these respects than generally was the case elsewhere in England. Indeed, greatest improvements to public health and mortality rates in Britain did not come about until late in the nineteenth century, not from advances in medicine but from an Act of Parliament resulting in the provision of efficient urban and domestic drainage and water supply systems.

An organization chart of an abbey's principal roles is set out in Appendix I.

St Benedict's rule (p. 201) laid the foundation for monastic communities which became established in countries throughout Europe. Benedict is now the patron saint of the European Union.

Redemption and indulgence (p. 205). The Church represented a substantial authority system, as those who transgressed it discovered: denying the Church's authority could be the ultimate crime. Redemption of past sins and other misdemeanours could be sought through prayer, and prayers usually were answered when combined with generous gifts to the Church. Indulgences extended this position, effectively by offering absolution in advance to those who gave lavishly for the privilege, for sins they had yet to commit.

Anchorite (p. 205). A reclusive hermit dwelling in a cell, which could be incorporated into a wall of a church. Such cells were cramped and usually had no door but instead, two small apertures, one permitting food to be passed inside, the other a narrow slit (termed a 'squint'), affording the anchorite sight of the altar. The anchorite lived walled up within.

Humiliati (p. 205) (or humble ones) were one of a number of schismatic groupings which arose outside (and implicitly in opposition to) the Church. They evolved during the twelfth century from an informal grouping of lay people. They wore simple, undyed clothing and chided those whom they considered neglected the Christian faith, which they preached publicly. They had to answer for this to Pope Lucius III (1181–5), who placed them under perpetual anathema.

Waldensians (p. 205). Severe famine in 1176 in the Lyonnais region not far from Cluny had given further emphasis to already existing disparities between rich and poor, made more striking by the ostentatious spending of the rich, while the sick and poor starved. Waldes, a rich merchant, experienced a religious conversion and vowed to give his wealth to the poor. Though the sight of a great burgher giving away his fortune in the streets alarmed the well-to-do, it brought Waldes followers: he became an Evangelical. The Waldensians preached in towns and villages, in public squares and sometimes in churches. In 1181, following the ascension of Pope Lucius III, Waldes was summoned before a synod presided over by Henry of Marcy, a cardinal experienced in dealing with heretics. However, in return for an agreement that though Waldes himself would remain poor, others need not do the same in order to be saved, tacit licence was given to Waldes and his followers. Earlier **Evangelicals** who had denied the authority of the Church had been less fortunate; in the previous century, they had been burned.

Kilmann–Saxton (p. 206): vide Kilmann, R.H. and Saxton, M.J. (1983) *The Kilmann–Saxton Culture Gap Survey*, Pittsburgh, PN: Organizational Design Consultants; also, Kilmann, R.H. (1988) *Beyond the Quick Fix*, San Francisco: Jossey-Bass.

Whalley Abbey (p. 208). Ownership of Whalley Abbey passed to Richard Assheton, one of the prosecutors who condemned its last abbot, John Paslew, to be hanged. Assheton adapted the structure, building himself an Elizabethan manor house with stone looted from the ruined abbey church. The estate changed hands several times during the nineteenth century and in 1923 the house and grounds were bought by the diocese of Manchester within the Church of England.

Appendix I Outline of an abbey's principal roles

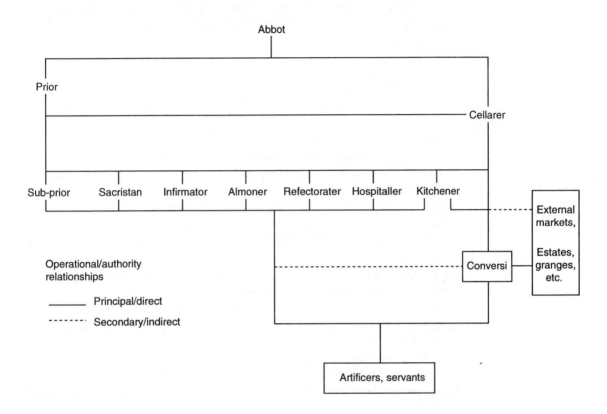

Deriving from a Benedictine model, a role structure could vary according to the size and wealth of a monastic establishment (ranging, for example, from a principal parent house to a small dependent subunit), while other orders might modify or dispense with certain titles or roles.

The:

- **Abbot** was the head of the house.
- **Prior** and **Sub-prior** were his principal assistants.
- **Cellarer** was the chief economic administrator (though contracts normally would be signed by the abbot).
- **Kitchener** was the cellarer's assistant, and was concerned with provisioning.
- Other **obedientiaries** (office-holders) took charge of various of the abbey's internal operational arrangements; for example,

  Sacristan: Church
  Infirmator: infirmary or sick quarters
  Almoner: poor relief

Refectorater/chamberlain: dining rooms, dormitories
Hospitaller: guest house/abbot's lodging

- **Conversi** were lay brothers. Often filling intercalary roles, they effectively were the abbey's commercial agents or intermediaries. They were responsible to the cellarer.

Further reading

Bowles, M.L. (1989) 'Myth, meaning and work organization', *Organization Studies* 10: 405–21.

Coppack, G. (1993) *Fountains Abbey*, London: Batsford.

Coulton, G.G. (1989) *The Medieval Village*, New York: Dover.

Gerth, H.H. and Mills, C.W. (eds) (1991) *From Max Weber: Essay in Sociology*, London: Routledge.

Knowles, D. (1966) *The Monastic Order in England*, Cambridge: Cambridge University Press.

McCann, J. (ed. and trans.) (1983) *The Rule of St Benedict*, New York: Darton, Longman and Todd.

Meyerson, D. and Martin, J. (1987) 'Cultural change: an interpretation of three different views', *Journal of Management Studies* 24: 623–247.

Penrose, E.T. (1995) *The Theory of the Growth of the Firm*, Oxford: Blackwell.

Roth, G. and Schluchter, R.G. (1984) *Max Weber's Vision of History*, London: California University Press.

Silber, I.F. (1993) 'Monasticism and the "Protestant ethic": asceticism, rationality and wealth in the Medieval West', *British Journal of Sociology* 44: 103–23.

Twining, W. and Myers, D. (1991) *How to Do Things with Rules*, London: Weidenfeld & Nicolson.

Weber, M. (1990) *Economy and Society*, London: Routledge.

Part six

Organizing the unknown

Case 6.1

Working in space: Skylab

Following the successful landing of the first human beings on the Moon in 1969, the US space programme entered a period of uncertainty and financial stringency. The Skylab missions, initially conceived as an experimental prelude to the establishment of permanent space stations, were undertaken in an atmosphere of cut-backs and constraints. Among the many unknowns attending the flights were the effects of lengthy exposure to zero-gravity conditions upon the physical and psychological well-being of the flight crews. Could humans survive under such conditions for months at a time?

The opening section of this case outlines the background to the Skylab programme, the technological environment, the characteristics of the crews, and the design of the work organization. The events occurring during each of the three manned flights are described, paying particular attention to the final mission. During this flight the crew staged the first 'strike in space'.

The second half of this case brings together some reflections and observations by the programme's managers and the Skylab 4 crew members on the events that had taken place. A brief account is also given of Carpenter's Mercury 7 flight during the early days of the space programme, and of the debates over the provision of on-board controls in space craft that occurred in both the United States and the Soviet Union at around the same time.

The case invites the reader to explain why the third crew resorted to a 'strike', to analyse the work organization and identify the assumptions and principles that appear to have underlain it, and to suggest possible alternative arrangements. Issues raised include conflict; management control; the management of professionals; group relations; organizational cultures and subcultures; sociotechnical systems; scientific management; power; communications; goals and priorities; environmental change; managing uncertainty; work design; selection and training; and motivation and leadership.

Case 6.1

Working in space: Skylab

ALAN B. THOMAS

The origins of the Skylab programme

In 1961, President J.F. Kennedy committed the United States to the goal of landing a man on the Moon by the end of the decade. When, on 21 July 1969, Neil Armstrong became the first human being to set foot on another world, that goal was achieved and the American space programme entered a new phase.

During the 1960s, the National Aeronautics and Space Administration (NASA) had enjoyed virtually unlimited government funding in its bid to win the 'space race'. But with the race won, and with the United States' growing involvement in the Vietnam War, both governmental and public interest in space exploration diminished rapidly. Although the Apollo lunar landing missions continued until 1972, by then space flights to the Moon had come to be seen as almost routine.

NASA pressed hard for the expansion of its manned space projects, but to no avail. Despite the pleas of NASA administrator, Dr Thomas Paine, and the rocket pioneer, Wernher von Braun, funding constraints were tightened. Both resigned from NASA in the early 1970s. When James Fletcher took over as NASA administrator in April 1971, he knew that its future depended upon its being able to devise programmes that could be seen to be both useful and effective.

Henceforth, continuation of NASA's space projects would depend less on political considerations and more on the ability to yield convincing scientific and economic returns.

NASA had been developing ambitious plans for an orbital space station since the mid-1960s, but by 1970 these plans had been scaled down. The new programme, designated as Skylab, abandoned the idea of building a purpose-built craft from scratch. Instead, the aim was to construct an orbital space laboratory based on hardware left over from the Apollo programme. Skylab would therefore consist of the shell of the third stage of the Saturn V booster, fitted out to enable a crew of three to live and work in space for extended periods of time. Access to the space station would be by means of the Apollo command and service modules, the same units as had been used for the lunar landing missions.

The Skylab missions, as originally conceived by William Schneider and his planning team, were envisaged primarily as experiments in living in space. The size of the space station and its semi-permanent status meant that the astronaut crews would be able to eat, sleep, work and play relatively free of the constraints imposed by the cramped conditions of previous craft. Seen as a 'house in space', the intention was to reproduce the pattern of normal life on Earth as closely as possible. For example, the crew would work an 8-hour day with regular meal breaks, prepare their own food, and have plenty of time for relaxation and leisure. Simply living in Skylab was the chief experiment. Could humans survive in extended conditions of zero-gravity for months at a time?

Previous experience was not especially encouraging. The longest flight prior to Skylab had lasted 14 days (Gemini 7). The astronauts had suffered a number of adverse physiological effects including the loss of muscle tissue, reduced calcium levels, loss of body fluids and changed blood characteristics, although these were less severe than had been feared. In the face of these uncertainties, the duration of the first Skylab mission was set at 28 days, a full month in space. The duration of subsequent missions could not be set in advance, but would depend upon the outcome of the first mission. But one thing seemed certain: Skylab's success was crucial to NASA's future.

The Skylab environment

Skylab was the largest structure ever placed in Earth orbit. Over 80 feet (24.4 metres) long and weighing nearly 100 tons, it provided a habitable area of around 10,000 cubic feet (283 cubic metres) (see Figure 1). The craft consisted of a capacious living area built within the Saturn third-stage shell to which a docking unit had been attached at one end. A large solar telescope, powered by four solar panels which gave the unit the appearance of a windmill, was mounted on the docking unit.

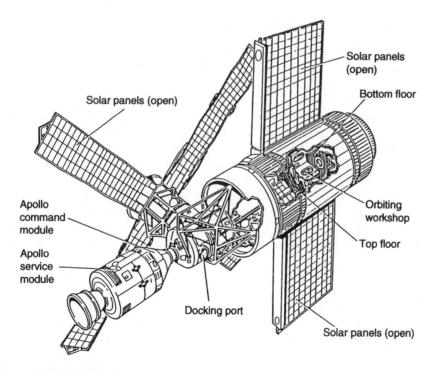

Figure 1 Skylab 1973–4

The living area, 48 feet long and 22 feet in diameter (14.6 × 6.7 metres), was divided into two levels separated by a mesh floor. The upper level housed the water and oxygen/nitrogen tanks and the main storage lockers. The lower level included an experiments room, sleeping compartment, bathroom ('waste-management compartment') and wardroom (dining and living area). By normal space standards, Skylab was extremely spacious, quite unlike the cramped cabins which had housed earlier astronaut crews.

A dominant feature of the Skylab environment was, of course, zero-gravity. Under these conditions, most everyday activities turned out to be much more difficult and time-consuming to carry out than might have been expected from the preflight simulations. Life was made more difficult by a variety of seemingly minor design failings. For example, at meal times the crews found that no pro-vision had been made to secure their cutlery to the food trays; spoons and forks tended to float off in mid-meal. Similarly, much of the astronauts' equipment was stored loose in locker drawers. When one of these was pulled open, the entire contents would spill out and float away. If a top drawer was opened, items in the drawer below would float up and make it impossible to close it again. Such niggling problems were, to say the least, irritating.

If eating was a problem, sleeping sometimes proved equally difficult. The astronauts slept in bags attached to the walls of the spacecraft. To ensure that they did not suffocate by breathing in their own exhaled carbon dioxide, cool air from the ventilation system was blown across their faces throughout the 'night'. Not everyone found this conducive to a sound night's sleep. And as the craft passed from the Earth's shadow into sunlight, the sudden change in external temperature brought noisy cracking and popping sounds as Skylab's outer skin responded. The crews also became acutely aware of the fact that the sleeping compartment was located on the lower level of the living area, at the furthest possible point from the docking unit.

Another problem area was communications. The atmosphere in Skylab con-sisted of a mixture of oxygen and nitrogen. In this 'thin air', maintained at low pressure, sound travelled slowly. Making oneself heard involved shouting, with the result that the astronauts tended to suffer from sore throats and hoarseness. Facilities for communication with the ground were also less than ideal. Skylab orbited the Earth once every 90 minutes, but direct communication with Mission Control, at the Johnson Spacecraft Centre near Houston, was possible for only a quarter of this time. Contact with other ground stations was even more limited, accounting for no more than a few minutes during each orbit. For most of the time, the Skylab crews were alone, much more so than the crews of previous manned flights.

The Skylab crews

NASA's flight crews were drawn heavily from the military. Although civilian scientists were included more frequently with the advent of the Shuttle programme, most of the astronauts who flew on the lunar and Skylab missions were highly-qualified Air Force or Navy pilots. Many of these men had been trained as military test pilots and they often had combat experience as well. Although they were accustomed to the constraints of military authority, they also cherished their independence as flyers.

These men looked on the prospect of flying in space as a 'once-in-a-lifetime' opportunity, the pinnacle of a flyer's career. Competition to join the space programme and be selected for a mission was correspondingly intense. Yet the astronauts also tended to be drawn together by their military backgrounds (although there was considerable rivalry between the Air Force and the Navy) and their shared love of flying.

The commanders of the first two Skylab missions, Conrad and Bean, were both from the Navy and had been room-mates. It was Conrad who first encouraged Bean to join the astronaut corps. Bean in turn had recruited Weitz (a Navy pilot), who became Conrad's second-in-command on the first Skylab mission. Lousma (a Marine fighter pilot), who became second-in-command to Bean on the second mission, had been with Weitz at the Naval Postgraduate School at Monterey, California.

Further details of the Skylab crews and the criteria used to select the first Mercury crews are shown in the appendices.

Skylab's work organization

The Skylab missions were under the overall control of the programme director, William Schneider, who was based in Washington. Operational control was in the hands of the flight director, Neil Hutchinson, who worked at the Houston Centre.

Hutchinson, an engineer by training, fitted well with the high-achievement culture that had developed at NASA. He took considerable pride in running a 'tight ship' and found any form of disorganization almost intolerable. It was well known that at NASA astronauts were expected to be motivated 100 per cent and to deliver 100 per cent. Hutchinson was determined that the astronaut's time in space would be used to the maximum.

The structure of the astronauts' day was planned as follows:

```
06.00 — crew woken
08.00 — start work
12.00 — meal break
13.00 — restart work
18.00 — main-meal break
20.00 — free time
22.00 — lights out
```

During the 'work' periods, the astronauts were to undertake four types of activity:

1 Medical experiments – the crew members themselves were the subjects of these experiments. For example, they were required to keep detailed records of their intake (and out-take!) of food and liquids; if they threw-up they were

to store the vomit in plastic bags for later analysis on Earth; and each day they had to spend several hours on the bicycle ergometer, a kind of electronically-monitored exercise bike.

2 Earth resources experiments – these involved photographic surveys of the Earth's surface using multiple cameras operating on different wavelengths.

3 Solar observations – using the large solar telescope to make photographic studies of solar phenomena.

4 Miscellaneous experiments ('corollaries') – in botany, biology, astronomy, optics, metals processing, etc. For example, the astronauts tried to manufacture the perfect ball-bearing, something impossible on Earth because gravity distorts the bearing as it cools. In the work schedule, these 'corollaries' tended to be used to 'fill in' gaps between the main activities. The crews also had to carry out a multitude of routine monitoring procedures as part of the day-to-day running of Skylab.

There were always many more experiments available than could be accommodated on the Skylab missions. The flight planners found themselves besieged by eager scientists, all wanting their pet projects to be included in the programme.

Each day's tasks were scheduled by Mission Control in much the same way as they had been for the previous manned flight programmes. Hutchinson described the process like this:

> *We're building a flight plan everyday as intricate as a lunar outing ... We send up about 6 feet of instructions to the astronauts' teleprinter in the docking adapter everyday – at least forty-two separate sets of instructions – telling them where to point the solar telescope, which scientific instruments to use, and which corollaries to do. We lay out the whole day for them, and the astronauts normally follow it to a T! What we've done is we've learned how to maximize what you can get out of a man in one day.*

The first Skylab missions

Skylab was launched on 14 May 1973. To fund the launch, NASA had had to cancel one of the Apollo series Moonshots. The craft went into orbit at the planned height of 271 miles (442 kilometres), and was joined ten days later by the first crew (Skylab 2).

The original plan was that the first crew would board Skylab the day after the launch. But during lift-off a meteorite shield had been ripped off the craft and destroyed. Without this protection the cabin temperature rose rapidly to 40°C, threatening to melt the plastic components within and render Skylab uninhabitable. One of the two main solar panels had also been lost and the second had become ensnared by loose debris and was only partially deployed. Even if this panel could be released, Skylab would only be able to function on half power.

At Mission Control, the engineers worked frantically to devise a rescue plan. After more than a week's delay, the first crew set out for Skylab with one key task in mind; to make the craft habitable and so save the whole programme. Equipped with a large folding sunshade and a set of special cutters, it took nearly two weeks for them to rig the sunshade over the exposed portion of the hull and free the jammed solar panel. Both tasks demanded considerable skill and initiative, not to mention courage. External maintenance had not been envisaged and no handholds had been provided on the outside of the craft. Despite these difficulties, the crew's efforts were successful. The Skylab programme had been brought back from the brink of disaster.

With half the mission-time gone, the crew had to work hard to catch up with the planned schedule. The crew were elated by their early success, but still complained occasionally that Mission Control was driving them too hard. Even so, by the end of the flight they had completed around 80 per cent of the planned solar observations, most of the earth resources surveys, all of the medical experiments and most of the corollaries. Although it had departed radically from expectations, the first mission to Skylab was considered a success.

A little over a month after the first crew's return, the second crew (Skylab 3) took up residence. As the first crew seemed to have reacted well to their month in space, the duration for Skylab 3 was set at 59 days.

After an initial bout of space sickness, the second crew settled in remarkably well and worked with great dedication and enthusiasm. On the solar observations alone they exceeded the scheduled hours by 50 per cent, producing over 75,000 photographs of the sun. The crew often worked 12–14 hours a day, taking their meals 'on the run' and sleeping for only six hours. They even asked Mission Control to give them extra tasks.

At Mission Control, the flight director, Hutchinson, was well pleased with the crew's performance. As he said later:

> Back at the first mission, we weren't good enough to schedule the guys tight, but by the time the second mission ended, we knew exactly how long everything took. We knew how long it took to screw in each screw up there. We could have planned a guy's day without leaving a spare minute if we wanted to – we had that ability. We prided ourselves here that, from the time the men got up to the time they went to bed, we had every minute programmed. The second crewmen made us think this way. You know, *we* really controlled their destiny.

By early November the third crew (Skylab 4) were ready to go. With few signs of physical deterioration in the second crew, the mission was scheduled to last 84 days.

The third mission and the 'space mutiny'

Everyone at NASA had high hopes of the third mission, not least the programme director, Schneider. In the light of the experience of the second crew, he instructed the Skylab 4 astronauts to take things easily and not go all out as they had done. Since the aim of the programme was to see whether humans could live a 'normal' life in space, he stressed that this should be their first priority.

As the third crew sat atop the Saturn 1B launcher eagerly awaiting lift-off, Mission Control terminated the countdown. Hairline cracks had been discovered in one of the tail fins of the launcher. Because a failure of one of these parts could cause the Saturn to disintegrate in flight, all eight of the fins had to be replaced. The launch was delayed by six days.

On 16 November, following a successful launch, the third crew reached Skylab, their home for the next three months. Although they had taken medicine to prevent the onset of the space sickness that had been experienced by the second crew, one member (Pogue) vomited soon after arriving. The crew decided not to report this to Mission Control. However, their deliberations were picked up by an automatic recorder and relayed to the ground. The crew were issued with a formal reprimand.

The crew's first task was to stow the several thousand items they had brought with them in the Apollo module as replenishments for Skylab. In the zero-gravity conditions, this proved to be a lengthy and irksome task. Before long the crew were complaining loudly that, as previous crew's had noted, quite a few of the facilities on Skylab didn't work well and some didn't work at all.

Finding things was a problem, partly because the previous crews had not always left equipment in its assigned location and partly because of design shortcomings. As Pogue put it to Mission Control: 'Locatability here is so bad that it almost looks like you had to go out of your way to design it that way!'.

Many of the new experiments, hastily conceived to fill the greatly extended schedule of the third mission, failed to run smoothly. A number of these were new to the astronauts who had not had sufficient time to practice them on Earth. Pogue probably voiced the feelings of the whole crew when he remarked:

> *Somebody thinks something up in an office, it sounds good, and then all of a sudden you find yourself trying to do it for the first time up here; never having done it before, you're gonna take probably four or five times as much time to do the task as the man who has been needling the flight planners to have it included said it would. 'Have 'em do my experiment; it only takes five minutes', he says, and you end up taking an hour to do it.*

On 22 November, Gibson and Pogue went outside the craft to repair a jammed antenna on the radiometer-altimeter. This difficult operation took over six-and-a-half hours to complete, during which they broke the record for the longest space walk. Their achievement brought praise from Mission Control but this was tempered by their forgetting to service some of the earth resources survey cameras. Valuable data were lost as a result. Next day, Skylab suffered a gyroscope failure. Although the craft could still be positioned using the remaining two gyroscopes, this could only be achieved at the cost of using extra fuel. If a second gyroscope were to fail, the mission would have to be terminated.

During the next two weeks, the crew became increasingly lethargic. They repeatedly fell behind schedule and seemed to lack any enthusiasm for the experiments. Two of the crew, Carr and Pogue, even gave up shaving; on their return to Earth they were barely recognizable even to their wives.

At Mission Control the crew's behaviour was giving rise to considerable concern. The flight surgeons argued that the planned schedule should be slackened, but they were told firmly by the flight planners that scheduling was a non-medical concern. As one medic put it: '... the engineers couldn't understand what we meant.' Hutchinson's view was that the crew were slacking and needed to be driven harder. He therefore decided to increase the workload and reduce the astronauts' free time.

On 25 December, Carr and Pogue took another 7-hour space walk. They went out again a few days later. Soon after, the crew took a momentous decision: they decided to go on strike.

For 24 hours, the crew refused to communicate with Mission Control and to carry out any of their assigned tasks. Gibson passed the time at the solar telescope while Carr and Pogue sat in the wardroom looking out of the window, one of the astronauts' favourite activities. Relationships between Skylab and Mission Control had reached breaking point. The upshot was another 'first' for the programme, the first space mutiny.

Aftermath

The costs of the 'mutiny' were substantial. Astronaut time was costed at $35,000 an hour which gave a total cost for the one-day strike of over $2.5 million. No work was done for 24 hours, crew morale was lowered and relationships with the ground were brought to an all-time low. And quite apart from the potential risks to life and limb, the future of the programme (which cost more than $2.5 billion), and perhaps of NASA itself, was put in jeopardy.

On 30 December, communications with Mission Control were restored. Carr told them that '... the problem we had at the beginning was that we started too high. A guy needs some quiet time to just unwind if we're going to keep him healthy and alert up here'. Pogue added, with unusual candour for an astronaut, that 'I'm a fallible human being. I cannot operate at 100 per cent efficiency. I am going to make mistakes.' And Gibson offered the comment: 'Off-duty activities? You gotta be kidding! There's no such thing up here. On day's off the only thing that's different is that we get to take a shower.'

Hutchinson was not greatly impressed by these sentiments. Nonetheless, the astronauts were given more time to carry out the experiments, although there was little increase in 'time off'. The crew responded positively and performance improved markedly. By the end of the mission most of the planned targets had been achieved.

When the crew finally left Skylab in February 1974, after more than 80 days in space, the craft was deteriorating rapidly. A second gyroscope was on the verge of failure, the sunshade had split, and the shower unit no longer worked. Skylab was boosted into a higher orbit in the hope that it might be revisited once the Shuttle came into service. But it was not to be. The NASA scientists had miscalculated the frictional effects of the upper atmosphere on the craft, and in July 1979 it disintegrated somewhere over Australia.

Reflections

We didn't want to repeat the experience of the second crew, which had taken its meals on the run and averaged 6-hours sleep a night. We had told the third crew we didn't want them to get tired or sick – that we wanted them to work on a plain 8-hour day, eat three square meals, and relax a bit. Having told them that, we increased the number of experiments aboard and gave them second-mission workloads – and the peak workloads of the second mission at that! (William Schneider, Skylab programme director)

The initial purpose of Skylab may have been to explore simply how to live in space, but the cost of the programme – $2.5 billion – caused us to change our minds.

Our system was designed to squeeze every minute out of an astronaut's day ... Suddenly, the system is asked to stop for a few hours, or a day, to give a man some time off. The system doesn't want to do it! Say, for example, there's a day off coming. But say that there's a perfect pass over an Earth resources target, and that the only chance to get that target is on that day. Now, are we going to say to the scientist whose experiment that is, 'no, goddam it, we're going to lose that real estate for the Skylab programme'?

So many jobs interfere with each other! What if a guy gets an instrument focused on a star, and just then his buddies in the docking adapter manoeuvre the vehicle around to look at the Earth? Or what if a guy starts riding the bicycle ergometer, jiggling the space station, while another guy is taking a long film of a solar flare? Now say that I gave the crew a rough framework of a schedule that said, for example, 'do five orbits of solar work followed by two orbits of Earth resources passes over Africa'. They might get so superinterested in the sun that they didn't get ready in time for the Earth resources passes and missed an important target on the ground. With so many constraints, I'd say they're bound to screw something up! (Neil Hutchinson, Skylab flight director)

Most of the guys come back with an interest in ecology, for they see how much snow and desert there is, and how hard it is for the people who have to live there. You come back feeling a little more humanitarian ... People in our line of work – a very technical type of work – are inclined to move along with the blinders on. You begin to get so involved with the details of what you're doing that I think you forget to look around you ... And I think this mission is going to do me a lot of good in that I think it's going to increase my awareness of what else is going on. (Gerald Carr, Skylab 4 flight commander)

I think in future the ground should give the astronauts the bare framework of a schedule, together with a sort of shopping list of things for them to do, and let the guys on board figure out the best way of doing them. (Edward Gibson, Skylab 4 crew)

I came to realize, during Skylab, that what we were doing was taking a human and making him function in a way he was not designed to. We were trying to function at a higher level of efficiency than we could ... When I tried to operate like a machine, I was a gross failure. Now I'm trying to operate as a human being within the limitations I possess ... I think a person needs to more or less recreate himself, to pause and reflect occasionally ... We've got to appreciate a human being for what he is. (William Pogue, Skylab 4 crew)

Autonomous behaviour in space: an example – and a precedent?

Mercury 7 (a one-man capsule) was launched on 24 May 1962 with Malcolm Scott Carpenter in the hot seat. Carpenter, a married man with four children, held a degree in aeronautical engineering and had flown for the US Navy during the Korean War. He later became a test pilot and then took up a post as an air intelligence officer on an aircraft carrier.

Carpenter excelled in tests of physical fitness. For example, on a test of lung capacity he was able to hold his breath for a record 171 seconds. He also displayed a more imaginative and less down-to-earth attitude to his duties than did many of his test-pilot colleagues.

Carpenter was expected to carry out a number of scientific experiments during his Mercury 7 flight, but he had been selected at only ten weeks notice, leaving relatively little time for detailed training.

The launch of the Mercury capsule went well, but problems developed soon after. Carpenter's pressure suit was overheating, he had trouble keeping up with the overloaded activity schedule, and, most seriously, when manoeuvring the spacecraft he began to use excessive amounts of fuel.

As the craft approached re-entry, the manual fuel reserves fell to a dangerously low level. A miscalculation could lead to the capsule bouncing off the Earth's atmosphere and into oblivion. The craft began to oscillate wildly, but this was brought under control by the release of the descent parachute. Carpenter got down safely, but he was 250 miles (402 kilometres) off target. A 3-hour wait in the life-raft ensued before he was recovered by helicopter.

Carpenter was given a hero's welcome on his return to the US mainland. He was awarded the Distinguished Service Medal by the President. But NASA ground staff were less impressed. The flight director and many of his colleagues regarded Mercury 7 as a near disaster provoked by Carpenter's arrogant behaviour and devil-may-care attitude. Carpenter had ignored repeated warnings about fuel consumption, had forgotten to carry out various checking procedures, and had failed to effect a correct re-entry. He had very nearly become the first US astronaut to be lost in space.

The flight director let it be known that, as he put it, 'that sonofabitch will never fly for me again!'

Space flight: the struggle for control

The first living creature to be launched into space by the United States was an ape called Ham. He was sealed into a small, windowless capsule and, of course, had no control over the direction of his flight.

Early designs for the Mercury capsule assumed that the astronaut would adopt an equally passive role. There were to be no manual controls fitted in the craft. Hence these missions were referred to derisively by the test-pilot fraternity as 'spam in the can'. Accustomed to having full, independent control of high-powered rocket planes which they flew to the edges of space, the prospect of merely sitting in a sealed capsule was regarded with considerable ambivalence.

A similar situation arose in the Soviet Union. Vostok 1, in which Yuri Gagarin made the world's first orbital space flight, was originally designed without manual controls. But objections from the Soviet astronauts resulted in manual backup systems being installed. Similar pressures from the US astronauts yielded similar results.

During the US missions, control over in-flight activities was a constant source of friction between the flight crews and the ground controllers. In 1959, two years before the first Mercury launch, a leading test pilot, Deke Slayton, publicly attacked the 'spam in the can' concept. Subsequently a repeated complaint of the astronauts was that their work schedules were overloaded. In particular, they sometimes seemed uncomfortable with the requirement that they carry out experiments devised by scientists in their laboratories on Earth. What, after all, did they know about the realities of space flight?

Questions for discussion

1 The case reports the experience of three missions. How can the behaviour of the third crew, culminating in the 'mutiny' be explained? What factors might have influenced the behaviour of the different crews?
2 What were the main features of Skylab's work organization? What were the assumptions underlying this design and why did the work organization take the form it did?
3 Can you suggest an alternative form of work organization that might have worked more satisfactorily?

Appendix I US manned space missions 1961–86

Name	Number of missions	Crew size	Dates
Mercury	6	1	1961–63
Gemini	10	2	1965–66
Apollo	12	3	1968–75
Skylab	3	3	1973–74
Shuttle	25	2–8	1981–86

Appendix II Skylab missions

Skylab 2 Launch date: 25 May 1973. Duration: 28 days.
Skylab 3 Launch date: 28 July 1973. Duration: 59 days.
Skylab 4 Launch date: 16 November 1973. Duration: 84 days.

Appendix III Skylab crew composition

Skylab 2
Charles 'Pete' Conrad (flight commander) – aged 43, degree in aeronautical engineering from Princeton University, Navy test pilot. Previous missions: Gemini 5, Gemini 11, Apollo 12.
Paul Weitz – aged 40, degree in aeronautical engineering, Navy pilot. Previous missions: none.
Joseph Kerwin – aged 41, degree in philosophy and medicine, qualified doctor. Previous missions: none.
Skylab 3
Alan Bean (flight commander) – aged 41, degree in aeronautical engineering, Navy test pilot. Previous missions: Apollo 12.

Owen Garriott – aged 42, degree in electrical engineering, doctorate in electrical engineering from Stanford University, university lecturer. Previous missions: none.

Jack Lousma – aged 37, degree in aeronautical engineering, Marines fighter pilot. Previous missions: none.

Skylab 4

Gerald Carr (flight commander) – aged 41, degree in mechanical and aeronautical engineering, Marines test pilot. Previous missions: none.

Edward Gibson – aged 37, doctorate in engineering physics, civilian research physicist. Previous missions: none.

William Pogue – aged 43, degrees in science and mathematics, Air Force pilot instructor. Previous missions: none.

Appendix IV Astronaut selection criteria (Mercury programme)

1 Under 40 years of age
2 Under 5 feet 11 inches tall
3 Excellent physical condition
4 Bachelor's degree or equivalent
5 Graduate of test pilot's school
6 Minimum 1,500 flying hours
7 Qualified jet pilot
8 Citizen of US.

Sources

This case is based on material drawn from the following sources:

Bond, P. (1987) *Heroes in Space: From Gagarin to Challenger*, Oxford: Basil Blackwell.

Cooper, H.S.F. (1977) *A House in Space*, London: Angus and Robertson.

Furniss, T. (1985) *Space Flight: The Records*, London: Guiness Superlatives.

Osman, T. (1983) *Space History*, London: Michael Joseph.

Schoonhoven, C.B. (1986) 'Sociotechnical considerations for the development of the space station: autonomy and the human element in space', *Journal of Applied Behavioral Science* 22: 271–86.

Yenne, B. (1986) *The Astronauts: The First 25 Years of Manned Space Flight*, London: Bison Books.

Further reading

Connors, M.M., Harrison, A.A. and Atkinson, F.R. (1985) *Living Aloft: Human Requirements for Extended Spaceflight*, Washington DC: NASA.

Cherns, A. (1987) 'Principles of sociotechnical design revisited', *Human Relations* 40: 153–61.

Fox, W.F. (1995) 'Sociotechnical systems principles and guidelines: past and present', *Journal of Applied Behavioral Science* 31: 91–105.

Gowler, D. (1974) 'Values, contracts and job satisfaction', *Personnel Review* 3: 4–14.

Gowler, D. and Legge, K. (1972) 'Occupational role development, part 1', *Personnel Review* 1: 12–27.

Harris, P.R. (1992) *Living and Working in Space: Human Behaviour, Culture and Organization*, Chichester: Ellis Horwood.

Huczynski, A.A. and Buchanan, D.A. (1991) *Organizational Behaviour: An Introductory Text* (Ch. 12 on scientific management), Hemel Hempstead: Prentice-Hall.

Maruyama, M. (1976) 'Designing a space community', *Futurist* 10: 273–81.

Maruyama, M. (1990) 'Organizational structure, training and selection of outer space crew members', *Technological Forecasting and Social Change* 37: 203–12.

Mumford, E. (1972) *Job Satisfaction: A Study of Computer Specialists*, London: Longman.

Pasmore, W.A. (1988) *Designing Effective Organizations: the Sociotechnical Systems Perspective*, New York: John Wiley.

Vaughan, D. (1990) 'Autonomy, interdependence, and social control: NASA and the space shuttle Challenger', *Administrative Science Quarterly* 35: 225–57.

Wolfe, T. (1981) *The Right Stuff*, London: Bantam Books.

Author index

Alvarez, J.L. 8, 9
Anthony, P.D. 147
Argyris, C. 1, 9
Atkinson, F.R. 225

Barker, R. 45
Barley, S.R. 122
Bate, P. 147
Batsleer, J. 196
Berger, M.A. 1, 9
Boddy, D. 147
Boeker, W. 32
Boje, D.M. 20
Boland, R.J. 45, 122
Bold, B. 196
Bond, P. 225
Bongiorno, L. 1, 9
Bowles, M.L. 212
Brindle, D. 180
Bromley, B.D. 3, 6, 9
Bryant, D. 77
Buchanan, D. 147, 226
Burrows, R. 96

Cameron, K.S. 32, 33, 45
Campbell, A. 95
Champy, J. 122
Cherns, A. 225
Clarke, W.M. 109
Collinson, D. 95
Collinson, M. 95
Connors, M.M. 225
Conti, R.F. 45
Cooper, C.L. 20, 109
Cooper, H.S.F. 225
Coppack, G. 212
Cordery, J. 19
Cornforth, C. 196
Coulton, G.G. 212
Crompton, R. 95
Curran, J. 32

Daft, R.L. 60, 109
Dandridge, T.C. 9

Davies, A. 180
de Varine Bohan, H. 131
De Wit, B. 95, 96
Deci, R.L. 20
Demarie, S.M. 45
Ditton, J. 19
Durham, K. 109

Easton, D. 10
Easton, G. 6, 9
Eisenhardt, K.M. 3, 9
Erskine, J.A. 5, 9
Evers, S. 196
Ezzamel, M. 147

Ferlie, E. 148
Flynn, N. 147
Ford, M.E. 20
Fox, W.F. 225
Frances, J. 148
Freeman, J. 32
Frost, P.J. 9, 180
Furniss, T. 225

Gaston, K.C. 60
Gerth, H.H. 212
Gibb, A. 32
Gibbons, P.T. 32
Gist, M.E. 20
Goffman, E. 76
Goodstein, J. 32
Goold, M. 95
Gowler, D. 225
Gragg, C.I. 5, 9
Gustafson, L.T. 45

Hakim, C. 6, 9
Halford, A. 147
Hall, E.T. 76, 77
Hammer, M. 45, 122
Handy, C. 109, 163
Hannan, M.T. 32
Harris, P.R. 226
Harrison, A.A. 225

Harrow, J. 180
Hassard, J. 180
Henne, D. 20
Hiltrop, J.M. 60
Hirschheim, R. 163
Hofmeister, K.R. 45, 122
Hogan, E. 6, 9
Hrebiniak, L.G. 32
Huczynski, A.A. 226
Hudson, K. 131
Huff, A.S. 122
Hull, B.B. 196

Isabella, L.A. 45

Johnson, L. 148
Jones, P.R. 131
Joyce, W.F. 32

Kahn, H. 109
Kaplan, R.S. 77
Kilmann, R.H. 180, 206, 210
Kimberly, J.R. 32
Knights, D. 95, 96, 163
Knowles, D. 212
Kohlt, A.K. 20
Kotter, J.P. 5, 9

Laughlin, R.C. 196
Leavitt, H.J. 20
Leenders, M.R. 9
Legge, K. 225
Levacic, R. 148
Lewis, B.N. 131
Lilley, S. 147
Locke, E.A. 20
Louis, M.R. 180
Lucas, H.C. 163
Lundberg, C.C. 1, 5, 9, 180

Mahler, S. 1, 9
Markus, M.L. 163
Mars, G. 77
Marsden, D. 180
Marsh, C. 96
Martin, J. 45, 122, 180, 212
Maruyama, M. 226
Mauffett-Leenders, L.R. 9
McCann, J. 212
McCardle, L. 180
McGivern, C. 33
McKee, L. 148
McNair, M.P. 9
Merchan, C. 8, 9
Meyer, M. 95, 96

Meyerson, D. 45, 212
Miller, D. 33
Mills, C.W. 212
Mintzberg, H. 1, 4, 5, 9, 33, 96, 109, 148, 163
Mitchell, J. 148
Mitchell, P. 77
Moore, L.F. 180
Morgan, Gareth 4, 9, 148
Morgan, Glenn 95, 96, 163
Morris, B. 131
Mullane, J.V. 45
Mumford, E. 163, 226
Myers, D. 212
Myerson, D. 122

Newman, M. 122
Newman, W.H. 33
Nicod, M. 77
Noble, F. 122
Norton, D.P. 77

O'Reilly, J. 96
Orwell, G. 77
Osman, T. 225
Ott, S. 60, 109, 148

Pasmore, W.A. 226
Paton, R. 196
Payne, R.L. 60
Pearce, J.L. 196
Penrose, E.T. 212
Perry, J.L. 180
Peters, T.J. 166
Pettigrew, A.M. 77, 148, 163
Pfeffer, J. 109, 163
Pollitt, C. 180
Pondy, L.R. 9, 20, 45, 122
Poole, M.S. 45
Procter, S. 180

Quinn, H.B. 33
Quinn, R.E. 33, 45

Reed, B. 196
Reger, R.K. 45
Reichers, A.E. 60
Reynolds, J.I. 5
Richardson, R. 180
Robertson, I.T. 20
Romanelli, E. 33
Romm, T. 1, 9
Roth, G. 212
Rowlinson, M. 180

Sackmann, S. 122
Sanderson, K. 95
Saxton, M.J. 206, 210
Schein, E.H. 109, 180
Schelling, C.S. 10
Schluchter, R.G. 212
Schneider, B. 60
Schneider, S. 122
Schoonhoven, C.B. 225
Schumacher, E.F. 6, 9
Scott, M. 32
Sheehy, P. 148
Silber, I.F. 212
Smircich, L. 8, 9
Smith, C. 96
Smith, G. 1, 9
Sparrow, P.R. 60
Spencer, B.A. 45
Spinelli, E. 4, 9
Sproull, L.S. 45, 122
Stanworth, J. 32
Steers, R.M. 20
Stewart, J. 148
Stewart, T.A. 196
Stonham, P. 1, 9

Taylor, J.A. 122
Taylor, M.S. 20
Thomas, A.B. 4, 9
Thomas, H. 45, 122
Thompson, G. 148
Thompson, L. 163
Tsoukas, H. 4, 9, 45
Tuckman, A. 45
Turner, R.H. 6, 10
Tushman, M.L. 33
Twining, W. 212

Van de Ven, A.H. 45
Van Maanen, J. 77
Vance, C.M. 9, 10
Vaughan, D. 226
Vroom, R.H. 20

Wall, T. 19
Walsh, K. 148
Walsham, G. 163
Warner, R.M. 45
Waterman, R.H. 166
Waters, J. 96, 163
Webb, G.H. 109
Weber, M. 212
Weick, K.E. 3, 10
Weiner, B. 20
Westenholz, A. 122
Whetton, D.A. 32
Whipp, R. 77
Whitley, R. 96
Whittington, R. 96
Whyte, W.F. 77
Will, L. 131
Willcocks, L. 180
Williams, H. 122
Williams, R. 131
Willmott, H. 96, 147
Wittlin, A. 131
Wolfe, T. 226

Yates, B. 131
Yenne, B. 225
Yin, R.K. 3, 10
Yorke, D. 131

Subject index

Abbey Life 82
Abbey National 90
adaptation 182, 207
Allied Bakeries 13
Allied British Foods 13
Allied Dunbar 82
Anchorite 205, 209
anti-case 8
anxiety 146
appraisal 125, 168, 169, 172
Asda 16, 29
Associated Tyre Services (ATS) 139
Audit Commission 134, 135, 136
authority 100, 145, 181, 182, 195, 197

British Bakeries 13
British Gas 82
British Museum 126
Business and Organizational Climate Index (BOCI) 51, 52, 54, 55
Business Process Re-engineering (BPR) 35, 80, 112, 118

career management 125
careers 53
case analysis, criticism of 4, 5
case method 1, 5
case teaching 1, 2
cases as texts 3
change 7, 11, 12, 19, 43, 44, 54, 79, 80, 81, 94, 123, 124, 129, 132, 134, 135, 136, 137, 139, 140, 141, 147, 149, 154, 160, 165, 167, 181, 182, 183, 195, 213
change agents 137
chaos 92
Church Commissioners 185, 187
Church of England 181, 183, 184, 185, 187, 189, 208, 209, 210
Citizen's Charter 135, 136
City of London 79, 81, 97, 105, 106, 107, 119, 120
coalitions 99, 206

communication 12, 30, 31, 35, 40, 41, 47, 80, 94, 98, 102, 103, 107, 116, 139, 153, 155, 157, 158, 161, 162, 213, 216, 221
Community Care Act 151
conflict 12, 79, 80, 86, 90, 107, 123, 124, 125, 213
construction of meaning 12
consultants 11, 12, 18, 34, 35, 41, 47, 50, 52, 54, 55, 88, 91, 179
control 23, 24, 53, 79, 80, 85, 89, 95, 97, 103, 106, 107, 133, 146, 153, 159, 161, 165, 166, 197, 213
convergent/divergent thinking 6
coping mechanisms 199
corporate speak 143
crisis 181
crisis management 181
Crown Prosecution Service 135, 141, 142
cynicism 146

debt crisis 98
decisions 31
Department for Education 191
Department of Social Security 149, 151
departmental perspectives 80
development 11
dismissal 79, 85, 94
divide-and-rule 146
drains 198, 199, 200, 209
drugs, drug dealing 76, 135

empire-building 106
ethnic cleansing 206
Evangelicals 205, 210

family firms 11, 12, 47, 98
family tradition 97
fear 94, 107
Financial Management Initiative 135
Financial Services Act 79, 86, 89, 95
Friends Provident 90
fun 95

futures markets 97, 103

glocalism 182, 207
goal displacement 182, 203
greed 87
Greggs 13
greenfielding 206
group think 31
groups/group relations 11, 80, 100, 101, 103, 105, 144, 213
growth 11, 12, 91, 182

Ham 223
Hambros 82
Her Majesty's Inspectors of Constabulary (HMIC) 134, 136, 147
Home Office 123, 134, 136, 145, 146, 147
Home Secretary 123
human relations 41
Humiliati 205, 209

information systems 88, 124, 153
information technology (IT) 80, 89, 91, 92, 94, 105, 112, 119, 124, 135, 149, 151, 154, 155, 156, 157, 160, 162
inter-agency approach 143, 145

Just-in-time (JIT) 34, 35, 44

leaders/leadership 11, 12, 53, 79, 80, 95, 100, 119, 123, 125, 143, 145, 165, 181, 182, 207, 213
Libraries Act 126
Lloyds 89

management control 11, 12
management education 1
management style 11, 21, 52, 53, 142, 165
management succession 12, 32
managerial bias 5
Marks and Spencer 14, 16, 17, 29
Materials Requirement Planning (MRP) 12, 34, 35, 44
McKinsey 166
Mergers and Monopolies Commission 48
metaphors 4
mission statements 49, 54, 99, 135, 145
morale 32, 90, 94, 142, 143, 146, 147
motivation 11, 19, 22, 32, 79, 80, 145, 157, 170, 171, 177, 178, 179, 181, 213

narrative fiction 8
National Aeronautics and Space Administration (NASA) 214, 215, 216, 217, 218, 219, 221

Natural History Museum 126
NatWest bank 90
new managerialism 135
new public management approach 139
Norwich Union 83

organization structure 11, 12, 31, 34, 48, 50, 54, 80, 95, 99, 133, 183, 184, 185, 195
organizational climate 47, 50, 51, 53, 54
organizational culture 12, 35, 40, 41, 44, 47, 49, 50, 51, 52, 53, 79, 80, 97, 106, 108, 119, 125, 153, 154, 161, 162, 179, 182, 198, 199, 205, 213
organizational politics 80, 119, 144
ownership 80

participation 53
patronage 103
performance evaluation 182
performance indicators 135, 140
performance management 124, 140, 141
performance marking 168
performance-related pay (PRP) 125, 135, 167, 168, 169, 170, 171, 172, 179
philistinism 126
polarization principle 89
policy research 6
power 44, 80, 90, 92, 99, 101, 107, 111, 133, 134, 135, 137, 140, 145, 146, 181, 182, 197, 213
power culture 198
private sector management 124, 125, 135
privatization 135, 164, 165, 197
Procter and Gamble 119
professionals/professionalism 53, 54, 89, 94, 123, 124, 125, 126, 128, 129, 130, 131, 160, 162, 165, 166, 168, 171, 213
Prudential 86, 88
public humiliation 145
public relations 41

ranks 133, 142
recruitment 80, 84, 105, 133, 151, 168
redundancy/unemployment 36, 39, 49, 94, 129, 147
regulation 79, 89, 94, 182
relativism 4
renewal 182, 203, 204, 207
reorganization/restructuring 11, 16, 50, 61, 62, 88, 91, 92, 93, 99, 132, 136, 137, 140, 145, 147, 149, 161, 167, 181, 182, 194, 195
reputation 182
research cases 3

resistance to change 153
rewards/reward systems 11, 24, 27, 29, 53, 84, 85, 90, 94, 99, 106, 125
RHM group 13
rightsizing 12, 35, 36, 38, 39, 40, 41, 44
rogue traders 79
role culture 199
rule culture 199
rules 31, 103, 142, 182, 199, 200, 201, 202, 209

Safeway 49
Sainsbury's 16, 17
salesforce 15, 16, 17, 18, 83, 84, 85, 86, 87, 90, 92, 93, 94
scientific management 41, 213
shareholders 99, 102, 106
Sheehy Report 135
sociotechnical systems 213
spam in the can 223, 224
specialization principle 90
staff turnover 28, 85, 87, 90
stakeholders 98, 111, 123
Standard Life 83
status 44, 100, 107, 133
strategy 12, 24, 25, 47, 48, 49, 51, 54, 67, 72, 79, 80, 88, 92, 95, 99, 100, 124, 135, 136, 139, 143, 144, 145, 147, 152, 154, 156, 158, 161, 162, 165

strike in space 213, 221
supervisory behaviour 11

teams/teamwork 21, 30, 35, 43, 44, 84, 111, 120, 124, 136, 137, 139, 142, 143, 145, 151, 152, 162, 166
technological change 80, 124, 154
Tesco 29, 49
Tomkins plc 13
total quality management (TQM) 12, 34, 35, 36, 37, 38, 39, 40, 41, 43
training 11, 37, 53, 80, 89, 101, 132, 133, 142, 156, 158, 159, 160, 162, 168, 169, 213
trust 52, 53, 106, 111, 119, 167

unintended consequences 161
unit trusts 81, 82, 83, 91
usable understandings 6

Victoria and Albert Museum 126

Waldensians 205, 210
Warburtons 13
Woolworths 29
workloads 124, 141, 142, 221, 222, 223, 224

zero-gravity 213, 215, 216